The Neoliberal Diet

The Neoliberal Diet

HEALTHY PROFITS, UNHEALTHY PEOPLE

Gerardo Otero

UNIVERSITY OF TEXAS PRESS ⟿ AUSTIN

Requests for permission to reproduce material from this work should be sent to:
    Permissions
    University of Texas Press
    P.O. Box 7819
    Austin, TX 78713-7819
    utpress.utexas.edu/rp-form

♾ The paper used in this book meets the minimum requirements of
ANSI/NISO Z39.48-1992 (R1997) (Permanence of Paper).

Library of Congress Cataloging-in-Publication Data
Names: Otero, Gerardo, author.
Title: The neoliberal diet : healthy profits, unhealthy people / Gerardo Otero.
Description: First edition. | Austin : University of Texas Press, 2018. | Includes
bibliographical references and index.
Identifiers: LCCN 2018004664| ISBN 978-1-4773-1697-9 (cloth : alk. paper) |
ISBN 978-1-4773-1698-6 (pbk. : alk. paper) | ISBN 978-1-4773-1699-3 (library e-book) |
ISBN 978-1-4773-1700-6 (nonlibrary e-book)
Subjects: LCSH: Food industry and trade—Social aspects. | Food industry and trade—
Political aspects. | Produce trade—Government policy. | Obesity—Social aspects. |
Food supply—Social aspects. | Food preferences—Economic aspects. |
Neoliberalism. | Globalization.
Classification: LCC HD9000.5 .O867 2018 | DDC 338.1/9—dc23
LC record available at https://lccn.loc.gov/2018004664

doi:10.7560/316979

For Alex, Paty, and our ever-loving memory of Rodrigo

Contents

Tables and Figures

TABLES

FIGURES

Acknowledgments

Most of the research for this book has been funded by the Social Sciences and the Humanities Research Council of Canada, which I thankfully acknowledge. Among other things, such funding has allowed me to bring on board several highly talented students and research assistants. Gabriela Pechlaner was among them during her doctoral studies with me (2002–2007). We have collaborated since then and long after her graduation. In fact, several chapters in this book originated as co-authored articles or book chapters, so I am heavily indebted to her. Other research assistants who helped with data gathering include Giselle Liberman, Anelyse Weiler, and most significantly, Efe Can Gürcan. Efe started his doctoral studies with me in 2011, and we have established a highly productive intellectual relationship. He contributed significant research for some of the chapters in this book, for which I am very thankful. Given the strong help I received from these assistants, especially from Gabriela and Efe, I could easily use the first-person plural "we" throughout the book. Yet, given all the major changes and updates I have done throughout, and to take full responsibility for this manuscript, my style here will be the first-person singular.

Part of my research and writing was done while I held the Highfield Fellowship at the Centre for Advanced Studies at the University of Nottingham in the United Kingdom (January–April 2012), with a project on food security. My thanks go to Adam Morton (then in the School of Politics and International Relations) and Wyn Morgan (School of Economics) for nominating me and for contributing to this exciting intellectual experience. Adam, now in the Department of Political Economy at the University of Sydney, was and continues to be a thoughtful interlocutor.

During the fall of 2014, I was fortunate to be back at my doctoral alma mater, the University of Wisconsin, Madison, as the Tinker Visiting Professor. I thank Alberto Vargas at the Latin American, Caribbean, and Iberian Studies Program for the invitation and friendly kindness during my stay. Many thanks also go to Jack Kloppenburg for supporting Alberto's nomination and offering me an academic home in the Department of Community and Environmental Sociology. Besides the rare sensation of having arrived "home" as the shuttle bus from Chicago approached Lake Mendota, the multiple seminars and conversations in Madison were highly stimulating for some of my writing in this book. Drafts of chapters 4, 6, and 7 were presented at several forums in which I got very useful feedback. These forums included the research seminar in the sociology of economic change and development in the Department of Sociology. It was great to see my former professors Erik Olin Wright and Jess Gilbert there and to find that, while most people were different from those in my times as a graduate student, the intellectual vibrancy was unchanged. I thank Gay Seidman for asking me to give a paper and for her friendship during my pleasant stay in Madison.

I made other presentations at the Rural Sociological Society and the Latin American Studies Association, two of my main academic reference groups. My discussions with Doug Constance, Horacio Mackinlay, Tony Winson, and Steve Zahnizer were particularly helpful. Horacio was especially helpful in clarifying some results of the 1992 agrarian reform in Mexico. In Vancouver, BC, I presented a draft of chapter 7 at a research colloquium in my new academic home as of 2015, Simon Fraser University's School for International Studies. I am deeply thankful to my colleagues for their critical feedback. Alec Dawson was generous in highlighting problems in the chapter during his introductory remarks, and John Harriss, Jeff Checkel, Liz Cooper, Chris Gibson, and Paul Meyer provided useful skeptical comments. Greg Feldman provided the sole sympathetic remark, which strengthened my determination to sharpen my arguments and presentation. Separately, Hannah Wittman and Juan Enrique Ramos Salas also gave me useful feedback on chapter 7.

Through the process of publishing other articles or book chapters, some of which served as the basis for this book, I got plenty of generous and constructive critiques from anonymous reviewers and other colleagues. Special thanks as book editors are due to Alessandro Bonanno, Larry Busch, María Vidal de Haymes, Geoff Lawrence, and Steve Wolf. For chapter 1, Christina Holmes, James Klepeck, and Karine Peschard provided useful comments, as did Liz Fitting. John Harriss and four anonymous reviewers for the *Canadian Journal of Development Studies*, which published an earlier version, also offered very valuable input.

A version of chapter 4 was presented at the plenary panel on NAFTA and other free trade agreements at the World Congress for Rural Sociology held in Toronto in August 2016. Along with the public, organizer Doug Constance and my panel colleagues, Hugh Campbell and Jennifer Clapp, posed provocative questions that helped me sharpen the argument.

An early version of chapter 5 was presented at a workshop entitled Migrant Rights in an Era of Globalization: The Mexico-US Case and held on 13 April 2011 at the University of Chicago. Javier Ramos Salas and two anonymous reviewers for the *Journal of Poverty* provided useful comments. My exposure to migration studies dates from my early days as a graduate student at the University of Texas, Austin, where I participated in seminars led by Bryan Roberts, Norman Long, and Juarez Rubens Brandão Lopes. At Wisconsin, the Mexican Student Association invited Jorge Bustamante for a lecture at a time when he was becoming the authority on the Mexican perspective in undocumented migration. Alejandro Portes has also been a central source for my understanding of migration, and I appreciate our exchanges in Madison and later in Zacatecas. My postdoctoral year at the Center for US-Mexican Studies at the University of California, San Diego, put me in contact with its director, Wayne Cornelius, one of the foremost US scholars on migration. From 2003 to 2012 I participated in the doctoral program in development studies at the Universidad Autónoma de Zacatecas in Mexico, invited by its founding director, Raúl Delgado Wise. Migration and development is the main strength of my colleagues there, and I learned much from all of them, including Rodolfo García Zamora, James Cypher, Humberto Márquez Covarrubias, Miguel Moctezuma Longoria, and Henry Veltmeyer. My work with Mexican farmworkers in Canada has been a critical encouragement for chapter 5, which started in collaboration with my former student Kerry Preibisch, who, sadly, passed away too early, in 2016. Her engaged scholarship is an inspiration.

Earlier versions of other chapters and sections were first published as journal articles as follows and listed in the bibliography: chapter 1, Otero

2012 and 2013; chapter 2, Pechlaner and Otero 2008; chapter 3, Otero, Pechlaner, Gürcan, and Liberman 2015; chapter 4, Pechlaner and Otero 2015; chapter 5, Otero 2011, Preibisch and Otero 2014; chapter 6, Otero, Pechlaner, and Gürcan 2013; chapter 7, Otero, Pechlaner, Liberman, and Gürcan 2018. They were all heavily revised, reorganized, and updated for this book. Yet my deep gratitude goes to my coauthors and the colleagues who served as anonymous reviewers for their critical engagement with our research, resulting in kind and generous help.

The Neoliberal Diet

Introduction

OBESITY AND THE NEOLIBERAL DIET

One of the principal puzzles in agrarian and food studies since the late 1990s has been the so-called obesity epidemic observed by US and World Health Organization (WHO) officials. Close to one billion people continue to face the challenge of not having access to sufficient quantities of food; they are food insecure in terms of a quantitative modality. But a larger and growing number now face the prospect of accessing mostly energy-dense foods that are nutritionally compromised. This is a new form of food insecurity that has less to do with quantity and more with quality. In other words, not all calories are made equal. Energy-dense foods or pseudo-foods are rich in fats and sugars that the human body may turn into adipose tissue or cholesterol. Michael Pollan (2006:91) calls energy-dense foods "the Western diet." Such edibles are particularly high in refined flour, saturated fat, sugars, and processed ingredients low in fiber (Popkin, Adair, and Ng 2012). Western diseases — obesity, type 2 diabetes, hypertension, stroke, and heart disease — have closely followed this diet (Popkin 2009). The obesity crisis and the rise of the industrial diet and its globalization are related to what I call "the neoliberal diet."

OBESITY

In 2000, the WHO warned about an "obesity epidemic." It followed a US official's use of that label a year earlier (Moss 2013). Since then, the scholarly and popular literature on food and weight has massively proliferated, with many observers giving advice to consumers on more healthful fare, such as Parisian food (Cohen 2013) and the Aztec diet (Arnot 2013). Most analysts, even many critical ones, contend that overweight and obesity can be modified if people pay attention to their good advice and make the right food choices, that is, "voting with forks" (Nestle 2013:372). The assumption is that what we eat is simply a matter of personal choice as part of a given lifestyle that may or may not include routinely engaging in physical activity and exercise.

Using the word "epidemic" for a condition that is not contagious is of course problematic. If obesity is not contagious, does causality then lie in individual food choices or in social structures of inequality and food production and distribution? Most policy and commentary regarding ways to stem overweight and obesity focus on interventions at the individual level (Christensen and Carpiano 2014; Koplan, Liverman, and Kraak 2005; Popkin 2009), a trend that exasperates sociologist Anthony Winson (2013). While Winson admires the rigor with which the medical and nutritional sciences have documented overweight and obesity, he regards the search for root causes as "pathetic" (2013:5). But without an adequate analysis of causal factors, it is practically impossible to outline solutions. Winson is particularly critical of what the likewise critical Julie Guthman (2011) labels "the energy-balance model." Winson summarizes this explanation as "too many nutrients going in and not enough energy expended"; the proposed solution, he says, is both "remarkably simplistic and entirely focused on individual responsibility: eat less and/or move more" (2013:6).

The individual focus raises the policy dilemma of whether to govern or not to govern (Vallgårda 2015), that is, to let individuals choose foods for themselves or steer populations toward foods by means of government policies (Calman 2008; Sparks 2011; Vallgårda 2015; Wiley, Berman, and Blanke 2013). Most scholars and governments primarily advocate interventions that aim to modify individual food consumption. If the issue were merely one of individual choice, then perhaps educational efforts and some regulation such as labeling and taxes intended to shape choice—"the conduct of conduct" (Vallgårda 2015)—would be in order. However, a Swedish study has confirmed results of earlier studies indicating that greater knowledge of food and diet is not enough to counter inequality (Håkansson, Andersson, and Grafeldt 2015). Marion Nestle has made the same point regarding food education (2013:392–393).

Winson may be frustrated with the solutions proposed by nutrition scientists, but he is not much happier with the explanations and solutions by other social scientists. Much of the literature, he contends, is dominated by writers in the social constructivist strand of thought: they see the so-called obesity crisis as overblown, when it is predominantly a social construct (2013:7). This critique questions the validity of the body mass index (BMI) used by nutritionists and health scientists to assess overweight and obesity. The BMI is derived by dividing a person's weight in kilograms by height in meters and squaring the result. If the BMI exceeds 27.3 for a man or 28 for a woman, the person is regarded as overweight. Obesity starts at a BMI of 30. For social constructivists, the BMI is flawed and unreliable, as it could, for instance, classify a weight lifter as obese. While Winson (2013:7) and many other scholars acknowledge the BMI's limitations, they see these as hardly grounds to dismiss concerns about population-wide weight gains.

Guthman's critique of the energy-balance explanation for overweight and obesity also aims at the focus on individuals. Finding that model and individual-level solutions wanting, Guthman searches for systemic causes so that solutions can be better directed toward the social structure. Her perspective is influenced by political ecology and food studies; the latter finds a mutually determining relation between knowledge generation and social relations (2011:1–23).

One of the main points of Guthman's critique of epidemiological studies of overweight and obesity is their use of the BMI, which she considers a crude measure of adiposity, or fatty tissue, in the human body: "The BMI makes no allowances for variations in bone mass and density, or somatic difference more generally" (2011:28). So, at least for assessing individuals, the BMI is not a reliable measure of body fatness, as it may account for 60 to 75 percent of the variation (29). Furthermore, Guthman strongly objects to labeling obesity an epidemic, as this assumes that being fat is a disease. She contends that obesity is not a disease, "much less a vector-borne one. At best it is a symptom of a disease—or a condition associated with a disease" (32). Guthman is understandably concerned about the health aspects of obesity but also about issues of justice and oppression. This is a main concern of social constructionists. People tend to judge based on socially constructed notions of what is "normal"; even researchers comparing twenty-first-century embodiments of perceived normalcy see them as deviations from historical norms (42). Guthman argues for rejecting the probabilistic and "natural" normativity and instead embracing human variation: "At least we must decenter thinness as the norm to which all should aspire" (43). She offers incisive questions about the measurement techniques used in epidemiological research and how they have led to the medicalization of obesity. Guthman does not deny that the US population has become fatter; rather, she questions how the discussion has proceeded around a notion that being thin and tall is normal. Difference is thus derided, possibly leading to discrimination and oppression.

New research into how to assess the health impacts of body fat has yielded a better measure than the BMI. The question is not so much whether people are overweight or obese but whether they have excess fat in their bodies. In fact, the prevalence of abdominal overfat has increased more quickly than the prevalence of obesity as defined by the BMI. Unlike BMI rates, which seem to be leveling or even declining in some rich countries, the rates of abdominal overfat have grown overall and more ominously, in children. The waist-to-height ratio (WHtR), therefore, "may be the single best clinical indicator of health risk as it can be used throughout childhood, into adult life, as well as throughout the world (in all ethnic groups)" (Maffetone, Rivera-Dominguez, and Laursen 2017:6). Given that comparative WHtR data are not yet available across time for my case study countries, I will use the BMI to test its correlation with the neoliberal diet risk (NDR) index. If anything, the BMI understates the prevalence of overweight and obesity.

In considering the health impacts of obesity, Guthman concedes that health is indeed important. But in her view, the rise of "healthism," directing individuals to consume fewer calories and exercise more, has led to pointing out "biological citizenship" and dumping the blame for obesity on individuals. Healthism also can entail "lifestylism," nutritionism, and other reductionisms that may lead to increased discipline and temperance (Guthman 2011:57–59). Guthman considers some questions inspired by Hannah Arendt: Who has the choice to have choice? Who has the right to have rights? These are good normative questions that point to structural issues as the main drivers of overweight and obesity in populations.

Guthman examines structural determinants of obesity, such as whether the neighborhood makes one fat: Is obesity a matter of the environment at large? She offers an excellent demystification of studies that aim to identify predictors of obesity such as those based on a structurally oriented "obesogenic environment" thesis. While the correlation of place with prevalence of obesity is established, the causality is inverted: people live in obesogenic places because their class status does not allow them to do otherwise. Class and race are key factors in determining where one can live; trying to resolve "supply side" issues may simply result in such unintended consequences as the gentrification of poor areas, says Guthman (2011:87–90).

Going to the heart of the energy-balance model, Guthman offers revealing data: "From 1980 to 2008, the prevalence of overweight in children ages two to five increased from 5.0 percent to 10.4 percent; for those ages six to eleven, from 6.5 percent to 19.6 percent; and for those ages twelve to nineteen, from 5.0 percent to 19.1 percent" (2011:92). The mainstream hypothesis is that people consume too many calories relative to expenditure, with some adjustments for genetic predisposition. Guthman presents a strong counterargument to the energy-balance model based on "endocrine-disruptive chemicals" as the main culprit of obesity: "The endocrine system is typically thought to comprise the glands and pathways that emit hormones, for example, the thyroid, pituitary, and the hypothalamus glands. *Endocrine disruption* thus entails interference with the action of these hormones" (2011: 101, original emphasis). Guthman starts by discussing the complex genetic pathways to obesity, which appear as multiple and interactive (96). But she critiques the attempt to elevate genetic predisposition to explain obesity, as doing so may "reinscribe the idea that race is biological" (97).

For Guthman, a geographer, it is important to think of place and how neoliberalism has "embodied" its diet in people: "It is critical to think about the body as a site where the biological and the social constantly remake each other. . . . This is true even for *class, the most indisputably social of all categories of difference*" (2011:97, emphasis added). Different classes have had differentiated exposures to "labor regimes, toxins, health care, diseases, nutrients and so forth" (98). Some of these exposures may involve intergenerational genetic changes through "epigenetic" effects that have been appreciated only since the 1990s. Epigenetics has to do with heritable changes in gene expression, that is, whether a specific gene is active, without necessarily changing the underlying DNA sequence. Similar BMI increases for black and white women, for instance, open the possibility of a shared source of change: class status (Guthman 2011:99). As Guthman puts it, endocrine-disruptive chemicals "can interfere with genetic expression in ways that permanently transform bodily form and function, and these changes can be passed on to offspring. Epigenetics could thus account for the genetic contribution of the abrupt increase in obesity" (102).

A downside of Guthman's argument on epigenetics is that she simply denies—without evidence—that people are eating more: "Empirically, the presumption that since 1980 people have been taking in more calories relative to those they expend has simply not been demonstrated" (2011:93). But data from FAOSTAT, the statistical database of the UN Food and Agriculture Organization (FAO), indicate that average per capita daily food caloric consumption in the United States was 3,178 kilocalories in 1980, reached a peak of 3,828 kilocalories in 2005, then declined to 3,682 kilocalories by 2013 (FAOSTAT 2017a). This represents a 16 percent increase between 1980 and 2013. Unless greater caloric consumption is compensated by more height, the BMI will increase.

Guthman helpfully points to environmental toxins that act as obesogens, but in vigorously seeking to discredit the energy-balance model, she falsely denies that the available evidence demonstrates an increase in dietary-energy consumption. Although she falters in studying obesity and social justice, probably because of the influence she has accepted from social constructionism, her structural explanations are welcome.

The most obvious reasons for the success of processed foods are that they are cheap and palatable for consumers and highly profitable for distributors. Winson refers to the business advantage by using the concept of "differential profit": "Where foodstuffs are very highly commoditized, some food and beverage products attract higher returns, or profits, for their sellers than others" (2013:190). PepsiCo's Frito-Lay products represented only 1 percent of US supermarket sales in 1998 but accounted for about 11 percent of operating profits and 40 percent of profit growth for the average supermarket in the same year (Winson 2013:191). Still, Michael Moss finds, industrial food can be sold very cheaply to final consumers: "The average kid who walked through the doors of these stores [in 2012] . . . scooped up chips, candy, and a sugary drink that came to 360 calories—all for just $1.06" (2013:343). A former executive of Pillsbury admits, "We're hooked on inexpensive food, just like we're hooked on cheap energy. . . . It costs more money to eat fresher, healthier foods. And so, there is a huge economic issue involved in the obesity problem. It falls most heavily on those who have the fewest resources and probably the least understanding or knowledge of what they are doing" (James Behnke, cited in Moss 2013:341). The 2008 financial crisis proved to be a boon for large parts of the food industry, "as shoppers pinching their pennies find it easier to buy soda, snacks and frozen entrees than more costly groceries, like fresh fruits and vegetables" (Moss 2013:108n). While there is no scientific consensus on the matter, a growing literature documents the addictive nature of sugar and the many foods with added sugar. Nora Volkow, who directed the National Institute on Drug Abuse, says that "processed sugar in certain individuals produces compulsive patterns of intake" and that overeating is as difficult to overcome as some drug addictions (in Moss 2013:342).

Thus, if larger social-structural and political forces are at work, among them inequality and agricultural subsidies, the point of intervention will be quite different. It takes a societal actor like the state to modify which agricultural products become the raw materials that shape food choices in the first place. I argue that social structure and not individual choice is the locus where interventions should be made. The main foci should be ameliorating social inequality and reshaping the system of agrifood production.

The individual consumption focus has been causally articulated by the UN Special Rapporteur on the Right to Food as follows: "The food we eat determines how we produce food" (De Schutter 2009:11). Many observers in critical food studies, including Pollan and Nestle, have followed the same view of taking the individual as the main agent or point of intervention to modify eating "one meal at a time" or by "voting with your fork." This is an illusion.

In this book, I suggest a different possibility about causality and points of intervention. In general, structural change in food choices will require broad policy change as a needed ingredient. I argue that food choices are structurally conditioned by income and wealth inequality and that we eat what oligopolistic food producers and distributors have on offer. The roots of social inequality are varied and include class, gender, and racial/ethnic constructions of difference. Income inequality in particular has been growing in the United States and other nations since the 1980s, which coincides with the neoliberal turn in the development model. Given data availability, I examine primarily income inequality and how it affects food consumption choices.

Guthman makes the point forcefully against the individual focus that is so prevalent in the literature: "I don't harbor the fantasy that individual, yuppified, organic, slow food consumption choices are the vehicles to move toward a more just and ecological way of producing and consuming food. To the contrary, I think that structures of inequality must necessarily be addressed so that others may eat well" (2007b:263). Therefore, to stem obesity, state interventions need to refocus on reducing social inequality and the societal determinants of food production and distribution.

Income inequality as well as food production and distribution are in turn shaped or facilitated by neoliberal state intervention. There is an intrinsic hypocrisy in wealthy nations, especially the United States, preaching free trade and keeping the state from intervening in the economy while giving agricultural subsidies. At the same time, many developing nations have been pressured to adopt policy recommendations of the International Monetary Fund that are meant to keep state intervention from subsidizing agriculture, while the World Bank promotes so-called nontraditional agricultural exports so those nations' foreign debts can be paid (Robinson 2008).

Reforming these structures could allow people to have affordable nutritional choices that are ecologically sustainable. Transcending individualistic and consumption-oriented approaches will help us appreciate that the state under bottom-up pressure from social movements is best positioned to implement change when it comes to food "choices" and production. Throughout the book, I use "the state" in a strict sense, to refer to what Antonio Gramsci (1971) calls "political society," the sphere of domination or the institutions of government. But Gramsci's expanded state also includes civil society, the sphere of hegemony or consent made up by private associations, unions, social movements, the family, churches, and so forth. The progressive sectors of civil society must mobilize to exert pressure on the state for it to become a societal actor in the wider public interest.

THE NEOLIBERAL DIET DEFINED

I set out to uncover the socioeconomic and political forces behind the production of processed, energy-dense foods that largely make up the neoliberal diet. Such foods were originally developed in the United States in the 1940s. It should be clarified that some foods like nuts and dried fruits also qualify as "energy dense" based on the calories per gram they contain, but I use the term primarily regarding processed foods. Covering this diet in 1998, a documentary from the PBS program *Frontline* is titled *Fat*. One snippet features Walter Willett, then chair of Harvard's Department of Nutrition, pointing the finger at food companies as the main culprits for the new health impacts of industrially processed food: "The transition of food to being an industrial product really has been a fundamental problem.... First, the actual processing has stripped away the nutritional value of the food. Most of the grains have been converted to starches. We have sugar in concentrated form, and many of the fats have been concentrated and then, worst of all, hydrogenated, which creates trans-fatty acids with very adverse effects on health" (in PBS 1998).

At least a few insiders in the food industry are well aware of the industry's role in promoting an unhealthful diet. Speaking to prominent food industry executives in 1999, Michael Mudd, a major adviser to Kraft's chief executive officer, warned them about the problem of child obesity. By that time half of

American adults were already considered overweight, and nearly a quarter—forty million—could be clinically defined as obese (Moss 2013:xvi). The US Department of Agriculture (USDA) promoted what it deemed healthful eating through its food pyramid, with grains at the base and far smaller quantities of sweets and fat squeezed into the top. Mudd told executives they were promoting "the *opposite* habits." He said, "We cannot pretend food isn't part of the obesity problem. No credible expert will attribute the rise in obesity solely to decreased physical activity" (in Moss 2013:xvii, emphasis by Moss). Through massive marketing campaigns, Nestle has argued, "the food industry changed society in ways that encourage us to eat more food, more often, in more places" (2013:xiv). Companies have gone to such lengths to defend their right to market industrial food that they even invoke their "First Amendment [free speech] right to market to children and to self-regulate rather than be regulated by government" (Nestle 2013:397).

Notably, ultraprocessed food has grown increasingly common since the 1970s. A 2012 study based on a 2001 national-level representative sample of households in Canada shows that almost two thirds (61.7 percent) of dietary energy came from ultraprocessed foods. This diet exceeds the World Health Organization's "upper limits for fat, saturated fat, free sugars and salt density, with less fibre than recommended" (Moubarac et al. 2012:2240).

A study of seventy-nine countries of varying income levels reveals several trends about the consumption of ultraprocessed foods. First, their consumption accounted for well over 50 percent of dietary energy in such high-income countries as Canada and the United States and more than 25 percent in upper-middle-income countries such as Brazil (Monteiro et al. 2013). Second, while the consumption of some ultraprocessed foods like soft drinks may have plateaued or peaked in high-income countries, the rate of increase in consumption in upper-middle-income countries was faster. These data confirm that the most processed components of the neoliberal diet are becoming globalized by a small, oligopolistic group of food-manufacturing multinational corporations (Monteiro et al. 2013; Popkin and Hawkes 2016).

There is thus the issue of intense concentration of market power by agri-food producers and distributors (P. Howard 2016). In the early 1970s, chickens were raised by thousands of farmers who supplied thousands of local and regional plants throughout the United States. In the twenty-first century, Nestle reports, "just a few gigantic corporations control every aspect of chicken production, from egg to grocery store" (2010:44). The concentration no doubt closely parallels the worldwide growth in chicken production that Tony Weis describes: "Chickens accounted for almost 53 billion of the more than 60 billion animals slaughtered in 2009, in comparison to 1.3 billion pigs

TABLE I.1. US and world changes in poultry meat production, 1961–2014, by animals slaughtered

	1961	1983	2014	% CHANGE 1961–1983	% CHANGE 1983–2014	% CHANGE 1961–2014
USA	2,366,872	4,496,170	8,938,222	90	99	278
World	7,014,581	21,534,133	66,234,895	207	208	844

Source: Constructed with data from FAOSTAT 2017b.

and 300 million cattle" (2013a:70). Meat can be regarded as one of the main processed foods of the neoliberal food regime, and the numbers involved are staggering, as Weis has shown:

> The average person on earth consumed 42 kg of meat in 2009, almost double the per capita world average in 1961 (23 kg), along with twice the eggs (from 5 to 10 kg). This transformation must also be set against the fact that human population leapt from three to seven billion over this time, which translates into a four-fold increase in world meat and egg production in a mere half-century. Amidst rising volumes, the relative share of total meat production that is internationally traded has also crept steadily upwards over the past century, from 5 to 13 percent. (2013a:67)

Meat production for export has expanded even in countries with food insecurity such as India, the leading exporter of beef (Winders 2017:157). Feeding those who suffer from hunger, Bill Winders points out (2017), is generally not as profitable as exporting to wealthy markets. By my calculation with data from FAOSTAT, as shown in table I.1, poultry meat increased the most in the United States and worldwide, even though meat from sheep and goats still was the meat most consumed in the world. Increases in meat consumption result from population growth but also from greater per capita consumption.

Behind the production of meat are the main raw materials to produce it: soybeans and corn, usually transgenic. The expansion in global meat production increased the demand for feed grains, as supply management policies were being phased out in the United States (Winders 2017). As a policy, the main goal of supply management was to "reduce production and raise prices by paying farmers to limit their production" (Winders 2017:37). During the 1920s, supply management had several stakeholders whose interests did not necessarily align. Hence it failed repeatedly, even when the government's goal was to support farmers. The government purchased surpluses to sell on the international market at world prices, and it protected domestic prices for farmers by imposing tariffs on imports even though consumers could be affected (Winders 2017:37). It was only in the Franklin D. Roosevelt administration that enough pressure from below generated the political will at the top to shape a proper supply management policy to defend farmers and working-class consumers; a coalition of the Left pushed government in the direction of protecting the popular sectors nationally (Winders 2017: 38). Internationally, however, such arrangements led to a surplus regime by which the US government tried to systematically dispose of grains on the world market in the 1940s and later; Winders has labeled this "the US food regime" (2009, 2012). The term may be appropriate in highlighting the nation whose policies have had a heavily determining role in the overall dynamic of capital accumulation. US policy has had that effect in the world economy, but other dynamics are in play as well.

Grains from the US regime of the 1940s to 1980s were destined largely for livestock feed rather than direct human consumption. The push to produce soybeans and corn fostered production of genetically modified (GM) or transgenic seeds by the 1990s. The US regime ultimately resulted in more demand for grains, greater supply, and the need to dispose of surpluses. With trade liberalization in the 1980s into the 1990s, there was broader adoption of GM seeds. By 2014 between 80 percent and 94 percent of US agricultural land surface was devoted to transgenic crops—soybeans, corn, and cotton (Winders 2017:113). Production on this technological basis grew 100 percent for maize and 200 percent for soybeans (Winders 2017:134). Crops of coarse grains, soybeans, and rapeseed (canola) grown for livestock took up one third of the world's harvested land area in 2009 (Schneider 2014). The global area in feed crops has expanded 30 percent since the 1960s; the area in maize has doubled, the area in soy has quadrupled, and the diversion of maize and soy for livestock feed has doubled (Schneider 2014). China imported 69 million tons of soybeans in 2013; that was 64 percent of global soy trade, mostly from Brazil and the United States. Imported soybeans accounted for 85 percent of domestic consumption, primarily for livestock feed, that year in China (Oliveira and Schneider 2014:5). Markets for rice and wheat are much more competitive than for feed grains and less subject to genetic modification, which farmers have resisted (Winders 2017).

Industry concentration, as calculated by economists, is the degree of competitiveness of a given industry. In standard economic theory, competitive industries offer lower prices; conversely, in more concentrated industries prices are skewed in favor of businesses and toward a disadvantage to consumers. A common indicator of concentration is the CR4, the concentration ratio or market share controlled by the top four firms in an industry. As Philip H. Howard (2016:7) puts it, "When four firms control 40 percent or 50 percent of the market it is no longer competitive." Howard's 2016 study of concentration in the food industry offers the CR4 for numerous sectors of the industry; I present a selection of them in table I.2.

Concentration in the agrifood industry is more pronounced than in most other economic sectors (P. Howard 2016). A study reported in *The Economist* found that of more than nine hundred economic sectors, two thirds were more concentrated in 2012 than in 1997: "The weighted average [market] share of the total held by the leading four firms in each sector rose from 26% to 32%" (O'Sullivan 2016:15). A traditional yardstick for excessive industry concentration, or oligopoly, is when four firms control 40 percent or more of the market. For agribusiness, Pollan has found "that percentage is exceeded in beef slaughter (82 percent of steers and heifers), chicken processing (53 percent), corn and soy processing (roughly 85 percent), pesticides (62 percent) and seeds (58 percent)" (2016:44). Furthermore, such concentration is leading to yet more concentration, which worsens inequality. Even the conservative London-based newsweekly *The Economist* (2016) warns, "High profits can deepen inequality in various ways. The pool of income to be split among employees could be squeezed. Consumers might pay too much for goods. In a market the size of America's prices should be lower than in other industrialised economies."

The problem is that the usual mechanisms of competition contained in economics books are no longer working. Adam Smith's invisible hand was presumed to lead new entrepreneurs into sectors that seem profitable and stabilize excessive profits. But in neoliberal capitalism, investment opportunities can arise precisely in markets that are highly concentrated and not competitive. In the same article in *The Economist* (2016), titled "Too Much of a Good Thing," two captains of US industry and finance advise as much: "Jack Welch, the boss of General Electric for two decades at the end of the 20th century, advised companies to get out of markets which they did not dominate. Warren Buffett, the 21st century's best-known investor, extols firms that have a 'moat' around them—a barrier that offers stability and pricing power." This general context of food production greatly shapes the configuration of what people eat, of what is most and least accessible, leading to class-differentiated diets.

The neoliberal diet in my usage consists of the globalization of the US

TABLE I.2. Concentration ratios (CR4) for various years between 2011 and 2014 by the top four firms in food industry markets

FIRM	MARKET SHARE %	FIRM	MARKET SHARE %
US grocery market		*US fast food*	
Walmart	33	McDonald's	18.6
Kroger	9	Yum! (KFC, Pizza Hut, Taco Bell, etc.)	12.6
Safeway	5	Doctor's Associates (Subway)	6.7
Supervalu	4	Wendy's	4.8
	CR4: 51 (p. 20)		CR4: 42.7 (p. 31)
US pork slaughtering		*US beer, 2012*	
Smithfield-Shuanghui	26	Anheuser-Busch InBev	46.4
Tyson	17	MillerCoors	27.6
JBS Swift	11	Crown Imports	5.8
Cargill	9	Heineken USA	14.0
	CR4: 63 (p. 83)		CR4: 83.8 (p. 55)
US bagged salad		*Soybean processors*	
Chiquita/Fresh Express	32.2	Bunge	25.5
Dole	22.2	ADM	21.4
Earthbound Farm	5.8	Cargill	21.2
Ready Pac	4.4	Ag Processing	11.7
	CR4: 64.6 (p. 66)		CR4: 79.8 (p. 74)
Global seeds		*Global pesticides*	
Monsanto (USA)	26	Syngenta (Switzerland)	23.1
DuPont Pioneer (USA)	18.2	Bayer CropScience (Germany)	17.1
Syngenta (Switzerland)	9.2	BASF (Germany)	12.3
Vilmorin/Groupe Limagrain (France)	4.8	Dow AgriSciences (USA)	9.6
	CR4: 58.2 (p. 107)		CR4: 62.1 (p. 107)

Source: Constructed with data compiled from several sources in P. Howard 2016. Page numbers for each industry are given in parenthesis, after the corresponding CR4.

industrial diet. I argue that larger social forces are shaping our food choices; one is accessibility. Not everyone can afford the fruits and vegetables or the time to prepare the foods that are generally regarded as the most healthful. The question of how the neoliberal diet interacts with growing inequality needs to be addressed in each of several countries I discuss and among countries globally. To specify the effects of neoliberal globalism, I give special attention to the international division of labor and trade in food and agriculture between the United States and Mexico, as this type of relation is becoming generalized on a global scale. I thus use the US-Mexico trade relation as the model of neoliberal globalism. The North American Free Trade Agreement (NAFTA) is the mechanism through which Mexico deepened its integration into the North American economy, including Canada. Neoliberal globalism, as ideology and practice, has expanded its reach through several other legal instruments such as the World Trade Organization.

Researchers in North Carolina projected that as of 23 May 2007, for the first time in history, the world's population would be more urban than rural (*ScienceDaily* 2007). Although some food is produced in cities, most of it continues to be produced in the countryside. Food is the most "intimate commodity" (Winson 1992), in that our reproduction as living beings depends on ingesting it and specifically on what we consume. Given market concentration, however, the great majority of humans have lost control over the production of food. A double issue emerges from this condition; one is the near-total lack of control over food production by the vast majority of the population, and the second is that only a very small minority of affluent people have the luxury of actually making choices of what to eat regardless of price. Most people are constrained by their budgets and/or time to eat what they can afford; the most accessible are energy-dense foods that can make them fat (Darmon and Drewnowski 2015).

In whose favor does the state intervene in the era of neoliberal globalism? By most accounts, state regulation (if any) and intervention such as subsidies are meant primarily to enhance the profitability of corporations and rarely to protect citizens. The problem starts in the structure of subsidies that shape agricultural production in the United States and the extent of influence that its agricultural and dietary models have in the world. It is in this nation that modern agriculture and the industrial diet were born and from which they have been diffused throughout the world in the form of the neoliberal diet. The crux of food import dependency is the combination of practicing subsidies and protectionism in the United States and other rich countries with prying open markets in developing countries (Friedmann 1982). Such a process has to do with the larger forces at work in the neoliberal food regime: the set of rules and regulations that account for capital accumulation in agriculture and the food industry. Because these are deeply entrenched structures, it will take social movements to change the character of state intervention in pursuit of the public interest in more healthful food.

Critical food scholars like Pollan (2006, 2008) and Nestle (2006, 2013) and journalists including Andrew Martin (2015), Moss (2013), and Michele Simon (2006) have amply documented how food companies resist any form of state regulation. Instead, "Big Food" promotes self-regulating and leaving it to consumers to decide what is best for them. Any state intervention is portrayed as a manifestation of the "nanny state" and a failure of individual responsibility. The nanny state is presumed to be the converse of individual freedom typical in any liberal democracy. But it so happens that food producers dominate the US agricultural lobby, shaping (non)regulation, support, and subsidies. Although hundreds of businesses are within the food industry, from producers to retailers, they jointly and individually lobby to promote policies that favor their profitability. The US agribusiness lobby spent about $65 million in 2011–2012; hence the interests of agricultural corporations remain heavily represented (Spark 2014:30).

Critical food scholars have done a fantastic job of uncovering how the food industry, to increase sales, promotes flavor at the expense of nutrition. They might thus expect that shaming food companies could enhance the business fashion of becoming good corporate citizens and assuming some corporate social responsibility. Even Walmart's CEO has advocated a "triple bottom line" of social, environmental, and financial aspects as the future of long-term capitalism (McLaughlin and McMillon 2015). This is a fine and respectable aspirational goal. But the reality about capitalist firms competing with each other is that most of them are just doing their jobs for the one bottom line by which they can live or die: maximizing profits in the short term, presumably within legal limits. A study by Rob Moodie and colleagues (2013) considers the rise in sales and promotion of tobacco, alcohol, and ultraprocessed foods globally in the context of rising rates of noncommunicable diseases. The authors address industry self-regulation and ask if transnational corporations, as major drivers of such sales and promotion, should play any role in prevention and control. They examine evidence on the effectiveness, or ineffectiveness, of the common reliance on industry self-regulation or public-private partnerships and of public regulation and market intervention by the state. The authors' resounding response is that "public regulation and market intervention are the only evidence-based mechanisms to prevent harm caused by the unhealthy commodity industries" (Moodie et al. 2013:670).

THE FOOD SYSTEM

We have a double-headed issue here. On one hand there is great inequality that leaves a large majority of the population unable to afford quality, healthful food; on the other hand the food industry has tremendous legal laxity to do as it pleases to maximize profits. By "food industry" I mean not only the producers and distributors of food but also those in the prior, agricultural phase of crop production. Much of the neoliberal diet can ultimately be traced to transgenic crops, the products of genetic engineering such as corn and soybeans, the most subsidized US crops (Pollan 2008:117). Most centrally, though, these crops are subsidized because powerful lobby groups get immense profits from them (Baines 2015; Winders 2009a, b). Agribusiness technology, agricultural policy, and agrifood processing are all inextricably linked in the industrial production of the food "choices" in the neoliberal diet. Ironically, most of the subsidized crops are not even produced for direct human consumption. Rather, they are used to produce livestock or processed food, as is high-fructose corn syrup.

I have examined diet in the larger framework of the neoliberal food regime (Otero 2012, 2013; Otero, Pechlaner, and Gürcan 2013; Pechlaner and Otero 2008, 2010) and the rise of the modern agricultural paradigm (Otero 2008). The food system has been changing around the world rapidly since the 1980s, reflecting changes that started in the United States in the early twentieth century. Central to these changes, called a "revolution" by Thomas Reardon and C. Peter Timmer (2012), is the increasing contribution of industrial processes that food is undergoing. In a simplified form, the food system can be represented as involving the following process:

Inputs → farming → wholesale buying → industrial processing → retail → consumption

Most of the major players in the world's top food and beverage processing firms are headquartered in the United States. In 2015 the ten largest US companies in this sector were, in order of largest sales, PepsiCo, Tyson Foods, Nestlé, JBS USA, Coca-Cola Co., Anheuser-Busch InBev, ConAgra Foods, Kraft Foods, Smithfield Foods Inc., and General Mills. Included in the top twenty are Kellogg Co., Cargill Inc., and Bimbo Bakeries USA, a Mexican multinational corporation (Food Processing 2015). Chandrasekaran and colleagues (2013) present data on Canada.

On a world level the market share of the ten top-selling food processors amounted to 28 percent of the total volume in 2009. With profits of around 15 percent to 20 percent for drink producers, the profit margins are among the highest in the food chain. The large food corporations make their enormous profits particularly by focusing on the expanding middle classes in emerging economies like those of Brazil, China, India, and Indonesia as well as the market segment of expensive branded goods. During the financial crisis of 2007–2009, food processors grew mainly through company acquisitions (Econexus and Berne-Declaration 2013:15). In Brazil, one of the major case studies I address in this book, the food industry's share of gross domestic product (GDP) has remained stable at around 10 percent. But the processing industry's share increased from 16.9 percent in 2004 to 20.2 percent in 2014 (Gomes 2015:2). Industrial food processing is an integral part of the food system. Located in the middle of the food system, food processing as an area of influence reaches other actors in several ways. Soybean processing companies fund farmers by financing the technological input packages, including transgenic seeds, in exchange for their products (Gomes 2015:2; Lapegna 2016).

A substantial and rising share of food in developing countries undergoes some degree of processing. The share of packaged food (a subset of all processed food) in food expenditures is roughly 7 percent in low-income countries, 30 percent in lower-middle-income countries, and 45 percent in upper-middle-income countries. The share of grains in the value added of processed foods varies by countries' income levels as well, but inversely; it is approximately 20 percent in lower-income countries and drops to 15 percent in upper-middle-income countries and lower-middle-income countries. The share of dairy climbs from 7 percent in lower-income countries to 10 to 13 percent in lower- and upper-middle-income countries. Processed meats, fish, fruits, vegetables, fats, and baked goods and noodles make up the rest of the processed food sector value added (Reardon and Timmer 2012:241–242). By 2000 Nestlé had a market share of 61 percent in Latin America for many packaged foods (confectionary, soups, pet food, baby food, dairy, and baked goods) and a market share of 26 percent in eastern Europe. In Brazil that share was 83 percent, while in the Philippines it was 37 percent. Unilever had similar dominance in other markets. Its market share in a set of packaged goods was 38 percent in Poland, 43 percent in Argentina, 37 percent in Indonesia, and 47 percent in South Africa (Reardon and Timmer 2012:452).

On the final link to consumers, when there is a single power as large as Walmart connecting food processors and food consumers, individual consumers are no longer the food-manufacturing industry's most important customer (Wenonah Hauter, cited in Spark 2014:29). The rapid growth of the retail sector globally is resulting in major dietary changes that will affect the food insecure as well as the food secure across rural and urban areas in lower- and middle-income countries. In Mexico City processed foods already make up about 58 percent of food-caloric consumption, compared with 30 percent in China (Popkin 2014).

Since the 1990s there has been heavy concentration of food processors as megamergers have resulted in their consolidation. Arlene Spark (2014) reports that the top four pork processors—Smithfield, Tyson Foods, Swift (JBS–Swift), and Excel (Cargill Meat Solutions)—slaughtered 64 percent of the pork in the United States. Similarly, Cargill, Tyson Foods, JBS, and National Beef slaughtered 81 percent of the beef; more than half of broiler chickens were slaughtered by Tyson Foods, Pilgrim's Pride Corporation, Perdue Farms, and Sanderson Farms (Spark 2014:56). Smithfield is the world's largest pork producer and controls all production stages from growing to slaughtering swine. Archer Daniels Midland is the largest corn producer and processor in the world and the leader in manufacturing high-fructose corn syrup, most of it produced from transgenic corn. These examples demonstrate the big business involved in food processing and the global reach of the corporations. Although it may seem that the variety of food products offered to consumers continues to increase, the reality is that most food is manufactured by a small number of companies.

In terms of value added resulting from a manufacturing process, the food and beverages industries are responsible for the largest shares of GDP in several of the emerging economies I analyze in this book, namely in the BRICS—Brazil, Russia, India, China, and South Africa. If we look at the full agribusiness chains, agriculture, auxiliary industries, and research and development services, we see that the national impact of food and beverage industries is even larger. Ruth Rama (2015) notes that most of the foreign food and beverage affiliates located in the BRICS that year were owned by large companies based in the United States (41 percent), the European Union (27 percent), and Japan (17 percent). BRICS capital accounted for around 4 percent of these foreign food and beverages affiliates. The only country where the presence of EU affiliates surpassed that of US affiliates was Russia. In China, affiliates owned by Japanese companies amounted to 27 percent, considerably more than the 17 percent in the BRICS (Rama 2015:300–301). The most important recipient of foreign food affiliates is China, followed at some distance by Brazil. India, Russia, and South Africa each hosted less than 10 percent of the foreign food affiliates located in the BRICS. Data on the distribution of affiliates provide valuable information on the consolidated position of multinational food firms over the years (Rama 2015).

SOCIAL MOVEMENTS AND STATE INTERVENTION IN BRAZIL

Despite the dominance of oligopolies in the food industry, states can intervene to redirect food production in more equitable and healthful directions. To put some flesh on the production-focused and inequality-alleviating approach proposed here, I outline an example of state policies that were implemented from 2003 to 2016 in Brazil, a large, middle-income country. Brazil's national-level experience came during the Workers Party (Partido dos Trabalhadores, PT) administrations. This was an effort to accomplish just what the Walmart executives proposed (McLaughlin and McMillon 2015): to strengthen smallholder farmers, promote ecological sustainability, and produce more healthful and accessible food for the poor. I must confess that I was hesitant to discuss the Brazilian case after the political events that led to President Dilma Rousseff's impeachment in 2016. Critical observers, including myself, consider the impeachment a coup d'état waged by the political Right based on legal technicalities. It was made possible by Brazil's coalitional electoral system; since their inception, the PT administrations were based on a fragile coalition with a right-of-center party. The coup underscores the fragility of Brazil's accomplishments in poverty reduction and food security, which may now be jeopardized. However, the Brazilian case shows that food systems and inequality are changeable through the political will of the state when it is nudged from below by social movements. One point should be clear, though: political outcomes regarding the food system and inequality are entirely contingent on the balance of social forces.

Two state policies that resulted from the PT's determination to reduce inequality and hunger were Bolsa Família (Family Allowance) and Fome Zero (Zero Hunger). The first program consists of cash transfers to poor families, conditional on sending their children to school; the second is intended to eliminate hunger by, among other measures, enhancing food provisioning at schools in coordination with smallholder farmers. The farmers, in many cases, are former beneficiaries of agrarian reform that resulted from social struggles led by the Movimento dos Trabalhadores Rurais sem Terra (MST, Movement of Landless Workers), the largest social movement in Latin America (Vergara-Camus 2014).

Bolsa Família has had positive effects on school enrollment and retention rates of children as well as completion rates in elementary school (Glewwe and Kassouf 2012). But it is not clear whether expenditures on the program compensate for the increased wages of new workers, which do not seem to be higher than the costs of the program over time. The question needs more research for proper calculation, but another issue is that increased education could also result in lowering the wage premium of education in the long term. Overall, there is not a clear picture regarding income redistribution. Still, Davide Rasella and colleagues, in a study published in the medical journal *The Lancet*, find that Bolsa Família "can greatly contribute to a decrease in childhood mortality overall, and in particular for deaths attributable to poverty-related causes such as malnutrition and diarrhoea, in a large middle-income country such as Brazil" (Rasella, Aquino, et al. 2013:57).

In another study, Simone Bohn (2011) tests the hypothesis that the former president Luiz Inácio Lula da Silva's government used Bolsa Família as a clientelistic, vote-getting strategy. Bohn's study disconfirms this critical view of the PT and shows instead that "poor voters vote differently across regions; BF recipients were already Lula voters in 2002 and cast ballots for him during his reelection at the same rate as nonrecipients" (Bohn 2011:54). Other researchers have found a negative correlation between Bolsa Família and crime: "Schools with a higher number of students between ages 16 and 17 in 2006 experienced larger declines in crime in 2008 and 2009, when the CCT [conditional cash transfer] coverage was expanded to include these age groups" (Chioda, Mello, and Soares 2016:15).

In his book about Fome Zero, Aaron Ansell (2014) confirms that most studies he reviewed conclude that both Fome Zero and Bolsa Família contributed strongly to reducing inequality and hunger. In a critique from the Left co-authored by the MST's spokesperson Joao Pedro Stédile and Horacio Martins de Carvalho (2011), the authors argue that while hunger was reduced, its causes were not, so people continue to go hungry. Reflecting on the politics of these programs, other scholars have found two main accomplishments: the broadening of participation vertically and the communication across communities horizontally (Sonnino, Lozano Torres, and Schneider 2014). Broader participation from the bottom up enhances the likelihood of promoting progressive policies centered on food production and redistribution.

Hannah Wittman and Jennifer Blesh (2017) have studied the involvement of resource-poor farmers in the Brazilian state of Mato Grosso. Those farmers who participated in public procurement programs that promoted Fome Zero favorably evaluated the program's influence on their transition to agroecology and their household well-being. Agroecology is a type of agricultural production that transcends the modern agricultural paradigm to make food production sustainable. A key point of agroecology is studying, designing, managing, and evaluating agricultural systems to make them productive while they also conserve resources. Interviews with actors along the food system reveal the potential for these programs to achieve goals related to food-system sustainability and social equity. Wittman and Blesh view this case as a model of innovation (within a highly unsustainable agricultural matrix) that can inform the scaling up of the larger and more ambitious food sovereignty program. Food sovereignty involves the right of peoples to healthful food that is culturally appropriate and ecologically sustainable. In the authors' view, much needs to be done to untangle critical bottlenecks in infrastructure and transaction costs before public food procurement programs can be considered a viable and scalable solution to global food crises. But these efforts are a start in articulating government procurement with smallholder farmers while addressing food inequality issues.

Finally, a study by Corinna Hawkes and collaborators (2016) describes the Brazilian government's policy efforts to coordinate school feeding and turn it into law in 2009 requiring a minimum of 30 percent of school food purchases from local family farmers. The authors evaluate the experience from 2009 to 2014 and conclude that about half the municipalities complied at least partially. Much research remains to be done on whether food sovereignty, strengthening of local farmers, and most importantly, nutrition goals have been met. Clearly, however, transcending the individual focus of intervention requires that social movements and the state as well as large supermarket chains collaborate on the mode of producing food and reducing income inequality.

These advancements are important, as they show how social movements from below can make their mark. But it is also necessary to put the optimism into perspective by assessing the antagonistic social forces. In Renata Motta's book *Social Mobilization, Global Capitalism, and Struggles over Food* (2016), she analyzes how the PT slowly capitulated to the *bancada ruralista*, the members of Brazil's Congress who are predominantly controlled by large-scale rural landholders. She shows how the governments of the PT, while providing food access to subaltern classes, did not change (and rather deepened) the neoliberal structures of food production in Brazil. With all its limitations, nonetheless, the Brazilian case shows that a change of focus into production and redistribution is possible, viable, and achievable.

Society's big challenge is thus to push for changes in state policies in a progressive direction. Whereas policies have primarily promoted the interests of large agribusiness corporations, the point now is to steer state intervention toward promoting agricultural and food production that enhances public health. Such a shift requires nothing short of strong social movements from below, of the type that seems to be building to convince governments to fight climate change. Climate change is perhaps the biggest challenge for humanity, but overweight and obesity are issues that also threaten the reproduction of healthy human beings; the present generation of children may have lower life expectancies than their parents. In both cases, powerful socioeconomic and political forces must be confronted to fundamentally change their ways.

ORGANIZATION OF THIS BOOK

My overall analytical strategy in this book is to zoom in and out from theory into empirical evidence or from lower geographical scales into larger ones. The goal is to gain greater understanding of the structural forces at work in shaping food production and consumption, driven primarily by agribusiness multinationals (ABMs) originating in the United States. Chapter 1 sets up the analytical and theoretical parameters of the book, including the rise of the modern agricultural paradigm and the neoliberal food regime. I outline four main dynamic elements in this food regime: neoregulation, a new form of state intervention that facilitates the dominance of agribusiness multinationals; ABMs as the dominant economic actors, with strong competitive advantages over others; biotechnology as the key technological form in the neoliberal food regime; and supermarkets, which since the 1990s have gone global in gaining larger shares of the food distribution system.

Chapter 2 elaborates on the state-determined aspects of the neoliberal food regime. "Deregulation" has been a buzzword used by observers on the Right and the Left since the start of the neoliberal turn in the 1980s. I argue that in contrast to deregulation, the concept of neoregulation underpins the neoliberal food regime based on a specific form of state intervention that facilitates the domination of agribusiness multinationals, or ABMs. While state intervention has in fact resulted in a withdrawal of the state from direct action in the economy, it nevertheless continues to be a key actor. In the chapter I discuss how the US state promoted specific legislative innovations with the goal of entrenching the protection and private ownership of intellectual property rights. This was a condition for biotechnology companies to thrive in the global economy. Legislative changes from the neoliberal era represent neoregulation at the suprastate level and in Canada, the United States, and Mexico.

The debate on obesity in the United States between individual and structural perspectives is discussed in chapter 3. The question is whether addressing overweight and obesity involves primarily how individuals choose their food or what food is produced in the first place. Siding with the structural explanation of obesity, I offer a detailed analysis of the evolution of the US diet since 1961 based on macrodata from the UN's FAOSTAT database. I consult FAOSTAT mainly because it uses official information from most countries in the world. I present comparative data on countries in later chapters; FAO provides useful estimates calculated in the same way for all countries, making this single source the best for appreciating global agrifood trends. I then analyze income inequality and food consumption based on official US data from the Bureau of Labor Statistics Consumer Expenditure Survey for 1972–1973, 1984, 1994, 2004, and 2014. This analysis highlights divergent class diets by showing that upper-income classes can afford an increasing diversity of luxury foods (meats, fruits, and vegetables), while lower- and middle-income classes are exposed to energy-dense diets based on sugars and vegetable oils. Illustrated in figures, the analysis splits the US population into five income quintiles and shows how each 20 percent spends on various types of food. The conclusion is straightforward: lower-income classes have decreasing access to higher-quality foods, and higher-income classes' diets are more diversified and nutritious. The data confirm many studies linking socioeconomic status with overweight and obesity, but they are offered on a national scale for multiple years so that the tendency toward the neoliberal diet's class divergence becomes quite clear.

Chapter 4 moves out from the United States into the international division of labor in the NAFTA region as a model of what further globalization may look like. North America is the first world region to experience substantial economic integration of two advanced economies with a developing country that began well before the implementation of NAFTA. The question is to what extent Canada, Mexico, and the United States have converged toward similar diets or in what ways they have diverged, if at all. My core argument, which I demonstrate with empirical macrodata from FAOSTAT and the USDA, is that NAFTA nations have experienced a class-differentiated convergence roughly mimicking what has happened in the United States, where upper-income classes are accessing more diversified luxury foods while lower- and middle-income classes are seeing more energy-dense fare in their diets.

Looking into the one developing country of NAFTA, I ask in chapter 5 how Mexico's countryside was affected by NAFTA and neoliberal globalization and what the working conditions have been for displaced migrants in US and Canadian agriculture. Mexico's asymmetrical integration into the North American economy, combined with neoliberalism, had a detrimental impact on its food self-sufficiency and labor sovereignty. These processes resulted in substantially greater outmigration. The main argument is that food self-sufficiency is the condition for a nation to also enjoy labor sovereignty—a nation's ability to provide living wages for a majority of the population. Of the three NAFTA nations, Mexico is the least self-sufficient in food and hence the one that has economically expelled the highest proportion of migrants. While most migrants to Canada enter that country as part of state-sponsored guest worker programs, the lion's share of migrants going to the United States do so as unauthorized workers. This imbalance raises significant issues of labor rights, discrimination, and exclusion in the United States. An overview of migration debates and working conditions reveals the precarious nature of work in agriculture. A North American union with free labor mobility that might enhance working conditions for all seems like a distant solution to these issues. Hence, in the meantime it is indispensable that Mexico restore its labor sovereignty, which will also require regenerating its food self-sufficiency and its countryside.

Leaving the NAFTA region, in chapter 6 I expand the discussion to a set of emerging nations (Brazil, China, India, Mexico, and Turkey) in comparison with the two traditional agroexporting powers of North America—Canada and the United States. One of my main goals in this chapter is to empirically test an argument made by Philip McMichael, that countries in the North and South become "mutually dependent" in food (2009a:287). Using FAOSTAT data from 1985 onward, I introduce a required nuance into his statement by showing that countries with the most neoliberal policies are the ones that have become dependent on the importation of basic foods. The wholehearted adoption of the free trade mantra of neoliberal discourse has exposed developing countries to increasing their exports to and imports from wealthier nations. My proposition is that the emerging countries that have resisted all-out neoliberal reform since the 1980s have retained significant levels of food self-sufficiency. Mexico, which fully adopted neoliberalism, has become the most dependent. Canada and the United States, in contrast, have become only minimally dependent on the importation of some luxury foods, such as fresh fruits, vegetables, and alcoholic beverages. My conclusion is that trade in the neoliberal food regime has resulted in a mutual but uneven and combined dependency.

Using the structural insights from previous chapters, in chapter 7 I set out to measure the risk of exposure to the neoliberal diet. I start with the acknowledgment that obesity is a complex factor that has multiple causes, including medical, genetic, and socioeconomic factors. Once I establish this multiple causality, I present the central socioeconomic causes that can be linked to the risk of exposure to energy-dense diets. The goal is to present a country-level index that measures this risk across time within each country and comparatively across countries. The neoliberal diet risk (NDR) index is a composite of five subindices. I offer NDR index measurements for eight emerging countries. Indonesia, Russia, and South Africa are added to those mentioned in chapter 6, plus Canada and the United States.

In the conclusion I wrap up the discussion on the neoliberal diet and its relation to obesity in theoretical and substantive terms. Because the socioeconomic causes of obesity lie well beyond individual choices, I outline the conditions for popular democratic empowerment to change those underlying causes. For better or worse, it will take much more than well-intended corporate or state policies from the top to modify the conditions for people as individuals to eat more healthful food. It will take social movements from the bottom up to change state policies that shift what is produced in agriculture. Social movements, however, are complex phenomena, and even those with popular grassroots constituencies do not necessarily have progressive or social justice goals. They may have complex relations with the state, which can easily co-opt and neutralize them. I look into such complexity, as concerted state policies will be needed to reduce or eliminate inequality so that healthful food becomes universally accessible.

CHAPTER 1

The Neoliberal Food Regime and Its Crisis

THE DYNAMIC FACTORS

Transgenic crops, the product of advanced genetic engineering techniques based on recombinant DNA, started to be commercialized in the mid-1990s. Since well before their commercialization, biotechnology in general and transgenic crops in particular have been touted as miraculous innovations (Cage 2008; J. Lee 2008; F. Harvey and Parker 2008; Russel and Hakim 2016); if only given a chance, they would make deserts bloom and do away with world hunger. The intensity of these assertions has not been tempered by the fact that most transgenic crops are not even intended for direct human consumption. Transgenic crops are sold in volatile global markets as raw materials to produce livestock feed, agrofuels, cooking oil, and sweeteners, among other products. The crops are grown in enormous, industrial, monocropping operations that amount to two thirds of global food production with biotechnology; predominant among them are soybeans, cotton, canola, and corn, which accounts for a fourth of all transgenic crops. A 2016 study by the National Academies of Science based on twenty years of implementation of transgenic crops concludes that there is no yield advantage to them, nor have they diminished the use of agrochemicals (Russel and Hakim 2016).

If a food regime is the articulation of a set of regulations and institutions making the accumulation of capital possible and stable in agriculture, the global food price inflation crisis of 2008 likely exposed the food regime's contradictions. The inflation crisis arrived after well over a century of declining food prices (Moore 2010) that made food, particularly the neoliberal diet, broadly accessible. Although the long-term trend in food prices was downward, there were a few fluctuations. Prices rose after World War II because of food shortages, in the 1970s because of oil price inflation, and in the mid-1990s. Since 1996, agricultural production of transgenics has expanded, but the narrow range of such crops is being fought over by economic agents with varying and antagonistic interests. Their clash is at the root of the crisis; I pay particular attention to the role of biotechnology. To understand what is behind the crisis we must also disentangle the central features of the neoliberal food regime: What are its principal dynamic factors, and how can they be modified to resolve the crisis in a progressive manner?

Four key dynamic factors of the neoliberal food regime are the state, which provides the political, legislative, and policy context through neo-regulation; agribusiness multinational corporations as the driving economic actors; biotechnology as the main technological form chosen to expand profitability for agribusiness firms; and supermarkets, which are increasingly becoming the dominant food distributors across the globe. I give special attention to biotechnology for two reasons; it has been the technology with the fastest adoption rate in the history of modern agriculture, and two of the four main crops produced with transgenic seeds—corn and soybeans—play a central role in the neoliberal food regime. Both crops could be designated as "flexible" in that they can have a variety of uses (Borras, Franco et al. 2015). Corn can be produced for direct human consumption, but most is used as livestock feed for meat, ethanol for biofuel, or high-fructose corn syrup, a ubiquitous ingredient in sweetened soft drinks, confectionary, and many other processed foods.

Overall, I argue that biotechnology is the continuation of the modern agricultural paradigm that started with the petrochemical, mechanical, and hybrid-seed revolution of the 1930s. This paradigm has also been called "intensive industrial agriculture" (S. Wolf and Buttel 1996).

NEOLIBERAL GLOBALISM AND INEQUALITY

To many readers, the word "neoliberal" will immediately evoke inequality. In case it does not, I will offer a brief discussion of the causal connection of the two concepts and their empirical realities. Let us start by defining what the word "neoliberal" is all about, as a concept that is increasingly used in the scholarly field of epidemiology with at least two meanings. In the political economy perspective, I use "neoliberal" to refer to the growing prominence of energy-dense diets and the political and economic actors involved in their promotion. Then there are "Foucauldian governmentality perspectives" that see neoliberalism as encouraging "the individual to take responsibility for his or her health by consuming more fruits and vegetables" (Bell and Green 2016:240). It has been argued that neoliberalism, or neoliberalization, involves both realms and even others. It is an ideology, a set of policies and programs, distinctive institutional forms, and a complex of normative conceptions of agency that consider individuals responsible for their own food choices (Schreker 2016:477).

Dani Rodrik (2017), an economist at Harvard, argues that neoliberalism has ultimately failed because of its bad economics. It has been closely associated with financial deregulation, which led to the crash of 2008, and to economic globalization and the proliferation of free trade agreements. The main emphasis has been on policy prescriptions for economic growth. But the emphasis on economics, argues Rodrik, sacrifices values such as equality, social inclusion, democratic deliberation, and justice. In another opinion article, Rodrik (2016) contends that "the elimination of barriers to trade and finance became an end in itself, rather than a means toward more fundamental economic and social goals. Societies were asked to subject domestic economies to the whims of global financial markets; sign investment treaties that created special rights for foreign companies; and reduce corporate and top income taxes to attract footloose corporations."

For the purposes of this book, neoliberal globalism consists of the ideology and practice that propose that the best way to achieve human welfare is through freedom and entrepreneurial abilities, all within a framework characterized by solid property rights, free markets, and free trade (D. Harvey 2005:2). The defining characteristic of neoliberalism is its reliance on market-based arrangements and norms in the interest of monopoly capitalism through active use of state power (Peck 2010). The withdrawal of direct state intervention in the economy is also essential for neoliberal globalism to allow the private sector to take hold of resource allocation through the market, presumably in a more efficient manner. The state has even played a critical role in the move toward financialization in agriculture (Clapp 2014).

Inequality has long been a concern in sociology (McAdam and Kloos 2014; Therborn 2013; Tilly 1998; Tomaskovic-Devey and Lin 2011) and a growing concern in economics in the 2010s, owing in part to the eruption of the Occupy Wall Street movement in 2011 in New York City and several major cities around the rich world (Atkinson 2015; Galbraith 2012; Piketty 2014; Stiglitz 2013). The most influential of these books has no doubt been Thomas Piketty's *Capital in the Twenty-First Century* (2014), with the rare distinction of becoming an academic bestseller on several top lists (Antonio 2014). Its earned influence derives from Piketty's elegant model and the most extensive and systematic data ever compiled on inequality in several rich countries — Britain and France but also Sweden and the United States.

Piketty's model is contained in the inequality of $r > g$, where r = the rate of return on capital, and g = the rate of economic growth. When r exceeds g, the trend is toward deepening inequality (Piketty 2014:27). That trend has continued generally since early capitalism in 1700; it gained momentum in the latter part of the nineteenth century but lessened with considerable redistribution after World War II. Since the 1980s, however, inequality is intensifying once again: "The fact that the return on capital is distinctly and persistently greater than the growth rate is a powerful force for a more unequal distribution of wealth" (Piketty 2014:361).

Piketty's conceptualization of capital differs in important ways from Karl Marx's (1977) even while arriving at somewhat similar conclusions. Marx built his critique of capital and capitalism on its exploitative nature; Piketty's critique is a moral one founded on the traditional capitalist and democratic values of the French and American Revolutions. One may or may not like the specific strand of economic thinking to which Piketty subscribes, institutionalist historical political economy, yet he supports his model well with massive empirical analysis in explaining inequality trends and reality. Given the centrality of his work, I will briefly sum up his main insights and data on the rise of neoliberalism and a renewed trend toward deepening inequality. I should clarify that Piketty does not use the concept of neoliberalism but clearly refers to its content in my usage.

It all started in the late 1970s and early 1980s with the rise to power of Margaret Thatcher in Britain and Ronald Reagan in the United States. They both promised to roll back the welfare state protections that emerged in the 1930s and were consolidated after World War II. The welfare state "had allegedly sapped the animal spirits of Anglo-Saxon entrepreneurs," so they set out to "return to pure nineteenth-century capitalism, which would allow the United States and Britain to regain the upper hand" (Piketty 2014:98). Perhaps the central feature of rolling back the welfare state was twofold: drastically reducing the top rates of income taxes while keeping wealth taxes low, and countering greater state indebtedness by cutting social expenditures

(138–139). In the United States, data compiled by the Federal Reserve for 2010–2011 indicate that the top decile, the richest 10 percent of the population, "own 72 percent of America's wealth, while the bottom half claim just 2 percent" (257).

Estimates for global inequality in the early 2010s were even more dire, similar to that of nineteenth-century Europe, says Piketty: "The top thousandth seems to own nearly 20 percent of total global wealth today, the top centile about 50 percent, and the top decile somewhere between 80 and 90 percent. The bottom half of the global wealth distribution undoubtedly owns that [sic] less than 5 percent of total global wealth" (2014:438).

So, what's wrong with inequality, if anything? Is it not merely a reflection that some people are working harder than others and that entrepreneurs, for instance, are adequately rewarded for their innovativeness and risk taking? The trouble is that inequality raises questions about the entire normative or value edifice of capitalism and democracy. French and US societies are founded on values that invoke equality as a central principle. Piketty convincingly argues that twenty-first century inequality far exceeds any rational justification of fairness. The US Declaration of Independence "asserts that everyone has an equal right to the pursuit of happiness" (Piketty 2014:479), while Article 1 of France's Declaration of the Rights of Man and the Citizen proclaims equal rights and prescribes that social distinctions be based only on "common utility" (479). Political democracies that do not also democratize their economies are inherently unstable, says Piketty, quoting British philosopher Bertrand Russell; they become plutodemocracies (508), democracies for the rich.

Inequality is a direct result of the tax cuts started in Anglo-Saxon countries in the late 1970s and early 1980s, and both phenomena are "perfectly correlated," says Piketty, in "the countries where the top earners' share of national income has increased the most (especially when it comes to the remuneration of executives of large firms). Conversely, the countries that did not reduce their top tax rates very much saw much more moderate increases in the top earners' share of national income" (2014:509). For Piketty the optimal top tax rate is 80 percent, but he is rather pessimistic that anything like this will be achieved anytime soon — except if there is a war. It was war, not universal suffrage, that gave rise to progressive taxation (514). However, I suggest that social mobilization from below could also hold the potential to nudge the state into progressive taxation and policies.

For now, though, let us see how inequality and neoliberalism have affected food and agriculture through financialization. "Financialization" is a term used in discussions about financial capitalism in the age of neoliberalism, both of which started in the 1980s. Piketty (2014) labels this phase "patrimonial capitalism" because the growth of inequality since the 1980s has had much more to do with regressive distribution based on existing wealth than on entrepreneurialism or productivity. Entrepreneurs are held in especially high regard in the system because of an "irrepressible need of modern democratic societies to make sense of inequality" (444). But in patrimonial capitalism many entrepreneurs become financiers, turning money into more money. A prime example is Bill Gates, who made his initial fortune as an entrepreneur but also enjoyed monopoly rents. He went on to multiply his wealth more than ten times as a financier. So, the patrimony or wealth itself accounts for growing inequality—hence Piketty's suggestion for heavy progressive taxation (493–514).

Geoffrey Lawrence describes how the "so-called 'financialization' of the agrifood sector has involved the intrusion of banks and other financial entities such as private equity firms in the purchase of farmland and the acquisition of food companies" (2014:421). This particular form of intrusion pertains to the productive aspect of the agrifood sector. But other implications have been identified as to whether farmland is seen and utilized, since 2007, as primarily a productive factor or as a source of speculative profits. The latter is increasingly the case with financialization (Fairbairn 2014:777). Furthermore, financialization has encompassed the distributive aspect of food, such as in restructuring the management and organization of retail companies like supermarkets. To the extent that supermarkets become dominant actors in the agrifood sector, they can have a feedback effect on the entire agrifood chain (Burch and Lawrence 2013:247).

Financial leveraging tends to lower the value of capital equity, and financial markets tend to dominate the manufacturing and agricultural industries invaded by the financial speculative logic. Thus, while the state's role in direct financing of agricultural endeavors has diminished since the 1980s, the state has nonetheless been central to promoting agriculture as an investment activity. Sarah Martin and Jennifer Clapp note, "The state, through its various interventions at the intersection of agriculture and finance, has shaped the conditions that today make agriculture an attractive site for investment by private financial actors" (2015:550).

One of the main arguments David Harvey makes in the discussion of neoliberalism is that it is a bourgeois project to restore the bourgeoisie's class power. Such power diminished during the postwar Keynesian years, when the welfare state developed and inequality declined. The welfare state conferred a greater purchasing power to working classes in that era, also called "Fordism" (D. Harvey 2005).

THE NEOLIBERAL FOOD REGIME

What was the food regime that emerged with neoliberalism in the 1980s and more specifically since the deployment of transgenic crops in the mid-1990s? From Franklin D. Roosevelt's administration to the late 1960s, economic development in the United States was predicated on mass production articulated to mass consumption, with a primary focus on the domestic market. This stage of capitalist development in the United States has been referred to as Fordism, based on Antonio Gramsci's analysis of 1920s mass production, and Taylorism (Gramsci 1971). As elaborated in the 1970s and 1980s in the French Regulation school (Aglietta 1979; Lipietz 1987), Fordism centered on a balance of mass production absorbed by mass consumption. Fordism consisted of a sort of economic pact between the state, unions, and corporations by which workers increased their productivity; its fruits were shared to an important degree with workers both through higher wages and the development of the welfare state. Women and minorities, however, were for the most part excluded from the benefits of Fordism, at least until the rise of the second wave of the feminist movement in the 1960s. Balancing mass production with mass consumption involved low unemployment rates (below 4 percent) until the late 1960s and gross national product (GNP) growth rates of about 5 percent (Otero 1995).

By the late 1960s, Fordism fell into crisis as the United States faced competitive pressures from Germany and Japan. In pursuit of lower costs, the US bourgeoisie searched for increased profits through cheaper labor. A trademark of neoliberalism as a class project has thus been to reduce working-class organizational power. This was achieved through the transfer of manufacturing production from the northern United States to its South starting in the 1970s and to low-wage countries such as Mexico and China through outsourcing in the 1980s.

In 1983 there were 17.7 million unionized workers who made up 20.1 percent of the US workforce, the largest number of them by far in the public sector. By 2016 the number of unionized workers was only 14.6 million, making up 10.7 percent of the US workforce. Public sector workers had a 34.4 percent unionization rate, while those in the private sector had a rate of merely 6.4 percent (BLS 2017a). One of the few remaining union strongholds is among state and municipal employees. Not only are these workers confronting cuts in their pay and benefits; they also are facing the stripping of rights to unionization. This drive has been led by Republican governors in at least seven states, starting with Wisconsin in 2011 (AP 2011).

Furthermore, a recomposition within the bourgeoisie, or capitalist class, took place with the merger of manufacturing, commercial, and financial capitals (D. Harvey 2005:31–36). David Harvey suggests that the divide-and-rule policies of the dominant class must be confronted by a political alliance of progressive forces interested in recovering the local spaces of self-determination (2005:203). The need for such a popular democratic alliance applies centrally to the production of food, which constitutes a fundamental component in working-class reproduction.

In a synthetic article about food and agrarian studies at the end of the twentieth century, Frederick Buttel (2001) observes that with the rise of globalization, the academic fields of the sociology of agriculture and food and the sociology of development were converging. Yet he laments that individual sociologists of agriculture remained specialists in developed country or southern agrifood systems: "Little groundwork has been laid for a sociology of agriculture that addresses simultaneously the agrarian change issues of both North and South" (177). I hope to bridge this gap by comparing several major emerging countries, including Mexico, with the region covering the two wealthier partner countries in NAFTA, Canada and the United States, which are also agroexporting powerhouses.

A good starting point to address the structural question of food production since the 1980s is the food regime perspective. As described by Buttel, "'Regime-type' work has proven to be one of the most durable perspectives in agrarian studies since the late 1980s, in large part because it is synthetic and nuanced." The world system logic of this perspective offers a view of the food regime as not merely an economic phenomenon, but also a political one: "It reflects periodic shifts in hegemonic regimes which are anchored in the politics of how commodity chains and production systems come to be constructed and coordinated over borders and boundaries" (2001:173). Henry Bernstein (2016) provides a rich and detailed critical summary of the food regime analysis that also acknowledges how this perspective has enhanced the study of agrifood systems in a world perspective.

The origin of food regime analysis may be traced to a 1982 article by Harriet Friedmann in which she proposes a way to understand the food crisis that arose after about two decades of stability, from the early 1950s to the early 1970s. The crisis was triggered by the US-Soviet Union trade deal through which a massive amount of US grain was sold to the Soviets. Friedmann develops a conceptual framework of the system that became consolidated in the post-World War II period and was now in crisis. She calls the system an "international world food order" in the 1982 article but renames it a "food regime" in the seminal 1989 article she co-wrote with Philip McMichael. The principal features Friedmann identifies in 1982 are

> (1) surpluses of grain, sustained primarily for domestic political reasons by the American government; (2) American policies, particularly food aid, designed to dispose of these surpluses abroad . . . ; (3) the conse- quent increase of the historically large American share of world grain exports; (4) a consequent downward pressure on world prices and, there- fore, on grain production in other export and import countries; (5) the opening of new grain markets, notably in the underdeveloped world; (6) "cheap food" policies of many Third World governments, encourag- ing the growth of urban populations dependent on food as a commodity; and (7) the resulting contribution to one condition for the penetration of international capital into previously self-sufficient agrarian societies. (Friedmann 1982:S254)

No matter how complex the mechanisms of determination—economic and political, national and international—Friedmann contends, *prices* are the immediate signals that guide and constrain states, enterprises, and individu- als (1982:S254). Therefore, complex mediations in international relations must work through prices, "through changes in relative prices" among coun- tries. And "wheat has been the overwhelmingly important staple food in world commerce throughout modern history" (S254). The most significant contribution of the surplus-producing international food world order com- manded by the United States after World War II was to widen and deepen capitalist relations within the world economy. Such deepening took place by "shifting vastly more of the world's population away from direct access to food and incorporating it instead into food markets" (S255).

For Friedmann (1982), the commodification of food is thus significant in two central ways—by the proletarianization of populations formerly en- gaged in subsistence farming and by extending capitalist relations of pro- duction to former colonies. The second point was crucial in the American strategy of "constructing the free world as an arena for the open flow of goods and capital" (S255). The shift in international power created the con- ditions for new relations between the United States and countries in Africa, Asia, and Latin America (S257). I build on Friedmann's insights about two crucial roots of inequality that affect food production and consumption—the proletarianization of the workforce and the ways developing countries insert themselves, through their states, into the world economy.

A food regime is a temporally specific dynamic in the global political economy of food. It is characterized by particular institutional structures, norms, and unwritten rules around agriculture and food that are geographically and historically specific. These dynamics combine to create a qualitatively distinct regime of capital accumulation trends in agriculture and food; the regime finds its durability in the international linking of agrifood production and consumption relations in accordance with global capital accumulation trends more broadly. Friedmann and McMichael (1989) identify two clearly demarcated food regimes. First was the settler regime throughout the empire of British hegemony that lasted from the 1870s until World War I. It was based on the expansion of the agricultural frontier for capital accumulation, as modern agriculture was not yet present. In a later work, Friedmann explains (2009:127), "The Settler-Colonial food regime thus unfolded via three mutually reinforcing effects of government policy: emigration from Europe, settlement of lands converted from indigenous use to commodity production of European staple foods, and long-distance shipment of low priced wheat and meat."

On the shaping of a global diet, Friedmann indicates that the settler-colonial food regime globalized wheat, primarily for the working class, and meat, which formerly was particularly for the elites. Ordinary people would eat coarse grains like barley, rye, and oats. Eliminating the wide variety of fruits and vegetables that may have once been available to European peasantries compromised their diets' nutritional value. In sum, Friedmann argues, "Workers had more to eat but the quality of their diet declined as white bread, industrial beer, sugared tea and jam, and (to some extent) canned foods, lowered its nutritional content" (2009:127). At least since the first food regime of global food production, therefore, quantity heavy on carbohydrates has been privileged over quality. Sugar, which provides calories empty of nutrients, is a food type that was globalized prior to the first food regime (Mintz 1985).

The second food regime, dominated by the United States, emerged after a transitional period between the two world wars and lasted until the 1970s. This second food regime, as theorized by Friedmann and McMichael (1989), was based on the modern agricultural paradigm that relies on petrochemicals, machinery, and hybrid seeds and has generated surpluses. Friedmann later describes the diet associated with the second regime: "Instead of the form that had characterized human diets for thousands of years, based on a starchy staple complemented by a variety of (mostly) plants providing flavours and proteins, the Mercantile-Industrial food regime introduced a manufactured diet whose main components are fats and sweeteners, supplemented with starches, thickeners, proteins, and synthesized flavours" (2009: 131). The second food regime is "mercantile-industrial" because of its protectionist trend, as "governments set prices and other conditions for domestic farmers, controlled the distribution (and prices) of food to the poor, and managed imports and exports" (129). Such conditions developed in the United States because, as Bill Winders describes in his 2017 book *Grain*, US farmers had become used to exporting, so the US push for reinstating free trade was limited.

Friedmann finds that by 1947 "a convergence of circumstances led to the adoption of a new set of implicitly mercantile rules, institutions and practices in agriculture" (2009:128). Mercantilism led to the shift from free trade to managed agriculture within the so-called free world. As explained by Winders (2017:16), supply management of grains could be in the form of acreage allotments, marketing agreements with other states, or other means to regulate and stabilize production and surplus. Each food regime has been grounded in relatively stable, albeit typically unequal, international trade relations and has been associated with a specific technological paradigm.

McMichael (2005) elaborates on the concept of the third food regime, which emerged after the crisis of Fordism in the United States. Central to the second food regime, Fordism involved accumulation focused primarily on the national economies, mass production and mass consumption, and the welfare state. Its crisis led to trying to extend capital accumulation well beyond national borders on a global scale. The third food regime is thus part of a global political project; McMichael argues that its central tension is between the globalization of corporate agriculture and countermovements wishing to pursue food sovereignty principles and a national focus for agriculture.

This characterization of the food regime perspective reflects the broad brush of the regulation school and world systems theory in which it was rooted. Such a macro view has raised critiques by other scholars regarding the original food regime perspective's structuralism (Goodman and Watts 1994), suggesting the need for more nuanced investigation and the call for a meso-level analysis (Bonanno and Constance 2001, 2008). While the perspective does acknowledge the role of the state, especially in advanced capitalist countries in maintaining their agricultural subsidies, McMichael, in my view, overemphasizes the main beneficiaries of the food regime—corporations—

and the North-South mutual dependency as a result. McMichael's 2005 formulation is clear that markets are politically constructed, through states as members of the World Trade Organization (WTO). This means also that states are therefore subject to resistance from countermovements that are part of the food regime dialectic and transformation. The trouble is that McMichael's analysis (2005, 2009a, b) remains primarily at the level of the world economy, in which states appear as black boxes, as units of analysis of the world economy. My goal here is to provide a friendly amendment that introduces some nuance at the national level of analysis, the point at which any food sovereignty program may even be attempted. Among others, Pablo Lapegna (2016) has also offered a subnational level of analysis while utilizing the overall neoliberal food regime perspective. The main idea here is that we must supplement the broadest world-system framing of the food regime to identify other significant social agencies, national and subnational, that can be tapped as points of intervention for change.

There is no doubt that corporations have become the dominant economic agents, especially after the neoliberal turn of the 1980s with its declining social welfare aspect; however, I argue that we must continue to take full and explicit account of the specific role of the state. One peril that we have witnessed of gauging the level of analysis—and action—at the world scale is that it condemns social movements to permanent mobilization against individual firms. One example has been the campaign against Nike for using sweatshops to produce shoes. With a better characterization of the structural determinants of the system, it is possible to identify ways in which the state, nudged by social movements, could better regulate multinational firms according to social needs and demands.

In contrast to McMichael's characterization of the "corporate food regime" (2005, 2009a, b), therefore, I subscribe to naming this the "neoliberal food regime" (Pechlaner and Otero 2008, 2010). This characterization considers national-level states and substate levels for contestation struggles. These are distinct, for instance, from the prominence that McMichael gives to one particular social movement, Vía Campesina, a transnational grassroots organization of peasants and farmers from fifty-seven nations (Desmarais 2007). Admittedly, this is the most important grassroots organization that wages much of its struggle for food sovereignty at the transnational level. What must be recognized, however, is that the struggles of constituent organizations of Vía Campesina are firmly rooted at the national level (Desmarais 2007, 2008); their objects of struggle are primarily their national states and subnational agencies and the states' involvement in local-level legislation as well as international regulations promoted and enacted by suprastate organizations.

Vía Campesina and affiliated organizations as well as the states of larger emerging economies have been quite successful in derailing the WTO's Doha Round of negotiations since the founding of Vía Campesina in 1997. The WTO's principal goal was to further liberalize agricultural trade, but the sector was already substantially liberalized through the passage of the WTO precursor's Uruguay Round of GATT (General Agreement on Tariffs and Trade) in 1993. That liberalization was highly uneven; it opened markets in developing countries while hypocritically reinforcing the rights of rich industrialized countries to continue subsidizing their own production. Therefore, the WTO's Doha Round, which started in 2001, has unsuccessfully tried to even the terrain. The extent to which liberalization has materialized in each country's agriculture largely depends on the interaction between states and domestic mobilization, resistance, and contestation (Holt-Giménez 2011).

Thus, it is not simply that the core principle has been displaced from the state to the market with the move from the second to the third food regime, as McMichael posits (2009a). Rather, the state continues to play a central role, even if it has changed to favor the predominance of ABMs in food production and distribution through supermarkets. Also, "the market" does not exist in the abstract; it is constructed in large part by states that also deploy some minimal rules of the market game and legislate, among other things, intellectual property rights, which are critical to biotechnology development. So, under neoliberalism the state apparatus has indeed contracted and cut social programs. In this sense, there is a crisis of the progressive social state. But the state continues to be a central actor in facilitating corporate domination. The most dynamic elements of the neoliberal food regime are the state, which promotes neoregulation, a series of international agreements and national legislation that impose the neoliberal agenda; large agribusiness multinationals, which have become the main economic actors; biotechnology as the key technological form that continues and enhances the modern agricultural paradigm of the earlier Green Revolution; and supermarkets, which have gone global as of the 1990s and constitute an oligopoly segment of the market, with vast buying power and massive influence to shape the agrifood sector. The dialectical counterparts of these factors are emerging social movements of resistance and contestation.

NEOLIBERAL GLOBALISM, THE STATE, AND NEOREGULATION

The neoliberal reforms that started in the 1980s had profound consequences for a large proportion of agricultural producers in Latin America. What can be considered "neoliberal globalism"? This ideology, which hypocritically vilifies state intervention and glorifies the private sector and free trade, emerged during the almost simultaneous administrations of Margaret Thatcher and Ronald Reagan. For Latin America, economic liberalization generally involved the unilateral end of protectionist policies; the opening of agricultural markets with the reduction or elimination of tariffs and import permits; privatization or dismantling of government agencies for rural credit, infrastructure, marketing, or technical assistance; the end or reversal of agrarian reforms; or the reorientation of food policies from domestic markets toward an export-oriented agricultural economy. Yet, the neoliberal reform was implemented in advanced capitalist countries' agriculture only partially, as they continue to subsidize and protect their agricultural sectors with billions of dollars per year, placing producers in Latin America and other developing countries at great competitive disadvantage.

Neoliberal globalism is considered an ideology here in the sense that the thought and policies associated with it are not inevitable. They can be modified with a different perspective that must be backed up by alternative social and political forces, such as bottom-up social movements, demanding that states implement a food sovereignty program. Given the national state's dominant role in promoting the new set of policies and regulations associated with neoliberal globalism, I use the term "neoregulation" rather than "deregulation" that is common in the food regime and other literatures (Ó Riain 2000; Weiss 1997). Despite the free trade rhetoric, the US state has made concerted policy and regulatory efforts to facilitate the development of its biotechnology-based industries (Kenney 1986; Kloppenburg 2004) and to keep other subsidies for its agrifood sector that mostly go to the largest farmers (Richter-Tate 2012) and benefit some processing industries that purchase most of the product. Although ABMs have become the principal economic actors in producing and disseminating agricultural inputs, their rise to dominance took place in close association with the US government through its Department of Agriculture and land grant universities that are heavily supported at the federal and state levels. The universities produced the science with public funds, and private firms developed the inputs for modern agriculture, including biotechnology (Pavitt 2001). The US state was also active in pressuring other states to homogenize patent laws so that US biotechnology companies would have enhanced intellectual property rights protection in the global economy. As stated in a major report by several US agencies, "Intellectual-property regimes, especially patents, play a substantial role in shaping the kinds of products available (and often therefore the planting decisions available) to farmers. Patent law, seedmarket concentration, and public-research investment can have various social and economic effects" (National Academies of Sciences, Engineering, and Medicine 2016:211).

Leland Glenna and Daniel Cahoy (2009) compare the concentration trends in three agribusiness industries—GM corn, non-GM corn, and biomass technologies. Biomass showed only a 33.5 percent concentration in the top three firms. But the trend toward concentration in the first two sectors, already high, was headed to much higher levels: 69.6 percent in non-GM corn and a whopping 85 percent concentration in the top three firms in GM maize (122). The three GM firms were Monsanto, DuPont, and Syngenta. Glenna and Cahoy attribute the concentration at the top to consolidation of intellectual property rights but also to lack of regulation: "Proponents of deregulation often pledge their allegiance to self-regulating markets. By this logic, there is no need for government oversight" (125). The authors err by pointing to deregulation, given that it was actually neoregulation that allowed for the strengthening of intellectual property rights in the first place. Jim Balsillie, one of Canada's few notable entrepreneurs internationally as a cofounder of Research in Motion (creator of the Blackberry smartphone), has made this point clearly about intellectual property rights: "In practice, companies commercialize knowledge not through open borders but through restrictions supported by the legal system" (2017).

Government or public support has not been limited to research and development funding. It has included new policies and legislation to protect intellectual property rights. Although US farmers also participated in this alliance, they never played a determining role in what technologies were to be developed or produced; they were simply recipients of technological innovations that responded to the profit-maximizing logic of ABMs (Pechlaner 2012a).

Other international agreements relevant to agricultural biotechnologies exist, but to date the most significant supranational regulatory body remains the WTO. Agriculture has featured prominently in WTO negotiations since it replaced and absorbed GATT in 1995 (Pechlaner and Otero 2010).

The most relevant point for my discussion here, then, is that states continue to be central agencies in the deployment of neoregulation and policies that enhance neoliberalism. Whether in agreeing (or not) to participate in suprastate agreements or developing national legislation, states have been the principal actors in implementing neoregulation. States are also the most visible point of struggle to counter neoliberal globalism, as illustrated in the following examples. James Klepek (2012) documents an example for Guatemala, which has resisted aspects of neoregulation; it has been able to resist the adoption of transgenic corn, given the great biodiversity of maize within its borders. Such resistance comes from the bottom up in the form of peasant and indigenous social movements. Yet, even in Guatemala there has been some informal flow of transgenic corn in its northern region (Grandia 2014).

Similarly, Elizabeth Fitting (2008, 2011) has shown that the Mexican anti-transgenic corn network has mobilized the symbolism around maize. It has garnered international media coverage and transnational NGO involvement because it raised the first case against "genetic pollution" in a crop's center of origin, as Kathy McAfee (2008) also reports. Initially, however, neoregulation moved right along in Mexico, and transgenic corn was deployed for pilot testing as of early 2013. But social struggles were successful in having a judge impose a moratorium on further use of transgenic corn a few months later. This was a grueling struggle that involved a tremendous legal fight with agribusiness multinationals and the federal government itself. Adelita San Vicente Tello, who legally represented the movement, and co-author Jaime Morales Hernández have described its main motivation, constituency, and legal obstacles it had to overcome (2015). The movement leaders contend that this has been a civilizational struggle. Peasants and indigenous peoples see in maize their own origin, their life and survival, so they claim their right to freely reproduce it. Similarly, other citizens of diverse political orientations see in maize their basic staple and a commitment to preserve it for future generations. In legal terms, the movement launched on 5 July 2013, a class-action suit called "Demanda Colectiva" in Mexico. Movement constituents included fifty-three individuals—among them activist academics and prominent environmentalists and artists—and twenty social movement organizations mostly in Mexico's countryside but also urban human rights and citizens groups.

The rural participants included some of the most prominent productive and social movement organizations since the 1980s, among them Alternativas y Procesos de Participación Social (Social Participation Processes and Alternatives), which produces *amaranto* (amaranth, a highly nutritious ancient grain produced by the Aztecs) in the state of Tlaxcala; the Asociación Nacional de Empresas Comercializadoras de Productos del Campo (National Association of Rural Products Marketing Enterprises), representing 60,000 maize producers in ten states and prominent in the earlier social movement

El Campo No Aguanta Más (The Countryside Can Bear No More); the Aso-ciación Rural de Interés Colectivo en Defensa y Preservación del Maíz Na-tivo del Estado de Tlaxcala (Collective Rural Interest Association in Defense and Preservation of Native Maize of Tlaxcala State), which gathers most of the collective *ejidos*, an important institutional and productive result of Mexico's agrarian reform of the state (Otero 1999); and Tosepan Titataniske (United We Win), the first cooperative constituted in the northern high-lands of the state of Puebla and encompassing 290 communities in twenty-two municipalities, with 22,000 Nahuatl and Totonac families.

The agribusiness and state legal defense against the class action suit to revoke the permit for transgenic corn was staggering. I offer some detail on the defendants' tenacity to impose their will, which ultimately failed. The ninety-three legal appeals included twenty-two writs of protection, sixteen recourses for revision, nine writs, eight revocations, seven impugnations against the suit's admissibility, seven appeals, five inconformities, one com-plaint, one annulment of action, one request for a Supreme Court hearing, and one request for the judge's recusal from the case. The scale of the fight extended to seventeen courts: one federal tribunal, one appellate tribunal, three writ tribunals, one administrative commission, ten collegiate tribunals, and one first hearing by the Supreme Court (San Vicente Tello 2015).

Irma Gómez González (2016) has offered a novel exploration of how the authorization of transgenic soybeans in the Yucatán Peninsula of Mexico had disastrous ecological effects on the surrounding forests, deeply impact-ing the Mayan beekeepers' economy. Beekeeping happens to be the main source of sustenance for a majority of Mayan peasants in the state of Cam-peche. GM soybeans represented a mortal threat to that economy after their authorization by the federal and state governments in 2011. At the same time, the European Union announced its new requirement for labeling honey containing transgenics. The circumstances highlight the contrasting regu-latory frameworks of Mexico and the European Union. Honey importers imposed a label indicating whether the honey was "transgenic-free." Gómez González documents the grassroots struggle, representing a broad alliance of Maya communities, beekeepers, civil society organizations, universities, and honey-exporting entrepreneurs. The alliance used astute media strate-gies and ultimately succeeded in pushing the judiciary power in Mexico to invalidate the authorization of transgenic soy production. The convergence of national and extranational regulatory policies presented specific oppor-tunities for mobilization that led to successful policy change at the level of the nation-state.

Until 2006 the Brazilian case was emblematic of a state that had resisted the marketing of transgenic soybeans for years (Jepson, Brannstrom, and Sousa 2008; Hisano and Altoé 2008; Motta 2016). In 2006 the Lula government caved to pressure from Monsanto's lobbying efforts and large-scale landowners who had in fact been smuggling transgenic seeds from Argentina (Motta 2016). In an ironic twist, the landowners, once the very promoters of the legalization and adoption of transgenic crops (Herring 2007), by 2011 were in an uproar against their resulting dependency on Monsanto, one of the world's leading ABMs; such dependency became economically disadvantageous, as Monsanto takes the bulk of the profits. Karine Peschard (2012) documents the resistance from Brazil's traditionally strong agrarian bourgeoisie. It remains to be seen whether the Brazilian state reverses neoregulation in view of the pressure.

AGRIBUSINESS MULTINATIONALS

Five agrochemical companies dominate biotechnology product development and production, while their customers are primarily mid- to large-scale farmers, well endowed with capital, whose main production logic is the profit motive. As highlighted in McMichael's characterization of the food regime, corporations are indeed the main economic actors. But states have regulated the markets even if such regulation has been mostly to corporations' advantage. Thus, corporations as an explicit feature of the neoliberal food regime have come to dominate such markets; the number of horizontally and vertically integrated corporations dominating agricultural production is diminishing. This concentrated—oligopolistic—market structure squeezes producers between few input sellers, processors, and food retailers, and it limits consumer options (Hendrickson and Heffernan 2005). The US Agribusiness Accountability Initiative put it sharply and succinctly:

> This [ABM-controlled] system isn't working for farmers. The power of large agribusinesses on the buying and selling sides means that farmers have less and less control over what they produce, how they produce it, where they can sell it, and what price they can get for it. The system isn't good for consumers and rural communities either: we are all affected when agribusinesses squeeze the rural economy or put profit above environmental and health concerns, community values, or fair wages. (AAI n.d.:1)

The pervasiveness of ABMs in the agrifood system is important with respect to their influence over neoregulation and their ability to deflect resistance to any socially undesirable features of the new regime, as some groups consider agricultural biotechnologies. The lack of labeling for genetically engineered (GE) content in North America is a case in point. It could be argued that farmers of all classes, including the agrarian bourgeoisie, have been subsumed under agribusiness capital.

BIOTECHNOLOGY, MODERN AGRICULTURE, AND NEOLIBERALISM

The biotechnology revolution coincided with the neoliberal reformation of capitalism and thus exacerbated the socioeconomic effects of the prior agricultural revolution in Latin America, the so-called Green Revolution of the 1940s–1970s. As defined by the Canadian Food Inspection Agency, "'Modern biotechnology' is used to distinguish newer applications of biotechnology, such as genetic engineering and cell fusion from more conventional methods such as breeding, or fermentation" (CFIA 2012). According to the same source, "mutagenesis" involves "the use of methods to physically change or 'mutate' the genetic sequence, without adding DNA from another organism." I focus on transgenic seeds, which involve the introduction of foreign genetic material into plant varieties, but I acknowledge that some forms of modern biotechnology do not involve such genetic alteration.

The Green Revolution was the incarnation of what had earlier emerged as the modern agricultural paradigm in US agriculture. The technological paradigm of modern agriculture encompasses a specific package of inputs made up of hybrid and other high-yielding plant varieties, mechanization, agrochemical fertilizers and pesticides, and irrigation. "Green Revolution" is the name adopted for this technological package when it was exported to developing countries. The Green Revolution technically began in Mexico in 1943 with a program promoting high-yield wheat varieties (Hewitt de Alcántara 1978), but its origin and initial development were located in the agriculture of the United States dating from the 1930s (Kloppenburg 1988). The exported package then became the technological paradigm for modern agriculture throughout the twentieth century.

A technological paradigm shapes the range of solutions to problems emerging in agricultural production, tending to address them within a narrow variety of options shaped by the paradigm. Offering an analogy with Thomas Kuhn's notions of "scientific paradigms" and "normal" science, Giovanni Dosi (1984) suggests that technological paradigms move along technological trajectories shaped by the "normal" solution to problems. Such technological paradigms not only select solutions but also tend to exclude alternative solutions that do not pertain to the paradigm. The technological paradigm, then, defines both the agendas for research and development and the technologies that are excluded from the frame of vision and imagination of engineers and, in our case, plant breeders and other agricultural researchers. It should be emphasized that there is not technological determinism here. Rather than merely responding to a social need, it is mostly the scientists and technologists, institutions and policy makers who promote particular technologies.

Problems emerging in agriculture will likely be solved along the lines determined by the technological trajectory. Other technologies that emerged in the 1990s, such as precision farming based on GPS, are also meant to optimize the use of "intensive industrial agriculture," made up mostly of "chemical fertilizer; synthetic pesticides; large-scale, tractor-based mechanization; and fertilizer-responsive, higher-yielding, genetically uniform crop varieties" (S. Wolf and Buttel 1996). Large-scale mechanization and monocropping have also become prominent features of modern agriculture. It is not surprising, then, that the application of agrochemicals has increased dramatically with the extension of the paradigm from its place of origin, the United States, to most regions of the world that practice capitalist agriculture. It should not be surprising, either, than the ABMs involved in their production have become dominant economic actors in world agriculture.

In what ways is biotechnology part of the modern agricultural paradigm? From its start at the laboratory stage in the 1980s, proponents have described agricultural biotechnology in general and genetic engineering in particular as potent tools for sustainable development and efforts to end world hunger, food insecurity, and malnutrition. It is well known that these problems are disproportionately concentrated in developing countries, where larger proportions of the population work in agriculture. But the technological profile of modern agriculture centers above all on improving the productivity of large-scale operations, those that are highly specialized in a single crop and intensive in the use of capital inputs rather than labor. Compared with this productive and technological model and bias, therefore, the majority of smallholder, peasant cultivators in developing countries have been rendered "inefficient."

In Henry Bernstein's (2016) analysis of the second food regime, he identifies six major trends. One is that the state comes to be subservient to the market and privatization of formerly public functions and services. Second is dispossession of peasant lands for corporate expansion; third, ecological destruction; fourth, the configuration of new diets in which biotechnology plays an important technological role. A fifth aspect is the "food from no-where" mantra, because globalization has virtually rooted out agricultural and food production from its locality. This is a central contradiction be-tween a world agriculture — as food from nowhere — and a place-based form of agroecology, or food from somewhere. Finally, a sixth point is food dis-tribution and hunger. The question of who goes hungry, where, and why is raised as an effect of the extreme inequality of income distribution in con-temporary capitalism, that is, its class basis, which has to do with the vola-tility in the prices of staple foods (Bernstein 2016:626–628).

Focusing for the moment on dispossession, in the FAO's calculation, twenty million to thirty million peasants were displaced by new policies and technologies in the 1990s (Araghi 2003). Some of the peasants were transformed into wage workers for large, capitalized farms, while count-less joined the unemployed. Many of those people have contributed to the growing trend toward internal and international migration, separating them from their communities and families for prolonged periods or permanently. Hence Stephen Castels and Mark Miller (2003) have called the rise of neo-liberal capitalism "the age of migration." In Mexico hundreds of thousands became redundant in agriculture (Corona and Tuirán 2006), and the rest of its macro economy was incapable of absorbing them (Otero 2004, 2011). As a result, Mexico became the number one sending nation in international mi-gration; between 2000 and 2005, Mexico economically expelled two million people, mostly to the United States but also increasingly to Canada; by com-parison, China and India sent fewer migrants abroad during this period even though those nations have more than ten times the population of Mexico (González Amador and Brooks 2007). My contention as to why Mexico has expelled so many migrants is that its government has followed one of the most aggressive neoliberal policies in the world (Cypher and Delgado-Wise 2010; Moreno-Brid and Ros 2009; Otero 2011).

What is the problem with the emerging domination of ABMs if they can produce food more efficiently for a growing population? Or can they, really? For millennia, peasants have been directly responsible for the preservation of immense plant diversity. In fact, given the vagaries of nature, develop-ing countries possess the greatest plant diversity on the planet (Fowler and Mooney 1990) as well as the greatest problems with soil erosion and ecologi-cal degradation (Montgomery 2007). Some of the degradation is related to global warming attributable mostly to advanced capitalist countries since the onset of the industrial revolution (Foster 2009; Jarosz 2009). Sreenivasan and Christie assert (2002:1), "All biodiversity is richer in the South than in the North. . . . This is as true for agricultural biodiversity as for wild or bio-logical diversity."

Capitalized and intensive farmers cannot preserve biological diversity, given modern agriculture's monocropping bias toward high-yield hybrid or transgenic plant varieties. That is to say, in order for large producers to stay viably in the market they must specialize, devoting large areas of land to single crops. Ironically, plant breeders, who require biological diversity as their raw material to keep the process of crop improvement going, depend on the availability of plant genetic diversity afforded by small peasant culti-vators. It is in these materials that plant breeders find the desirable traits to improve crops. If peasants disappear, the same fate awaits the raw materials for future plant breeding (Fowler and Mooney 1990; Kloppenburg 1988). Combined with neoliberal globalism, agricultural biotechnology can only exacerbate the tendencies to social polarization and ecological degradation, given its immersion in the modern agricultural paradigm.

Beyond ecological concerns, the productive logic of modern agriculture contrasts with that of smallholder petty commodity producers. Rather than producing to generate profits, petty commodity producers supply themselves and local, regional, and national markets. By definition, petty commodity producers provide commodities for human consumption to generate reve-nues for the simple reproduction of their household units. Such production may occasionally generate income above and beyond simple reproduction needs. In that case, the income may contribute to improving their living stan-dards or even setting the conditions for bourgeoisification. Most of the time, however, petty commodity producers are in economic survival mode, given the structural constraints in which they operate (Chayanov 1974; Otero 1999; E. Wolf 1966). The European Union considers the support of petty com-modity producers a safeguard of the environment and recognizes them at the institutional level.

The point here is to transcend a dichotomous way of classifying agri-cultural producers. As I have argued elsewhere (Otero 1998), there is the possibility for petty commodity producers to become peasant entrepreneurs successfully incorporated into modern markets. These are family farms and farmers whose activities may include export-oriented monocropping as well as mixed farming for local, regional, and even national markets. These pro-ducers are embedded in the market without being capitalist corporations. Jan Douwe van der Ploeg (2008) has offered a three-way categorization of agri-cultural producers that places "entrepreneurial farming" between peasant and capitalist production. Entrepreneurial farmers may be best suited to engaging in a food sovereignty program, as such agriculture can also be ecologically sustainable. Their production is oriented to the market, but their logic of production is still imbued with a moral economy (140). In this moral economy, the market will no doubt represent an ongoing and harsh context in which only a few will win. Because entrepreneurial farmers are content with recovering costs and gaining the equivalent of self-attributed wages, however, their numbers could be much greater than only capitalist farms; they seek simple rather than expanded reproduction, as in capital accumulation.

Capitalist farmers, by contrast, must produce primarily exchange values based on salaried workers, whether the products are sold for human use or otherwise. Their main goal is to produce a profit above and beyond their simple reproduction needs in order to stay competitive (van der Ploeg 2008:2). Thus, although capitalist farmers must also operate in a continuous economic survival mode, their productive logic allows them—indeed compels them—to look beyond producing use values for human consumption. To the extent that ABMs increase their domination of agricultural research and production, the exchange value and profit logic comes to prevail, whether it is to produce food or agrofuels (Bello 2009:15).

The capitalist mode of producing food crops is consequently not the most adequate to fulfill human needs. It is neither ecologically nor socially sustainable. Nevertheless, the global food price inflation that started in 2007 unleashed a return to the rhetoric of faith in biotechnology and transgenics. These technologies have been posed once again as the necessary solution to the food crisis (Cage 2008; J. Lee 2008; F. Harvey and Parker 2008). According to this perspective, world hunger can be eradicated in poor countries only with greater yields and cheaper and more efficient crops, and transgenics are supposed to bear out this promise. A particularly relentless observer, Bjorn Lomborg (2009), contends that it would be criminal to sidestep the hope offered by biotechnology to the worst-fed people in the world. Critics of the position that biotechnology offers a solution to the world's poor, however, have multiplied their voices with empirically based research in the social sciences (Glover 2010a, b, c, d; Hisano 2005; Jansen and Gupta 2009; Scoones 2002, 2008).

The idea that we can solve the food crisis simply by increasing yields is problematic in a world where hunger is present in the midst of plenty. The world produces enough food for everyone on the planet, but the hungry simply cannot afford it. The core issue is one of inequality and lack of access to food rather than not producing enough of it. Since the 1960s the world has seen a reduction in the numbers of people affected by famine, even as the numbers of the food insecure has risen relentlessly. We have the phenomenon of obesity combined with hunger on a planetary scale (Patel 2007). Importing transgenic crops produced at low costs failed to protect Mexicans from high corn prices once the crisis struck, given Mexico's inequality; when price inflation for corn reached 15 percent in December 2007, consumption plummeted by 30 percent (Notimex 2009).

Whatever level of transgenic crops is adopted in Mexico or other Latin American countries, it is doubtful that this will help feed their peoples. On the contrary, US-based ABMs sell their seeds to farmers each agricultural cycle, always as part of a package that includes herbicides and other agrochemicals and all under contract (Peschard 2012). More direct adoption of transgenic crops leads to greater dependency on imports of capital-intensive inputs and lower demand for labor, further threatening peasant agriculture. The trend will exacerbate the socially polarizing effects brought about by the Green Revolution (Hewitt de Alcántara 1978; Pearse 1980), ultimately expelling more workers from the countryside (Cypher and Delgado-Wise 2010; Otero 2011).

Adopters of transgenic crops to produce soybeans or corn for the export market, which may be more lucrative than domestic markets in Latin America, are large-scale farmers with substantial capital endowments. Export agriculture takes agricultural land away from production for the domestic market. Hence we had the Argentine paradox at the turn of the twenty-first century (Teubal 2008). Until it was displaced by Brazil, Argentina was the second soybean exporter after the United States and one of the leading agricultural exporters in the world, yet Argentina experienced substantial growth in the number of people going hungry.

Peasant agriculture is not highly productive in economic terms, that is, in generating profits for producers, but at the very least it can produce food and subsistence for those who depend on it for their livelihoods, even though it does not save peasants from the occasional drought, pest, and so forth. On the other hand, peasants have scarce alternative job opportunities in an economy that does not offer sufficient or adequately paid employment to urban migrants or rights or dignity to international migrants (Cypher and Delgado-Wise 2010; Otero 2011). Substituting peasant farming for export-oriented industrial agriculture forces many in the rural population to depend on dollar remittances from migrant relatives; it increases food insecurity at the family level even if the nation's total agricultural production increases. Besides producing subsistence foods, peasants offer gratis to society the service of plant biological conservation, as they do not engage in the monocropping of large-scale cultivators (Bartra 2004).

The social polarization trends brought about by the Green Revolution and then by biotechnology and the neoliberal reform were exacerbated with the food price inflation crisis of 2007–2008, which resurfaced in 2010–2011. Excluding a process of bottom-up technological innovation, one that builds on the actual needs of smallholder farmers, the reaction of some suprastate institutions like the World Bank has been to promote industrial agriculture (Akram-Lodhi 2012). Based as it is on the profit motive, this approach can hardly help mitigate the food crisis. Several studies have shown the limits of ABM-promoted biotechnology, including strong doubts about its effective economic performance, the tendency to favor ABMs, and the limited benefits for smallholder producers or the hungry (Friends of the Earth International 2009; McAfee 2008; Otero and Pechlaner 2005, 2009; Otero, Poitras, and Pechlaner 2008; Pechlaner and Otero 2008, 2010).

THE CRISIS OF THE NEOLIBERAL FOOD REGIME AND GLOBAL FOOD PRICE INFLATION

The neoliberal food regime entered a period of protracted crisis in 2007, at which point there was a reversal of nearly a century of diminishing food prices, with a few spikes in the 1970s and 1990s. The crisis was generated primarily by new economic actors focused on the exchange value rather than the use value of food. Prominent among them were finance capital in agricultural futures markets and state policies related to the geopolitics of oil and energy dependency, such as US and EU public policies to expand the production of agrofuels that divert land from food production (Bello 2009; McMichael 2009a). Modern agricultural production has also precipitated climate change by contributing about 30 percent of greenhouse gas emissions.

A critical point of cleavage that arises with capitalist-dominated agriculture is that several for-profit interests are competing in the same crops. The most dramatic example is corn. Driven by hefty state subsidies on one side or another, contenders include industrialists who process corn to make ethanol for fuel or high-fructose corn syrup, livestock growers who use corn as feed, and financial speculators who invest in corn futures. The speculators are interested in higher prices of corn, while all others want lower prices of corn as a raw material. But whether corn is used to produce ethanol or food has vastly different consequences. In fact, producing ethanol rather than food also has a big impact in overall food price inflation (Turrent Fernández, Wise, and Garvey 2012). And the many who think ethanol is green are wrong; ethanol made from corn actually produces more greenhouse gas emissions than even gasoline (Otero and Jones 2010), and it is unsustainable without subsidies. A 2012 drought in the United States heightened the cleavages and tensions among the various groups with high stakes in corn. Consumers of corn products are at the mercy of the oligopolistic competition over a food that is also used to produce fuel or straight financial profits. Only the state can provide agency to regulate these forces in a different direction. In the United States, the question is whether corn will continue to be controlled by strong lobby groups.

My goal here is not to engage in a detailed discussion of the global food price inflation crisis of 2007–2008; that has been discussed by many scholars (Bello 2009; Holt-Giménez, Patel, and Shattuck 2009; McMichael 2009a). Rather, I want to highlight the role of food import dependency as the crisis affected a sample of Latin American countries and a few others for comparison. All the data come from the UN Food and Agriculture Organization's FAOSTAT database. In general, rich economies of the Organization for Economic Cooperation and Development (OECD) experienced accumulated inflation rates no higher than about 35 points above 2000-level prices (2000 = 100) through 2011. A comparison of the United Kingdom, France, and Germany clearly shows that the United Kingdom was the most sharply affected, with a price hike of about 35 percent by 2010, likely due to its early wholehearted adoption of the neoliberal reforms, in contrast to Germany (18 percent) and France (23 percent). Also, Germany and France are more self-sufficient than the United Kingdom. In spite of this inflation level, the UK as well as the rest of western European countries except Spain and Portugal were considered at "low food security risk" (Carrington 2011).

In contrast, a sharp disparity in food inflation rates in Latin American countries and advanced capitalist countries is accompanied by a higher food security risk in all Latin American countries (Carrington 2011). Argentina's food inflation skyrocketed to more than 200 percent in 2006 and more than 300 percent accumulated food price inflation by 2011. Brazil also experienced considerable food price inflation, but its rate in 2011 was about 100 points below that of Argentina (figure 1.1). On the American continent, the United States and Canada were at the bottom, with the lowest accumulated food inflation rates since 2000 of about 36 and 37 percent, respectively, while all the developing countries had rates three to four times higher. The notable exception is Cuba's inflation, which has been below that of even advanced capitalist countries, likely reflecting the concerted food sovereignty policy its government has pursued.

A slightly different selection of countries for which inflation data are complete through 2014 is presented in figure 1.2, in comparison with general

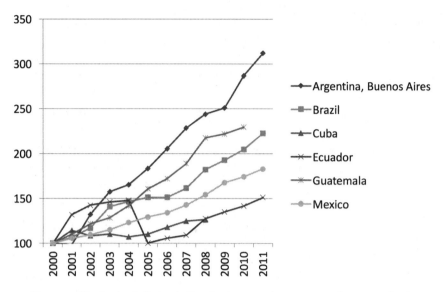

Figure 1.1. Food price inflation indices in six countries, 2000–2011 (2000 = 100).
Source: FAOSTAT 2012a.

price inflation. Except for Bolivia and Ecuador, which had state policies oriented toward food self-sufficiency, food inflation in the rest of the countries was higher than general price inflation.

SUPERMARKETS IN THE GLOBAL ERA

Supermarkets as vehicles for food distribution have been around since about the 1930s in the United States (Burch and Lawrence 2007; Markin 1968), but their globalization is a relatively recent phenomenon, dating from the 1990s (Lee, Gereffi, and Beauvais 2012; Reardon, Barrett et al. 2009; Reardon, Timmer et al. 2003). Supermarkets can be distinguished from former local stores in that they are much larger, manage large lines of products, and have food as their central sales revenues. Individual buyers generally engage in self-serving of goods from open displays and must pay in specific locations (checkouts). Supermarkets tend to be part of larger chains or cooperatives (Burch and Lawrence 2007:3). Supermarkets emerged as a response to growing demand resulting both from urbanization and the entry of women into the workforce outside of the home. In tandem, the same forces that motivated shopping convenience also became an incentive to produce processed foods (Reardon, Barrett et al. 2003:1141). As we will see, besides distributing food, supermarkets are playing a growing role in shaping the structure and

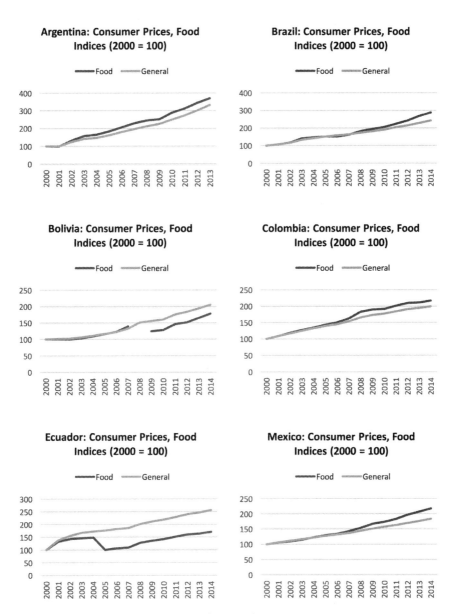

Figure 1.2. General and food price inflation indices in six countries, 2000–2014.
Source: FAOSTAT 2012a.

conditions of the agrifood system, including agricultural producers and food processors. Hence they could become a critical point of intervention for the state and food-justice social movements.

For my purposes, a discussion of supermarkets must be framed by the kinds of commodity chains in which they are involved in the production and distribution of food and agricultural products. One of the most incisive sociological theorizations to think about this issue for the era of globalization has been provided by Gary Gereffi and collaborators (Gereffi and Korzeniewikz 1994; Gereffi, Lee, and Christian 2009; Lee, Gereffi, and Beauvais 2012). In the mid-1990s they proposed that two main types of global commodity chains articulate production and capital accumulation processes across nations: producer-driven and buyer-driven commodity chains. The naming of each type of commodity chain is meant to capture the economic actors with the greatest control of the capital accumulation process in the given chain, the main buyers or the main producers. An example of a producer-driven chain is the automobile industry; by the late 1980s a Ford Taurus was built with parts manufactured in sixteen countries. It was thus labeled the first global car. By the 1990s, other commodity chains emerged such as that driven by Nike, a shoes seller; as a buyer and distributor of huge numbers of shoes, Nike controlled the production of multiple manufacturers. The 1990s also saw the globalization of supermarkets, which command buyer-driven commodity chains.

For the specific case of the agrifood industry, Gereffi has offered a useful conceptualization of commodity chains that further specifies his initial duo, depending on market structure. Reformulated as "global value chains," Joonkoo Lee, Gary Gereffi, and Janet Beauvais (2012) arrive at a typology of four main types of chains based on the levels of concentration among farmers and producers on one hand and sellers on the other; they are traditional markets with loose and fragmented competitive markets, buyer-driven chains controlled primarily by supermarkets, producer-driven chains, and bilateral oligopolies. There is hardly any room for smallholders in producer-driven and bilateral oligopoly chains except as contract farmers, much more in traditional markets, and some in buyer-driven chains. Examples of these are, respectively, local fresh produce markets (traditional), fresh fruits and vegetables (buyer-driven), coffee and cocoa (producer-driven), and bananas and pineapples (bilateral oligopolies).

Supermarkets, then, act in both buyer-driven and bilateral oligopoly global value chains. Some data on the rise of supermarkets give an idea of their oligopoly and rising power in conjunction with their key food-manufacturing suppliers, which also constitute an oligopoly. It was only in

TABLE 1.1. Four-firm concentration (CR4), 2007, by region and product category

| | | | | | TOTAL PRODUCT SALES IN VARIOUS CATEGORIES OF TOP FOUR FIRMS (PERCENTAGE SHARE) | | |
REGION	SOUP	BREAKFAST CEREAL	BABY FOOD	PET FOOD	CONFECTIONERY	CHEESE
Africa, Middle East	71.5	55.9	55.7	60.4	38.3	28.2
Asia Pacific	42.9	61.9	43.3	29.9	26.0	43.1
Australasia	91.1	87.8	91.5	59.0	74.1	70.1
Eastern Europe	66.5	40.0	55.2	58.2	36.6	17.5
Latin America	75.0	75.0	84.1	51.3	42.3	15.0
North America	68.3	82.3	88.0	48.6	56.8	43.2
Western Europe	55.6	61.3	73.9	45.5	37.8	21.5
World	50.4	62.3	60.0	45.8	32.9	20.2

Source: USDA 2017d.

Note: Four-firm concentration (CR4) is the sum of the sales shares of the leading four suppliers in each market.

1991 that Walmart started in Mexico, as Walmex. By 2008 Walmex revenues accounted for well over a third of Walmart's foreign operations (Gereffi and Christian 2009). It is in the advanced capitalist countries that supermarkets have the greatest concentration and control the largest share of food distribution compared to, say, traditional commodity chains. By the early twenty-first century, global food retail sales represented about $4 trillion annually, and supermarkets accounted for the largest share of sales (USDA 2016). The leading global companies are based in the United States or Europe. The top fifteen supermarket chains in 2016 captured 30 percent of total food sales globally (USDA 2016). Another trend in tandem with the growth and dominance of supermarkets is that food processing companies are also gaining dominance by focusing on a handful of products and brands. Food manufacturing concentration is not evident on the global scale, but firm concentration exists in specific product lines and regional markets (USDA 2016). Table 1.1 captures the CR4, that is, the index that measures industry concentration by the top four firms. It reveals the considerable extent to which food processing firms have become concentrated by focusing on specific brands.

CONCLUSION

The central dynamic factors of the neoliberal food regime are the state, ABMs, biotechnology, and supermarkets. States continue to be the principal if not the sole societal agency to implement neoregulation, the specific form of state intervention in the time of neoliberal globalism, since the 1980s. Neoregulation translates such globalism into laws and policies that create market conditions to favor ABMs. Neoregulation has consisted, for instance, of the type of legislation best suited to protect the intellectual property rights of ABMs and their coming to prominence in the economy. ABMs plainly dominate the markets shaped by the state; biotechnology is the central technological form, enabling the continuation of the modern agricultural paradigm, and supermarkets have become the dominant distributors in advanced capitalist countries and beyond.

The state has been posited as a central agent in the neoliberal food regime for its deployment and principal means for its transcendence. Even if neoliberalism has involved a reduction of the state's direct intervention in the economy and its social policy aspects, the state continues to play a critical role in providing hefty subsidies and setting up the conditions under which the private sector enters the market through neoregulation. Having a fuller picture of the key dynamic factors puts us in a better position to develop strategies for resistance and perhaps transcend the neoliberal food regime by targeting the state and corporations that deal directly with consumers, that is, supermarket chains. Thus, emphasizing only the corporate aspect of the food regime detracts from a more dialectical engagement with the analysis of the state and how it operates not just to impose the logic of capital but also to respond to mobilization and pressure from below. The state itself is a set of relations rife with contradictions (Jessop 2007). Subordinate classes can thus use these contradictions to advance a popular democratic cause such as food sovereignty. In fact, even the agrarian bourgeoisie would benefit from having a clear picture of where to put its mobilization efforts, not just against specific ABMs but also against and through the state. While ABMs are the key economic agents, they are not almighty. States can control them, and states can be influenced from below. Even a small state like Guatemala can keep corporations and their technologies at bay if the state faces sufficient pressure from organized social movements (Klepek 2012).

Biotechnology emerged in the 1980s as an industry in its own right, driven as it was by the association of venture capitalists and academics with promising products based on molecular biology and genetic engineering (Kenney

1986). Yet, biotechnology was eventually absorbed by the existing giant firms in the chemical and pharmaceutical industries and turned it into an enabling technology. Biotechnology enabled the industries to extend the modern agricultural paradigm in which they were so deeply invested.

While the technology itself may indeed theoretically contain unsuspected promise to alleviate human and ecological issues, the question is one of who actually drives technological development for what technological problems and in whose interests. The research agendas driven by the modern agricultural paradigm and their main economic actors—large ABMs—have served primarily the goal of maximizing their own profits. It is not clear that even heavily capitalized farmers can benefit from the technology, let alone peasant or entrepreneurial farmers. Given the role of ABMs in agrifood production, it would seem that the great majority of cultivators who come into the orbit of biotechnology throughout the Americas have become contract managers to deploy biotechnology products. Even the agrarian bourgeoisie is becoming subsumed under agribusiness capital.

Food price inflation, which reemerged in 2011–2012, motivated resistance movements like Vía Campesina, which has a presence globally and in each of the nation-states of its constituting organizations. I suggest that the state can be a critical target to steer the food regime in a progressive direction domestically, at national and regional scales, and in suprastate organizations. At a time when the cheap food era seems to be over, enhanced food dependency resulting from the neoliberal food regime has made most developing countries in Latin America much more vulnerable to food price volatility. The food sovereignty program strongly advocated by Vía Campesina (Desmarais 2007) is the safest policy route for developing countries to take, raising small-scale and entrepreneurial peasants to a central productive and environmental role. The neoliberal food regime's crisis was brought on because neoregulation favored the private sector almost exclusively. Progressive forces may continue to press the states to transcend it into a postneoliberal regime. Supermarkets, which must deal directly with consumers and are dominant actors in buyer-driven commodity chains, also emerge as potentially vital actors in the food system to be pressured by popular democratic movements. With the impetus from civil society organizations, the state and supermarkets could become determining forces in promoting better food quality production, distribution, and access. Let us now explore how neoregulation has been shaped at the national and suprastate scales as the contextual terrain for agribusiness operations.

CHAPTER 2

Neoregulation of Agricultural Biotechnology at the National and Suprastate Scales

One of the main features of post–World War II agriculture was its nation-centeredness. Yet, agriculture has a strong history in global trade despite the contentiousness in World Trade Organization negotiations at the turn of the twenty-first century. A more novel aspect of agriculture's position in international trade is its thorough incorporation under supranational trade agreements and national neoregulation spurred by neoliberal globalism. The resulting regulatory dynamic is accompanied by the rapid adoption of agricultural biotechnologies since the 1990s. Biotechnology has given significant empirical indications that it could be transformative for capitalized agriculture (Kloppenburg 1988; Otero 2008; Pechlaner 2012). Facilitated by evolving regulatory structures, agricultural biotechnology forms the basis of the neoliberal food regime.

The main hypothesis I defend here relates to the role of biotechnology as the principal technological form in the neoliberal food regime; biotechnology will entrench and exacerbate inequalities between nation-states, particularly between developed and developing countries. I question, however, whether neoregulation and corporate biotechnology will inevitably reorganize agricultural production relations in the somewhat homogeneous manner suggested by food regime proponents. Speculation abounds as to how power struggles over international regulations will affect the global development of biotechnology; the US-WTO challenge of the European Union is a case in point. However, little attention is given to the influence of decisions in individual nation-states, that is, more or fewer policies with neoliberal globalist content.

The mitigating impact of resistance to agricultural neoregulation on the food regime is acknowledged to some extent; McMichael (2005), for example, considers the potential impact of the international organization Vía Campesina. But I believe the greatest effect will come from the cumulative neoregulatory decisions in individual nation-states. These decisions, in turn, will be highly influenced by the force of local-level resistance. Despite prevailing trends, sufficient local resistance to agricultural biotechnology could modify or even derail its role within nations and accordingly in the neoliberal food regime as a whole. Guatemala and Mexico serve as examples of successful resistance to the deployment of transgenic soybeans (Gómez González 2016) and maize (Klepek 2012). Preliminary evidence suggests that the adverse impacts of biotechnology and neoregulatory restructuring in agriculture are likely to be greater in less-developed countries. The reason for this is straightforward: developing countries have much larger proportions of the labor force in agriculture than developed nations. Therefore, to the extent that biotechnology favors larger-scale agriculture, smallholder farmers will be adversely affected. The demographic and economic profile of developing countries sets the conditions for greater consequences. Unless displaced farmers are successfully absorbed into gainful employment in industry or services, the potential increases for social and political unrest and mobilization or outmigration.

To explore this hypothesis I compare the use of agricultural biotechnology products in Canada and the United States as advanced capitalist countries with that in Mexico as a developing country. My two main points of comparison are the role and effects of national and international regulations in the development and adoption of the technology, and local-level resistance to the technology and its effects.

AGRICULTURAL BIOTECHNOLOGY AND ITS SUPRANATIONAL REGULATORY CONTEXT

North America provides a unique opportunity for empirical study of the role of agricultural biotechnologies. Agricultural biotechnology is a US-dominated project, and the United States has considerable influence on the global stage. Consequently, the way in which the technology has unfolded in the country will determine its further global dissemination and adoption. Canada provides an example of the introduction of the technology into a developed country with some interest in a domestic biotechnology sector but involvement and international influence that are far weaker than in the United States. Canada falls in the middle, between being a "taker" and a "promoter" of agricultural biotechnology. Mexico is a developing country that can provide insight into how nations with little influence on biotechnology's development are affected by its dissemination, either directly or indirectly, that is, by adopting transgenic crops or importing them. Through this three-country comparison, I investigate the differential impacts of the new technology's introduction in nations with differing power relations to the technology as well as the social resistance to it that has emerged. The comparison offers valuable empirical insights into biotechnology's broader role in structuring the neoliberal food regime.

Agricultural biotechnologies were first commercialized in the mid-1990s. By 2016 there were 185.1 million hectares planted with transgenic or genetically modified (GM) crops in twenty-eight countries. In the initial period, 1996 to 2010, seven industrial countries, predominantly the United States and Canada, accounted for most of the planted surface (James 2014:1). By 2011, however, developing countries had surpassed them, reaching 54 percent of cultivated area by 2016, concentrated in nineteen countries and most heavily in Brazil, Argentina, and India (ISAAA 2016:5 and table 1). The production of transgenic crops entails two prominent traits—herbicide tolerance (HT) and insect resistance (IR). HT accounts for 47 percent of global hectarage, IR 12 percent, and stacked HT and IR, 41 percent. Four GM crops predominate: soybeans, maize, cotton, and canola; soybeans make up 66 percent and maize 32 percent of global biotechnology (ISAAA 2016:92–93). Although the number of transgenic agricultural crops is still relatively limited, their adoption has been dramatic, increasing sixtyfold, from 1.7 million hectares in 1996 to 90 million hectares in 2005 and then more than doubling to 185.1 million hectares by 2016 (ISAAA 2016:93).

The United States has been the undisputed leader in development and adoption of biotechnology, with 72.92 million hectares (39 percent of the global total) in 2016 and 93 percent US average adoption in the main crops: maize 93 percent, soybean 94 percent, and cotton 96 percent of cultivated area in those crops (ISAAA 2016:8). We can see that biotechnology dissemination is increasingly important in developed and developing countries, with the latter surpassing the former in GM crop surface area. The number of adopting countries and the land area dedicated to GM crops are on the increase. In growth rates of GM crops, Brazil was first in 2014 and Argentina third. Canada was fifth, at 11.6 million hectares, and had 96 percent adoption of GM canola by 2014. While certainly not proceeding free of impediments, adoption of the technology occurred rapidly enough that Clive James, in a 2006 report of the International Service for the Acquisition of Agri-biotech Applications (ISAAA), would proclaim it "the fastest adopted crop technology in recent history" (ISAAA 2006:1).

Given the capital intensity and novelty of biotechnology, two regulatory factors feature prominently in its adoption in addition to those that affect agriculture and food more generally: the intellectual property regime in place to protect the technology developer's interests, and the regulatory regime that oversees GM crops once adopted. These legal and regulatory frameworks are found in national and supranational laws. While other international agreements relevant to agricultural biotechnologies exist, to date the most significant supranational regulatory body remains the WTO. Agriculture has become salient in WTO negotiations since that organization replaced GATT in 1995. Starting with the next round of WTO negotiations in 2001, with meetings in Qatar's capital, Doha, the issue of reducing trade distortion in agriculture has become increasingly important. Disagreement over the topic led to the stagnation of negotiations, and the future of the Doha Development Round, as it is known semiofficially, remained uncertain by the end of 2017. This round brought to a head tensions over agriculture between developed and developing countries. Representatives of the latter argue that agreements supported protectionist practices of developed countries such as the United States while development goals fell to the wayside. Despite the heated controversy and the failure of negotiators to agree on the next wave of agricultural trade liberalization strategies, a number of agreements that were reached during GATT's Uruguay Round of negotiations by 1993 are already in place, many of which have had significant impact on agricultural biotechnology. Most notable are the Sanitary and Phytosanitary Measures (SPS) agreement and the agreement on Trade-Related Aspects of Intellectual Property Rights (TRIPS).

The SPS agreement covers issues of food safety and animal and plant health standards. Given the controversy over the safety of novel transgenic technology, this agreement is important for the technology's dissemination. The SPS is intended as a means for member states to regulate the safety of food products and establish guidelines to prevent regulations from acting as nontariff trade barriers. The primary means of striking such a balance is to insist on scientifically justifiable safety regulations and apply them "only to the extent necessary" for the protection of human, animal, or plant life or health (Codex Alimentarius 1995, article 2.3). Because what is considered scientifically justifiable in one nation may not be in another, members are encouraged to use international standards such as the Codex Alimentarius of the WHO and FAO: "To harmonize sanitary and phytosanitary measures on as wide a basis as possible, Members shall base their sanitary and phytosanitary measures on international standards, guidelines or recommendations, where they exist, except as otherwise provided for in this Agreement" (Codex Alimentarius 1995, article 3.1).

Through TRIPS the WTO aims to establish a regime of minimum intellectual property rights protection common to all its members. With respect to plant life, however, such protection does not have to be in the form of patents but can be provided for "either by patents or by an effective sui generis system or by any combination thereof" (WTO 1994, article 27.3b). Seemingly even more open to debate than what constitutes scientific justification for safety regulation is the question of a suitable sui generis system of intellectual property rights protection. Once again, members subscribing to international standards reduces subjectivity and the need for dispute resolution.

The Convention of the International Union for the Protection of Plant Varieties (UPOV) provides a framework for acceptable intellectual property rights protection; the strength of protection depends to a certain extent on which year's convention a member adopts. Like the agreement on agriculture itself, TRIPS presides over similar tensions between developed and developing countries, given the protection it offers technology developers (mostly in developed countries) and the lack of protection for genetic source material (primarily originating in developing countries). A number of developing countries are agitating for amendments to TRIPS such that patent applications relating to genetic resources and traditional knowledge provide evidence of benefit sharing with countries of origin or face revocation (Concheiro Bórquez and López Bárcenas 2006; TWN 2005). The proposal for amendments was presented by Bolivia, Brazil, Colombia, Dominican Republic, Ecuador, India, Peru, and Thailand at the TRIPS council meeting in 2005 under the agenda item of the relationship of TRIPS to the UN Convention on Biological Diversity (CBD) (TWN 2005).

The CBD and its supplementary Cartagena Protocol on Biosafety are international agreements on the conservation, sustainable use, and fair and equitable sharing of benefits of genetic resources; they provide greater credence to precautionary conduct and support the exchange of science and information. The CBD had more than 150 signatories at the time of its inception in 1992. However, there is considerable debate about how the CBD meshes with WTO agreements and which takes precedence in cases of conflict. Further, the CBD is less appealing to those who have the most to lose from the equitable sharing of genetic resources. Consequently, the United States signed but never ratified the CBD and did not sign the Protocol on Biosafety. Canada and Mexico signed and ratified the CBD and signed the protocol, and Mexico ratified it in 2002. In short, developing countries lobby for the incorporation of CBD values into TRIPS as it currently stands, while TRIPS appears to remain more influential in the international regulatory context for agricultural biotechnology.

BIOTECHNOLOGY AND NEOREGULATION IN THE UNITED STATES, CANADA, AND MEXICO

As should be obvious, the adoption of GM crops needs to be considered in the context of the role that agriculture plays in each country. Only about 2 percent of the economically active population (EAP) in the United States and Canada is engaged in agriculture; the proportion in Mexico is almost 20 percent. The ratio of agricultural GDP to agricultural EAP in 2005 US dollars was $39,993 in the United States, $48,557 in Canada, and only $2,692 in Mexico (Zahniser, Young, and Wainio 2005:5). In other words, a much greater percentage of Mexico's population is engaged in agriculture, but the income returns for those engaged are far lower than in the United States and Canada. These differences also reflect the capital intensity of US and Canadian agriculture compared to Mexico's, in which the large majority of producers are small-scale, peasant farmers with very limited capital endowments. Such differences need to be kept firmly in mind when considering the contexts in which these countries have made their regulatory decisions.

The United States

As noted, the United States is the top global producer of transgenic crops, accounting for over 39 percent of the global GM crop production area by 2016. The country grows a number of transgenic crops: soybeans, maize, cotton, canola, squash, papaya, and, since its 2006 approval, alfalfa (ISAAA 2016). The country not only is the top adopter but has a heavy investment in biotechnology and undisputed global dominance in it. The success the United States has enjoyed in its agriculture sector under a highly favorable international regulatory context for trade liberalization appears to have had complementary success in agricultural biotechnology under likewise favorable WTO agreements such as TRIPS. Given the country's early involvement in the development of biotechnology, securing worldwide patent protection was critical. Once TRIPS was in place, the United States adopted the most stringent version of intellectual property protection available under the agreement for its agricultural biotechnologies: patents. This approach is consistent with the country's long history of support for the patentability of life forms, as evidenced by court rulings through the second half of the twentieth century. As early as 1952 the congressional approach to the Patent Act was that patentability could be extended to "anything under the sun that is made by man" (Vaver 2004:158). Not to overstate the case, the patentability of life forms was subjected to a number of challenges over the years, and only in 1980—in the Supreme Court case of *Chakrabarty* over an oil-eating bacterial culture—did proponents find unambiguous judicial support for the patentability of life. That support extended to multicellular organisms a few years later in subsequent court cases.

Specifically with respect to agricultural biotechnologies, the United States adopted UPOV 1991 as the framework for its intellectual property protection. This version of UPOV provides intellectual property protection on plants for twenty years, but it does not strictly require the use of patents, which would restrict seed saving. Rather, UPOV 1991 leaves it to national prerogative whether to adopt patents on plants or another system that would still allow for farmers and plant breeders to be exempt from restrictions on seed saving. By adopting TRIPS in 1994, the United States chose to adopt patents and forgo the continuation of UPOV exemptions. Consequently, the traditional rights of farmers to save and reuse their seeds from year to year are voided once they adopt patented agricultural biotechnologies; then they must purchase new seeds for every crop.

The US position on patents is consistent with its overall regulatory approach to biotechnology; patents and regulation are intended to maximize the potential for growth in the sector. Citizen opposition arose in the 1980s against the first open release into the environment of GE organisms, "ice minus" potatoes and strawberries (Marchant 1988), but the US government ultimately decided against creating a separate regulatory agency to oversee agricultural biotechnology applications. Rather, the Coordinated Framework for the Regulation of Biotechnology was created in 1986 to designate the roles that existing agencies—notably the USDA, FDA, and EPA—would play in regulating the new technology.

The regulatory thrust in all these agencies is based on the concept of substantial equivalence, which assumes the products of agricultural biotechnology to be substantially equivalent to conventionally bred products. The products of biotechnology are given no special consideration for the process in which they were developed (and for any potential deviations that might arise specific to this process) but are essentially judged on the basis of their face value. The FDA requires that GE foods "meet the same rigorous safety standards as is required of all other foods" (EPA 2003). The FDA does not require premarket approval for most GE crops; they fall into its category of substances deemed "generally recognized as safe." This approach is consistent across the agencies that regulate biotechnology.

Regulatory weaknesses are clearly indicated in the highly pro-biotechnology development stance of the United States. In 2005 the USDA Office of the Inspector General cited the USDA Animal and Plant Health Inspection Service's lax regulatory approach and overall failure to adequately perform its duties. Despite an audit over a decade prior, the inspector general's report found that "the agency continued to lack an effective, comprehensive management information system to account for all inspections and their outcomes" (USDA 2005:iii). Practical evidence of regulatory failure also has appeared. The Starlink corn incident in 2000 entailed GE corn that was approved only for animal feed, not for human consumption, but was not properly segregated. The resulting contamination of food products brought a plethora of lawsuits that Aventis, the producer of Starlink corn, ultimately paid approximately $120 million to settle (Gunther 2007). The health repercussions of the failure were uncertain. Yet, subsequent failures to contain GE pharmaceutical crops—cultivated species used to extract or prepare therapeutic substances—in 2002 (Wright 2005) and unapproved Bt10 corn in 2005 have shown that regulatory laxity persisted. Bt10 corn is a variety based on *Bacillus thuringiensis*, soil-dwelling bacteria commonly used as a biological pesticide. It was engineered by Syngenta to resist an insect pest and, without a permit, deployed in four US states from 2001 to 2005. This corn line had been developed along with Bt11, which did have approval, and it was mixed in export shipments to many countries around the world (Potato Gene 2005).

In January 2006, no GE rice was yet commercially sold in the United States, but GE rice was found to have contaminated US rice shipments to Europe (Gunther 2007). Once again, the legal machine was rolling, with estimates of hundreds of millions of dollars in damages from not determining how the GE rice had spread from a research station where preventive measures were taken such as 120-foot buffer zones rather than the contracted 30-

foot ones. Despite the incident, the USDA still granted another company's application for 3,200 acres of pharma rice to be grown in Kansas (Gunther 2007).

For the most part, the United States' seemingly lax regulatory approach appears to have had the desired effect on biotechnology development. Agricultural biotechnology is reportedly one of the fastest-adopted agricultural technologies, and the United States has a significant share in the profits of that adoption globally. Monsanto posted only one year of losses from 1996 to 2007. Profits have varied since then, as can be expected from a capital-intensive technology and particularly a highly political one; profits stabilized and increased from 2003 to 2007. Monsanto posted the following profits a few years into the millennium: $68 million in 2003; $267 million in 2004; $255 million in 2005; $689 million in 2006; $993 million in 2007 (Monsanto 2005, 2007). Indications are that the 2007 drive for corn ethanol helped increase Monsanto's sales in its corn technology and hence in its profits (Gillam 2007). In 2016 the German chemical giant Bayer bought Monsanto, creating one of the largest agribusiness corporations in the world (Bayer 2016).

The rapid adoption, strong intellectual property protection, and weak regulatory oversight of agricultural biotechnologies in the United States have not gone without challenge. No doubt largely because of the lack of labeling, consumer opposition in the country appears weak. Opposition to the technology has appeared in the United States over strong intellectual property protection on life forms, marketing issues, environmental and health implications, and weak regulatory oversight of the substantial equivalence policy approach.

The prohibition of seed saving that accompanies the patentability of agricultural biotechnologies has created conflicts with farmers and nongovernmental organizations concerned about the traditional rights of farmers and concentration of ownership over the food supply and food security. By 2004 Monsanto had filed ninety lawsuits against farmers across the country for infringement of its patent rights (CFS 2005:31). Many of the farmers signed settlement agreements with the company, but others chose to fight their cases in the court system and had some limited successes in curtailing the rights of biotechnology companies (Pechlaner 2007). Even when such cases have not led to these limited successes in the legal forum, many of them have garnered publicity around the issues and consequently fortified the resistance efforts of those opposed to the technology. Organizations such as the Center for Food Safety, with offices in San Francisco, Portland, Oregon, and Washington, DC, and the Farmers Legal Action Group in Minnesota have worked to publicize the effects of patents on plants and the impacts on farmers caught in litigation.

Perspectives on the impact of the technology on US producers in general are mixed and highly dependent on the crop and the GE event at issue. Roundup-ready cotton is a genetically engineered cotton variety that makes the plants resistant to Monsanto's Roundup herbicide, but its higher input costs create added financial pressure for farmers. In India adoption of Bt cotton has slowed since 2012 (ISAAA 2016). A pharmaceutical crop has the potential of yielding higher incomes for its producers but creates greater risk for nonpharmaceutical producers of the same crop. In whichever case, crops that are destined for sensitive international markets with greater aversion to genetic engineering, such as the EU and Japan, are likely to garner much more resistance. Incidents like these involving Starlink corn and GE rice have raised resistance and had substantial economic impacts on producers because of such market issues and contamination fears (Greenpeace 2007).

Monsanto ultimately pulled GE wheat after the corporation encountered organized opposition, an example of resistance that succeeded prior to a product's commercialization. Federal support for the industry is high, but some subnational governments have resisted the technology, in part because of such marketability concerns. Maine proposed a ban on the use of the technology. Mendocino and Marin Counties in California successfully banned GM crops. The resolution of marketing issues has yet to be determined, and the ultimate place of GE crops will depend to a certain extent on changes in their acceptability in foreign markets. The introduction of pharmaceutical crops will create another hurdle, and improvements in containment will need to be assured before marketability issues cease to be a point of resistance.

Another important form of resistance in the United States has arisen from NGOs concerned about the environmental and health impacts of GE crops, with some interesting local-level experiences (Hendrickson and Heffernan 2002). This sort of resistance is rampant on the internet, and an international campaign of resistance to the technology's environmental and health impacts and the lack of labeling is evident in the proliferation of anti-GE information and propaganda. Protests and other forms of resistance are seen across North America and beyond, spearheaded by organizations such as Greenpeace, Sierra Club, Friends of the Earth International, Grain, Center for Food Safety, Organic Consumers Association, and Council of Canadians. Many campaigns have been organized by these and other organizations, as can be seen on websites like that of the Organic Consumers

Association's Millions against Monsanto (organicconsumers.org/campaigns/millions-against-monsanto).

Given the legal culture of the United States, lawsuits have provided another resistance venue for some groups. The Center for Food Safety, representing itself and several other organizations, filed a lawsuit requesting that the court rescind the USDA's 2005 approval of Roundup-ready alfalfa (Common Dreams Progressive Newswire 2006). In March 2007 a US district court judge vacated the approval of the alfalfa, agreeing that the USDA "failed to abide by federal environmental laws when it approved the crop without conducting a full Environmental Impact Assessment" (Heller 2007). Such lawsuits may not ultimately prevent the further commercialization of GE crops, but they could go some way toward changing the rate and manner in which the plantings are commercialized. In an ironic turn, Monsanto was forced to drop its first genetically modified product, rBGH (recombinant bovine growth hormone), a drug that enhances milk production in dairy cows; it was banned in Canada and most of Europe but approved for use in the United States in 1993. Given the enormous pressure of consumer groups to access organic milk instead, rBGH was silently withdrawn from the market by around 2007. Monsanto did not give up without a fight; it funded a group called the Center for Global Food Issues, proclaiming on its website that "milk is milk." Still, by 2011, the USDA estimated that organic milk could be bought at 20,000 establishments in the country, so it had become conventional once again (Escobar 2011).

Canada

Canada does not have the same crop area dedicated to agricultural biotechnology production that the United States has; in a 2016 report, Canada had 6.3 percent of global production area and the United States 39 percent (ISAAA 2016:93). Nor is Canada as quick to adopt the range of transgenic crops that are increasingly commercially available in the United States. The main transgenic crops grown in Canada in 2016 were canola, maize, soybeans, sugar beets, and alfalfa (ISAAA 2016).

The regulatory context for agricultural biotechnologies in Canada has come to bear some distinct similarities to that in the United States. Similarities extend to its approach to intellectual property rights and regulation more generally. In compliance with its WTO TRIPS obligation, Canada chose to become a member of UPOV as a signatory to the 1978 version of the agreement. Doing so was consistent with the country's history of protections for intellectual property rights, which have generally been weaker than those of the United States. UPOV 1978 retains the exemptions for farmers and plant breeders to save seeds for their own use. Industry groups have lobbied for the upgrade to UPOV 1991, thus far unsuccessfully. Nonetheless, other methods of restricting seed saving are employed in Canada—such as the use of contracts—that critics charge make a mockery of the right to save seeds (Beingessner 2004). Canada has a long history of legal struggles over whether life forms are patentable.

The chronology of patenting life forms is not as unambiguously pro-patenting in Canada as in the United States. In 2002 the Supreme Court of Canada denied a patent on a cancer-prone mouse ("Harvard mouse") on the basis that higher life forms were inappropriate subject matter for patents. The Harvard mouse was patented in the United States in 1988. In part because of uncertainties around the strength of patents in Canada and in part because of the drastically smaller size of its industry, Canada has had nowhere near the litigation between farmers and biotechnology developers over seed saving that has occurred in the United States. Canada did have one landmark case—*Monsanto v. Schmeiser*—that changed the context for patenting life forms in the country. In that case the Supreme Court of Canada ruled that while life forms were not patentable, the genes within a life form are patentable. The practical outcome for farmers wanting to save seeds was no different than in the United States; the impact on farmers is that they must purchase seeds anew each year, which increases their overall input costs to produce crops with biotechnologies as the dominant input.

Canada's regulation of agricultural biotechnologies in general shows a number of similarities to the US system. The Canadian regulatory framework for biotechnology was slower to develop than the American one, ultimately manifesting in the 1993 Regulatory Framework for Biotechnology. As in the American system, this framework designated the regulation of biotechnology under existing agencies and legislation. The three main agencies responsible for biotechnology regulation in Canada are Health Canada, the Canadian Food Inspection Agency (CFIA), and Environment Canada. An "arms-length" advisory board made up of multidisciplinary experts and members of the public was formed; it is the Canadian Biotechnology Advisory Committee (CBAC). Despite claims by the committee that regulatory oversight in Canada was triggered by "novelty," the policy approach to biotechnology in various agencies reveals an implicit concurrence with the same concept of substantial equivalence that underwrites the US policy approach. Further, assessments of biotechnology are again conducted on a product rather than a process basis. Health Canada's assessment strategy was premised on the comparison of the biotechnology product with its conventional counterpart, to compare it with "traditional foods that have an established history of safe use" (CBAC 2002). Essentially, this approach is no different from Monsanto's argument that "milk is milk" regardless of how it is produced or whether it contains traces of recombinant growth hormone.

Given the similarities between the US and Canadian regulatory systems, it is not surprising that they have similar critiques and evidence of regulatory failures. In Canada, public pressure led to a Royal Society of Canada review in 2001 that resulted in thirty-three recommendations for strengthening biotechnology regulation. In 2002 the CBAC issued another report with recommendations. Despite those recommendations to strengthen Canada's regulatory stance, the CBAC complained in a 2004 follow-up memorandum that there was "little evidence of government action to implement recommended improvements" (CBAC 2004).

Although Canada's biotechnology industry is not on the same scale as its US counterpart, Canada has a strong intellectual property rights framework and relatively lax regulatory regime around agricultural biotechnology. Also consistent with the United States, the emphasis on development appears to have been quite successful. Maxime Bernier, Canada's minister of industry in 2007, asserted that Canada had one of the highest biotech expenditures among member states of the OECD. Its global ranking was "third in the number of biotechnology firms, third in biotechnology revenue and R&D [research and development] spending, and fifth in inventions" (Bernier 2007).

Once again, the neoregulated biotechnology scenario did not go unchallenged. There are some differences in the resistance efforts in Canada and the United States; Canada appears to have fewer subnational government initiatives against GE and fewer legal challenges by NGOs (nongovernmental organizations) and ENGOs (environmental nongovernmental organizations) than in the United States. But the two have more similarities than differences. In Canada and the United States, an enormous amount of the resistance occurs through NGO lobbying, campaigns, and other initiatives that are designed to put pressure on governments. Some of the pressure can involve producer groups as well. Like alfalfa growers in the United States, organic producers in Canada are a reliable source of opposition to the technology. They are not the only source of opposition, however.

Resistance to the attempted introduction of Roundup-ready wheat in Canada in 2004 involved organic farmers, conventional farmers, producer organizations, and environmental organizations. Resistance was so widespread that it eventually forced Monsanto to withdraw its application, even though the Canadian federal government was a partner in the GM wheat's development (Scoffield 2004). While certainly the resistance was a communal effort, the robust opposition by non-GM wheat producers on the basis of marketing considerations was a large factor (Eaton 2013). Emily Eaton's 2013 book *Growing Resistance* is a tribute to the community efforts that stopped Monsanto from deploying GM wheat. Interestingly, the proponents of GM wheat, among them the Canadian Food Inspection Agency, made their arguments based on the neoliberal, individual-focused stance that consumers can make their own choices to consume GM wheat or not. The resistance was against neoliberalism and corporate control of food and advocated for a food sovereignty and food security program instead.

It is also interesting to note that one of the greatest opponents of the Roundup-ready wheat, the Canadian Wheat Board, later came under attack from proponents of the neoliberal restructuring in the agricultural sector. It was ultimately dismantled by the Conservative government of Stephen Harper in 2012 (Magnan 2016). Established in 1935, the Canadian Wheat Board was a farmer-controlled marketing cooperative with monopoly control over wheat and barley marketing in western Canada. Consequently, it was accused, particularly by American farmers, of lending an unfair trade advantage to Canadian farmers and distorting fair trade practices (CBC 2006). Producer factions in Canada such as the National Farmers Union and the Canadian Wheat Board struggled to retain the protections that supply management and single-desk marketing offer farmers in products such as wheat, dairy, and eggs. While not explicitly associated, the linkages between neoliberal neoregulation, international marketing, and corporate biotechnology became increasingly evident (Magnan 2016). The linkages become even more explicit when considering the case of Mexico.

For her part, Abby Kinchy in her book *Seeds, Science, and Struggle: The Global Politics of Transgenic Crops* (2012) challenges the conventional argument that regulatory decisions about biotechnology must be based on science and considering anything else politicizes the issue. She provides a detailed study of how social movements engaged in the scientization of public debate about contamination of conventional crops by pollen drift from GM crops. Participants called on international experts and conducted their own research, questioning regulatory science in court. A central demand was that governments consider the social and economic impacts of transgenic crops and their technological packages to avoid marginalizing alternative rural livelihoods such as agroecology and sustainable food production. Kinchy shows that subordinate actors in Canada and Mexico like small-scale farmers, environmentalists, and members of urban civil society organizations resisted GM crops, but she also exposes the pitfalls of their resistance. Their small victory in challenging GM crops in the courts put the issue to rest, dampened continuous pressure to enforce regulation, and discouraged further resistance. The story highlights the complexity of social movements and unintended consequences from the point of view of movement actors.

Mexico

In comparison to the United States and even to Canada, Mexico has remained a small player in the global adoption and development of transgenic crops. In 2016 Mexico ranked seventeenth of the twenty-six countries that have adopted the technology, with 0.1 million hectares, 0.1 percent of global crop area. Transgenic cotton and soybeans are grown in Mexico (ISAAA 2016:93). The large Mexican transnational corporation Grupo Pulsar has a competitive biotechnology arm. Pulsar has bought several smaller US biotechnology firms, and its detractors call it Mexico's Monsanto, as it tries to push its seeds and trees south of the central state of Puebla. Using the Plan Puebla Panamá, a trade agreement between Mexico and Central American countries, Pulsar also planned to tap the vast biological resources on indigenous communities' lands (Carlsen 2004:68).

Mexico's intellectual property protection evolved considerably toward convergence with the United States since the 1980s, although it stops short of affording patent protection for biological processes, plants, animals, and humans. Yet, microorganisms, proteins, genes, cellular lines, antibodies, pharmaceutical products, and microbiological processes may be patented. Furthermore, property rights over plants may be protected through the Ley Federal de Variedades Vegetales (Federal Law of Plant Varieties) (Cámara 2012).

Mexico has played a relatively minor role in biotechnology development and adoption but was one of the first adopters of rBGH in the early 1990s, before it was even approved for use in the United States (Otero, Poitras, and Pechlaner 2008). Despite Mexico's minor role, GE technology has had an enormous indirect impact on its agrarian social structure by liberalizing its farm trade (Fitting 2008). Moreover, Mexico keenly engaged in the process of neoregulating its farm structure. In 1992 Mexico deeply revised its agrarian reform legislation that dated from 1917 as a result of the Mexican Revolution (Otero 1999). The country joined its two northern neighbors in the North American Free Trade Agreement in 1994 and regulated biotechnology according to the same corporate-driven impetus as in the United States and Canada. The 2005 Law of Biosecurity of Genetically Modified Organisms, derisively called "Ley Monsanto" (Monsanto Law) by its detractors, is guided by a combination of North American- and European-style principles. It articulates both the precautionary principle that is central to EU legislation and the substantial equivalence to natural products that inspires US and Canadian law.

After Mexico joined GATT in 1986, its first major legislative transformation was the New Agrarian Reform Law of 1992. The law ended the state's obligation—set in the postrevolutionary 1917 Constitution—to redistribute land through an agrarian reform process. The land tenures under the older law (agrarian communities and *ejidos*) were initially intended to restore indigenous communities' lands from which they were dispossessed in the latter part of the nineteenth century. By the end of the 1980s, "social property" emanating from the agrarian reform process amounted to about 50 percent of all agricultural, forestry, and grazing land in Mexico. The 1992 law allowed the possibility of selling the formerly inalienable land tenures in order to open them to the market and promote their concentration (Otero 1999). In the logic of peasant households, access to land is a resource among others at their disposal that can help minimize food insecurity, given that Mexico's macro economy has been unable to offer secure jobs with living wages. *Ejido* land has been privatized in those places where the land has acquired a high value, such as in urban centers, beaches, golf courses, and tourist and recreation attractions.

In the rural sector, land concentration has also emerged but in this case through informal means of exchanging land rather than actual property transfer. Rentals of *ejido* lands with irrigation facilities have grown considerably, even encompassing whole *ejidos*, especially in the highly developed commercial farming regions of the north (Pérez Castañeda and Mackinlay 2015). This trend toward concentration of former or current *ejido* land has taken place in parallel to another trend to *ejido* land fragmentation resulting from the agrarian regularization program PROCEDE (Programa de Certificación de Derechos Ejidales y Titulación de Solares) throughout the country; most *ejidos* form part of this process. Actual sales of the highly fragmented lands in small plots have taken place all over Mexico. A dual tendency both renews concentration into de facto *latifundios* (large concentration of landed property) but also further splits *ejido* land into *microfundios* (tiny properties).

The precise figures of privatization are hard to assess, as land transfers continue to take place by informal means in spite of the legal possibility of privatization (Concheiro Bórquez and Diego Quintana 2001). Juan Carlos Pérez Castañeda and Horacio Mackinlay (2015) argue that the dual process is indeed a reality, of reconcentration on one hand and further fragmentation on the other. The concentration could result in more lands being incorporated into the logic of modernization and capitalist production, while the fragmentation could keep some peasant farmers making meager subsistence that might be incorporated into the formal sector if an opportunity arises. This economic status puts small- or micro-scale peasants in a highly vulnerable situation economically and politically, as their "votes" can easily be bought in a less than democratic country like Mexico.

Mobilization against the 1992 agrarian law was widespread, but it was passed swiftly (Cornelius and Myhre 1998; Otero 1999). Two years later, however, on 1 January 1994—the day of NAFTA's official start—the Zapatista National Liberation Army launched an armed insurrection in the southeastern state of Chiapas (Gilbreth and Otero 2001; Harvey 1996, 1998). NAFTA would subsequently be indelibly linked to the main oppositional cries of the peasant movement. After the insurrection, Subcomandante Marcos, a noted Zapatista spokesperson, said NAFTA amounted to a death sentence to Mexico's indigenous ethnicities. It was on the heels of this very specific and volatile context that new agricultural biotechnologies and neoregulation were introduced.

Between 1995 and January 2005, thirty-one agricultural genetically modified organisms (GMOs) for human consumption were approved for commercial use in Mexico. Products included varieties of alfalfa (one), soybeans (two), tomatoes (three), potatoes (three), canola (four), cotton (nine), and maize (nine). Although a total of nine companies developed the varieties, Monsanto alone accounted for sixteen of the thirty-one varieties. Not surprisingly, eight of the varieties developed by Monsanto were resistant to its Roundup herbicide (COFEPRIS 2005). Because Mexico is a center of origin of corn, the country holds an important reservoir of biological diversity of this crop. The Mexican government initially had a cautious approach toward the release of transgenic corn, but by 2002 Mexico's Department of Agriculture started awarding permits for its commercial use. Presumably these were for use in northern Mexico, away from the central and southern regions of greatest biodiversity.

In view of the haphazard approach to awarding permits, the Mexican Congress finally issued the Law of Biosecurity of Genetically Modified Organisms (Ley de Bioseguridad de los Organismos Genéticamente Modifica-dos) on 18 February 2005. The law's goals include an adequate and efficient level of protection of human health, the environment, biological diversity, and animal and plant health; definition of principles and national policy; competencies in various government agencies; a permits regime; and con-trol measures. Salient among the goals is singling out maize as a crop to be treated as a special case, in contrast to the government's practice of liberally awarding permits since 2002.

Interestingly, permits for commercial release also imply import permits for the same GMO, thus introducing a clearly market-oriented criterion of economic feasibility; interested parties must be better off producing a GMO in Mexico compared with importing it, as there is no protection for GMO production against foreign trade. Imports must be submitted to the same permit process as producing GMOs domestically, and in most cases, one of the requirements is that the relevant GMO be permitted for commercial re-lease in its country of origin.

A special section of Mexico's 2005 biodiversity law is devoted to restricted zones for the protection of centers of origin and biological diversity as well as to GMO-free zones, which may be designated at the request of local com-munities. The zones may involve, for instance, communities that seek to pro-tect organic farming practices and markets. Such community requests, how-ever, must be backed by both state and municipal governments, a caveat that raises the question of the extent to which such governments have sufficient autonomy from local ruling classes and large transnational corporations.

With respect to labeling GMOs, the law takes a combined approach between the precautionary (European) and the substantial equivalence (North American) approaches, with the latter ultimately prevailing. For di-rect human consumption, labeling is required only if the product is "signifi-cantly different" from conventional products. With regard to seeds, however, the law follows a stricter labeling approach, as Mexico must honor its trade agreements not only with the United States and Canada but also with the European Union. To comply with this commitment, article 101 of Mexico's biodiversity law entrusts the Departments of Agriculture and Economy with following general labeling rules and specifically identifying products that contain GMOs, their features, and the implications. In the case of GMO im-ports, the law leaves it up to the various agencies involved as to labeling re-quirements, but these must include the product's intended final destination, for human food or animal feed.

As in the United States and Canada, biotechnology adoption in Mexico has garnered substantial resistance. Resistance in the United States and Canada has focused on legislative and judicial systems, and in Mexico it has also spilled into the streets in the form of social movement protest and even armed insurrection. Three reasons explain the difference. First, as mentioned, biotechnology and neoliberal globalism have not had as grave an impact on the agrarian social structures of either Canada or the United States. In contrast, the neoliberal turn has been notably more devastating for Mexico's agrarian social structure than for its northern neighbors. Clearly, the impact has much to do with the sheer numbers of people whose livelihoods depended on agriculture in Mexico and have been made redundant since the mid-1980s, when the country entered GATT. This was the first major indication that Mexico was moving from an inward-looking country focused on its internal market to one newly attempting to focus its economic growth on exports. In 1990, when President Carlos Salinas proposed discussions toward building NAFTA, close to 30 percent of Mexico's labor force worked in farming. By NAFTA's fourteenth year, in 2008, when all remaining protections for four crops were finally phased out, that proportion had decreased to less than 20 percent (Otero 2011).

A second reason behind protests in Mexico is that corn happens to be the country's main staple and a special cause of concern (Fitting 2011). Corn has had a central importance in Mexico's economy, diet, and culture. Given a similar importance of beekeeping for Mayan peasants in Campeche, resistance to the deployment of transgenic soybeans was strong and effective (Gómez González 2016). There, it was not that peasants were producing soybeans but that the pesticides used to cultivate the transgenic version by modern, capitalized farmers were devastating the bees.

A third reason that explains different resistance responses in Mexico is that its democratic institutions are much weaker and less developed than those in the north. Until 2015 or so, Mexican courts had a rather insignificant presence in adjudicating contentious issues and showed little if any political independence from the holders of executive power. It took strong social movements, usually alliances of peasant organizations with academics and environmentalists, to have some tribunals rule in their favor (Gómez González 2016). For its part, the legislature has been readily dominated by pro-neoliberal, pro-agribusiness concerns, and their lobbying groups have exerted determining pressure in issuing new laws.

Corporation-friendly biotechnology regulation and agrarian reform detrimental to peasants created a conspicuous double attack on peasant agriculture. Resistance movements in Mexico have consequently explicitly linked the issues of agricultural biotechnology and neoliberal agricultural restructuring to NAFTA's agricultural chapter and have demanded its renegotiation in their opposition statements. That has been the case since 1994, but their demands came to a head at the end of 2002, just before most crops would be opened to free trade with Canada and the United States at the start of NAFTA's eighth year. At that time, the largest peasant movement—measured by the number of peasant organizations and political allegiances it represented—was mobilized into the oppositional coalition El Campo No Aguanta Más. The coalition initially achieved a promise from President Vicente Fox's administration (2000–2006) to renegotiate NAFTA's agricultural chapter or introduce some compensatory measures, but the movement eventually became fragmented as some organization leaders accepted short-term promises for their constituencies (Bartra and Otero 2005; Celis 2004).

Massive mobilization and even armed insurrection had not managed to modify neoliberal policies to any great extent by 2006, and Mexico's political system was shaken to its roots in that year's highly questioned presidential elections (Otero 2007). The campaign by Fox and the Entrepreneurial Coordinating Council, an organization of the capitalist class, against the left-of-center candidate Andrés Manuel López Obrador was found to go against the electoral law but insufficiently to annul the election. A series of communication errors by the Federal Electoral Institute led to a widespread belief that electoral fraud had occurred. Some hoped that the electoral tribunal of the federal judiciary would rectify the situation by ordering a recount or even nullifying the election, but it ultimately only ordered a vote recount for a little over 9 percent of the balloting boxes, setting off a tremendous amount of uncertainty in the entire institutional process. Despite the considerable irregularities found, the tribunal decided that these did not change the final results. According to public opinion polls at the time, 46 percent of respondents believed that the elections were fraudulent. Thus it is no surprise that considerable mobilization took place after the 2006 elections and again after the 2012 elections.

An important issue in the mobilization was the preservation of Mexico's food sovereignty around maize; it entailed keen opposition to the use of transgenic crops because of their direct and indirect effects on peasant livelihoods. The battle cry of opponents in 2007 was "Sin maíz no hay país" (Without corn, there's no country). The movement was energized by the end of NAFTA's phase-out of protections for the last four agricultural commodities: maize, beans, sugar, and milk. A massive demonstration of 200,000 peasants, urban workers, and other sympathizers took place in Mexico City on 31 January 2008 in protest of NAFTA's full opening of agricultural trade. Whether resistance could successfully alter the trajectory remains uncertain but certainly possible. The 2018 elections could mark a watershed moment in Mexican politics, as the major political parties have lost credibility among many citizens, and a new political formation, Movimiento Regeneración Nacional (MORENA), is led by López Obrador in his third presidential campaign.

CONCLUSION

All in all, the least developed and least economically powerful country in the NAFTA trio is suffering the brunt of social impacts with the introduction of biotechnology in the neoliberal context. The policy expressions of neoliberal globalism—trade liberalization, neoregulation, and corporation-friendly intellectual property rights—have provided important linkages between the neoliberal regulatory thrust and biotechnology. In sum, the term "third food regime" could aptly be changed to "neoliberal food regime." It is centrally characterized by biotechnology and so-called life sciences multinational corporations as key economic actors operating in an international context of neoregulation. The neoliberal food regime has shown significant evidence of becoming entrenched. Still, it has depended on state support for trade liberalization and regulations important to the technology, such as intellectual property rights. Resistance efforts directed specifically at biotechnology (as in the United States and Canada) or at the conjunction of biotechnology and the neoliberal paradigm (as in Mexico) will yet affect the food regime's future shape.

With respect to agricultural biotechnology, specifically, the drive to develop and disseminate the technology has taken precedence over more precautionary approaches in Canada and the United States. An official pro-biotechnology stance has not been free of adverse impacts, yet the development drive has outweighed those considerations. In Mexico, which has a much weaker biotechnology sector, indirect effects of biotechnology through trade liberalization have been more devastating and social resistance has been much greater (Gómez González 2016; Poitras 2008). Resistance to biotechnology in Canada and the United States, except on the issue of intellectual property rights, is not as explicitly linked with neoliberal restructuring or international trade rules as it is in Mexico. There is a marked qualitative difference in the nature of resistance in these countries. The livelihoods of US and Canadian organic growers and some others within the small percentage of the farming population in those countries may be in danger. But the neoliberal food regime is certainly not as detrimental to them as in Mexico or the repercussions on their compromised livelihoods as dire (Otero and Lapegna 2016).

The neoliberal food regime threatens to reinstate a form of neocolonialism by external economic agents—hence the more vigorous resistance in Latin America. While in Mexico social resistance has been confined mostly to civil society with some gains through judiciary tribunals, the situation is markedly different in some countries of Latin America. In these nations, strong indigenous movements have been among the most vigorous opponents of the privatization and commodification trends of neoliberal globalism, and they are also ones that have a considerable biological diversity to defend. In Bolivia, Ecuador, and Venezuela, opposition to neoliberal globalism gained state power by 2007, and it has spread to other nations including Nicaragua. Middle-of-the road countries like Argentina, Brazil, and Uruguay with left-of-center social democratic governments have remained for the most part working within the confines of an overall neoliberal perspective. Argentina and Brazil are two large adopters of biotechnology, namely transgenic soybeans (Gras and Hernández 2016; Legizamón 2016; Motta 2016).

Generally speaking, then, the regime arising from neoliberal globalism is already increasing the inequality between North and South. The presumed or implied inevitability of the neoliberal food regime is questioned by resistance in Mexico and beyond, however. One empirical question that future research could tackle is the extent to which resistance in Mexico will succeed, given its proximity to the United States and the strength and authoritarian tendencies of its right-wing ruling class and politicians. How will any change affect food trade and diets across the NAFTA nations? US-based ABMs have been NAFTA's prime beneficiaries, at least in agricultural production and trade. Before turning to comparing the food performance of NAFTA partners, however, I will first examine how the neoliberal diet has evolved in its country of origin, the United States of America.

CHAPTER 3

Food and Inequality in the United States

T he United States dominates the modern agricultural paradigm and its associated dietary patterns while also generating an acute dilemma within its own borders. On one hand, it has the most profitable and successful agribusiness multinational corporations. On the other, it is exacerbating the neoliberal diet, composed of what is popularly known as "junk food" but also a range of highly processed and convenience products that is broader than the chips, pop, and candy traditionally associated with the term. A watershed decision came in 1973 under President Richard Nixon when the Food and Drug Administration repealed a 1938 law requiring the food industry to include the word "imitation" when a natural food was adulterated. The new requirement stipulated only that such edibles be "nutritionally equivalent" to real food. Michael Pollan says of the moment, "Adulteration had been repositioned as food science" (2008:36). The industrial, edible commodities that nutritionists identify as energy-dense foods are usually highly processed and have low nutritional value and high contents of fat, often transfats, and empty calories (Drewnowski and Darmon 2005; Drewnowski and Specter 2004; Nestle 2006; Popkin 2009). The health repercussions of that dietary shift became apparent as obesity was labeled a national epidemic with mounting costs; by 2012 the United States was spending about $190 billion a year on obesity-related illnesses (Nestle 2013:393).

In 2004 an estimated 12 percent of the US population faced food insecurity, a figure that was just above 10 percent in 2001. After the 2008 recession, food insecurity rose to a peak of 15 percent in 2011, then declined to 12.7 percent by 2015 and 12.3 by 2016 (Coleman-Jensen et al. 2017:vi). These percentages represent a sizable and disturbing number of food-insecure people in a rich country. And yet I argue that the core nutritional issue in the United States is not whether people have sufficient access to food but what quality of food is accessible to most. The global food crisis set off in 2007–2008 made even the US working classes vulnerable to price fluctuations and food insecurity and increased their exposure to the energy-dense, nutritionally compromised food that typifies the neoliberal diet. This type of food is the most accessible to lower-income groups, whose numbers and proportion rise with greater levels of income inequality. Worsening income inequality in the United States has drawn much public and scholarly attention after the Occupy Wall Street movement of 2011–2012 (Galbraith 2012; Piketty 2014; Stiglitz 2012).

Classes or socioeconomic strata in the United States have increasingly differentiated diets. Upper-income groups have had growing access to higher-quality and value-added foods that are profitable for capital such as meats, imported fresh fruits and vegetables, and wines and other alcoholic beverages, while the diets of low- to middle-income classes are heavily weighted toward the energy-dense pseudofoods associated with the proliferation of obesity in the United States. The neoliberal diet is the nutritional expression of the neoliberal food regime. It is the industrial diet as it becomes globalized under the impetus of neoliberalism, the international realignments and historically and geographically variegated national and local regulatory trends in global political economy since the 1980s.

The US government and those of other wealthy nations have acted inconsistently in terms of neoliberalism and state intervention. The US government continues to heavily subsidize domestic agriculture while promoting trade liberalization for the rest of the world. It also selectively practices trade protectionism for sectors and industries including some agricultural products (McMichael 2009; Otero, Pechlaner, and Gürcan 2013). Neoliberal capitalism has represented a frontal attack on working-class rights in the market by means such as undermining unions and citizenship rights of even market-dependent, liberal welfare states (Coburn 2004:44).

Much of the literature on class and inequality dynamics of dietary consumption focuses on the individual as the leading locus to address obesity, as if consumers had equal economic chances of choosing their food.

My major goal here is to contribute to the literature by providing data and analysis highlighting the structural determinants of food choice. My analysis of macro data from the UN FAOSTAT demonstrates how the US diet has changed since 1961 toward an increasing emphasis on fats and high-calorie foods. Comparing patterns of US household food consumption by income levels for selected years can help illustrate the consequences of inequality. My analysis shows that food systems and social inequality constitute structural realities, placing most solutions well beyond individual choice. I find that the state is the only social agent that can ameliorate deteriorating food quality and security as well as inequality and the health risks they generate.

THE LITERATURE ON CLASS AND INEQUALITY IN DIETARY CONSUMPTION

There is general support in the academic literature for the correlation between various socioeconomic variables and diet (Darmon and Drewnowski 2008; Dixon 2009; Drewnowski 2009; Drewnowski and Specter 2004; Dubowitz et al. 2008; Harrington, Fitzgerald, et al. 2011; Larson et al. 2009; Lee 2011; Thirlaway and Upton 2009). In the United States the history of racialized populations and their cuisines is tightly linked to work regimes. The diets of enslaved African Americans often consisted of high-fat, energy-dense foods that were required in the past, given the amount of physical labor that many had to undertake. Eventually, "soul food" became commonly defined as traditional black American dishes that originated in the rural South such as chitterlings, pig knuckles, turnip greens, and cornbread. Soul food tends to be fried, pork-infused, and sugary. Much of this food has carried over to new labor conditions that require less energy expenditure (Miller 2013; Williams-Forson 2006). Changing to more healthful diets, however, is constrained by class.

The social class dimension and its correlation with food is encapsulated in Andrea Freeman's term "food oppression" as a "form of structural subordination that builds on and deepens pre-existing disparities along race and class lines" (2007:2245). Freeman finds that government support of the fast food industry—through industry-friendly subsidies for animal feed, sugars, and fats—serves to reduce the cost of fast food and create a structural constraint on dietary choices. A 2010 report produced by the USDA's Economic Research Service discusses how government policies helped make corn sweeteners less expensive than sugar through mechanisms such as "investments in public research that raised yields for corn, sugar production allotments and trade restrictions, and subsidies for corn production" (Morrison, Buzby, and Wells 2010:17). Consequently, the availability of sweeteners increased from 113.2 pounds per person between 1924 and 1974 (excluding the war years) to 136.3 pounds per person in 2008. No doubt the ease of access and affordability has something to do with the increase in soft drink consumption.

Guthman contends that the current problems in the US food system—and thus the source of their resolution—have to do with the nature of capitalism (2011:16). More specifically, Kathryn Thirlaway and Dominic Upton (2009) show that "people living on a low income have higher rates of diet-related diseases than other people" (58). Most notable of the health impacts is the proliferation of obesity that disproportionately affects the poor (Dixon 2009; Drewnowski 2009; Drewnowski and Specter 2004; Popkin 2009). Drawing on an extensive review of existing literature, Hedwig Lee (2011) concludes that social inequality is closely linked to obesity in the United States at the individual, family, school, and neighborhood levels. Katherine Mason (2012) has shown that obesity itself has become a new basis for discrimination that furthers inequality and affects women more severely than men.

An important mediating factor between socioeconomic status and diet is that highly processed, high-fat, high-sugar, energy-dense junk food is usually more affordable than fresh fruits and vegetables and leaner proteins (Lee 2011). In Adam Drewnowski and S. E. Specter's 2004 analysis of food energy and cost the authors find an "inverse relation between energy density and energy cost . . . [suggesting] that 'obesity-promoting' foods are simply those that offer the most dietary energy at the lowest cost" and "dry foods with a stable shelf life are generally less costly (per MJ [megajoule]) than perishable meats or fresh produce" (9). Thus, the energy cost of cookies or potato chips in 2009 was roughly 20 cents/MJ but about 95 cents/MJ for carrots (9). Nicole Darmon and Adam Drewnowski's 2015 meta-analysis of the literature on the price of energy-dense foods concludes unequivocally that energy-dense foods are cheaper per calorie than nutrient-dense foods. The findings were the same in multiple countries.

Not only is healthful food more expensive, but it also may be more difficult to obtain for lower-income individuals and racial minorities because of accessibility issues. This issue is explored in the food deserts literature (Gordon et al. 2011; Guptill, Copelton, and Lucal 2013; Shaw 2006; Walker et al. 2010), with its inconsistently defined concept of some form of exclusion or impediment to access to food or particular types of food. Notably, supermarkets and chain stores are more likely to have cheaper high-quality food than convenience stores and small grocery or neighborhood stores, which are more likely to stock processed items. A study of low-income populations in the United States (Rose and Richards 2004) concludes that neighborhood food availability such as easy access to supermarket shopping is a significant factor in determining household fruit consumption. Food costs are usually higher in such deserts, reducing available funds for the more expensive fresh fruits and vegetables even where they are available.

Other variables—culture, education, and gender, to name a few— complicate the relation of socioeconomic status to obesity (Christensen and Carpiano 2014). In the United States and other higher-income countries, there is broad general evidence of an inverse association between socioeconomic status and obesity. The neoliberal diet is being exported internationally, however, and is well on its way to forming the basis of a global diet. This dietary globalization occurs through the dissemination of agriculture and food industrialization, supermarketization, proliferation of fast food outlets, cultural shifts, and various marketing processes. Export mechanisms of the neoliberal diet are familiar, but again, it should be noted that the diet's correlation with class manifests with notable differences outside of the United States and other high-income countries.

Most notably, although the basis of the neoliberal diet is the proliferation of cheap processed foods, these foods are still prohibitively expensive for many in lower-income countries. Those at greatest risk in these countries are thus initially the middle and upper classes. A growing body of evidence supports the contention that the class-diet relationship is reversed in lower-income countries but transitions as a country economically develops. Through a systematic assessment of sixty-seven nations (Pampel, Denney, and Krueger 2012), the authors specifically assess and find support for this "reversal hypothesis" (with some variations by gender), whereby the relation between socioeconomic status and body weight reverses with a change in a country's GDP. The global replication and/or reversal of US patterns of dietary inequality provides a powerful incentive to understand the dietary dynamics of the United States.

MAKING SENSE OF THE EVOLUTION OF THE US DIET

The United States has been a disproportionate consumer among nations, with an average per capita caloric consumption well above the world's average. Tables 3.1 and 3.2 present a comparative perspective with a small sample of emerging nations. As may be seen, there has been a process of upward convergence toward US levels since 1962, but not on a uniform basis. Brazil and China closed the gap with the United States, while Mexico reached

TABLE 3.1. Total food supply (kcal/capita/day), world, USA, and four emerging nations, 1962–2012

	1962	1972	1982	1992	2002	2012
USA	2,858	3,062	3,191	3,559	3,783	3,687
Brazil	2,271	2,397	2,643	2,771	2,927	3,248
China	1,547	1,848	2,339	2,468	2,836	3,098
Mexico	2,286	2,574	3,132	3,000	3,103	3,049
World	2,243	2,352	2,531	2,610	2,728	2,874
India	2,052	1,985	2,029	2,333	2,285	2,435

Source: FAOSTAT 2017a.
Note: Order is by 2012 data.

TABLE 3.2. Total food supply, world and four nations, as percent of US supply, 1962–2012

	1962	1972	1982	1992	2002	2012
USA	100	100	100	100	100	100
Brazil	79.5	78.3	82.8	77.9	77.4	**88.1**
China	54.1	60.4	73.3	69.3	75.0	**84.0**
Mexico	80.0	84.1	**98.2**	84.3	82.0	82.7
World	78.5	76.8	**79.3**	73.3	72.1	77.9
India	**71.8**	64.8	63.6	65.6	60.4	66.0

Source: Calculations from table 3.1, based on FAOSTAT 2017a.
Notes: Order is by 2012 data. Bold numbers are world and four countries' highest percentages reached relative to US totals.

TABLE 3.3. US average caloric food supply in excess of the
world's average (%), 1961–2011

CALORIC SOURCE	1961	2011	2011–1961	PERCENTAGE CHANGE
Alcoholic beverages	205.7	229.0	23.3	11.3
Fruits, excluding wine	156.9	118.1	–38.8	–24.7
Sugar, sweeteners	266.8	247.4	–19.4	–7.3
Vegetable oils	244.2	252.2	7.9	3.2
Vegetables	145.5	74.2	–71.3	–49.0
Animal products	298.8	195.9	–103.0	–34.5
Animal fats	280.3	165.6	–114.7	–40.9
Eggs	372.2	151.4	–220.8	–59.3
Meat	304.5	187.0	–117.5	–38.6
Milk, excluding butter	324.6	268.3	–56.2	–17.3
Total	131.1	126.8	–4.4	–3.3

Source: Constructed with data from FAOSTAT 2016.
Note: For each food-caloric source the world's average per capita
daily consumption was subtracted from the US average, which is
always greater.

its highest point in food-caloric consumption in 1982, well before NAFTA.
India has remained below the world's average, which is in turn lowered by
the least developed countries. In spite of the different paces of convergence,
I am arguing that a globalized neoliberal diet is emerging, if not in total calories, at least in the energy-dense and meat composition of industrial foods.

Table 3.3 compares the change in caloric contribution from the main
food sources for the US average and the percentage by which it exceeded
the world's average. As the percentage change in the grand total indicates,
there has been a mere 3.3 percent reduction in the US average caloric consumption compared with the world's average per capita food-caloric consumption. The change can also be seen as a gain in the world's average food
consumption; except for alcoholic beverages and vegetable oils, in which US
consumption far exceeds the world's average, the world is converging toward
US food-caloric levels in all other categories. It may well be that much of
the average increase in the world's food consumption is accounted for by the

rising middle classes in emerging economies like Brazil, China, and Mexico. A crucial point, though, is that this dietary move is going in the direction of adopting a US type of diet.

Let us break down the sources of increased caloric intake in the United States since 1961, for what matters most is not only the quantity but the quality of increased calories. The *proportion* of calories contributed by animal products has declined, although *absolute* figures have remained stable. The increase in total food intake is due primarily to three categories of food, all part of the larger category of "vegetable products" defined by the FAO as cereals, vegetable oils, and sugars. I am not referring to fresh vegetables. Rather, these are primarily processed or industrialized vegetable products. All of these caloric sources have a strong link to overweight and obesity.

Historically, we have seen a clear correlation between high income levels both for countries and individuals, with higher-fat diets coming from meat and milk products. The globalization of US dietary patterns has involved a sharp decline in the consumption of complex carbohydrates such as those from whole grains and fresh fruits, vegetables, and legumes. The relation between GNP and fat consumption was high and direct in the 1960s but declined by the 1990s, when high fat consumption became less linked to GNP levels and more linked to rates of urbanization. Adam Drewnowski and Barry Popkin (1997) observe, "Although the availability of animal fats continued to be linked to income, but less strongly than before, vegetable fats now accounted for a greater proportion of dietary energy, and their availability was virtually independent of income" (33). The authors highlight the strong relevance of the rise of vegetable oils. Soybean oil was an important component, accounting "for about 70% of the production and consumption of edible oils and fats in the United States, and . . . for the bulk of vegetable oil consumption worldwide" by the 1990s (34). Urbanization is an important indicator of neoliberal diet pressures and one of the five components of my NDR index.

Figure 3.1 depicts the rise or decline of the four main contributors to caloric intake in the United States: cereals, sugars including high-fructose corn syrup, vegetable oils, and animal products. Clearly, animal products continued to make up the lion's share of US caloric intake. In absolute terms, animal products remained high and stable throughout the period 1961–2013. Sugars increased as a caloric contribution from 515 calories a day in 1961 to a high point of 660 in 2004, then declined to 569 by 2011. Cereals increased from 627 calories per capita per day in 1961 to a high point of 871 in 1997 and declined to 798 by 2011, still a 27 percent increase for the entire period. The United States experienced a more pronounced increase in cereal supply than

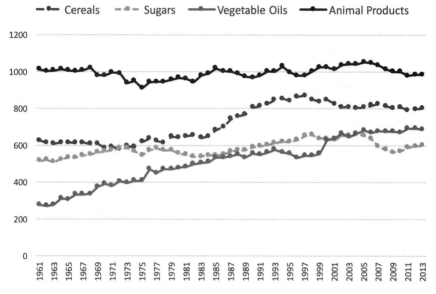

Figure 3.1. US main food caloric sources, 1961–2013 (kcal/capita/day).
Source: FAOSTAT 2017c, d.

the world average increase of 19 percent. Yet the US per capita average consumption of cereals pales in comparison to the world average of 1,296 kilocalories in 2011. Cereals continue to be the main component of basic foods in most of the world; in the United States, animal products are the predominant dietary feature. A large share of corn and soybeans produced in the United States is used as feed for livestock.

The most dramatic caloric increase, 154 percent, was in US consumption of vegetable oils by 2011, compared with a 148 percent increase worldwide. This climb is consistent with my understanding of the importance of vegetable oils in the prevalence of processed, energy-dense foods that typify the neoliberal diet. It is also related to what Pollan identifies as the dietary move from leaves (for feed and food) to seeds (2008:124–132); the former contain more micronutrients, while the latter undergo considerable processing. The trend is in keeping with a broader one of nutritional loss through what Winson calls the "simplification" of our diets (2013:30). The word "simplification" here has to do with reducing whole foods to their simpler elements, but that involves considerable industrial processing and a complex food delivery system. The history of the US diet is one that is being replicated in a global "nutrition transition" (Popkin 1998). Similar historical changes can be seen in a sample of other high-income countries presented in table 3.4.

Table 3.4 presents changes between 1961 and 2011 in the caloric (kilo-

TABLE 3.4. Changes in main food supply sources in the world and five rich countries (%), 1961–2011, by kcal/capita/day

	ANIMAL PRODUCTS			CEREALS			SUGARS			VEGETABLE OILS		
	1961	2011	%	1961	2011	%	1961	2011	%	1961	2011	%
World	338	507	**50**	1,086	1,296	19	192	229	19	113	280	**148**
Canada	1,069	913	-1.5	628	770	**23**	471	443	-6	159	582	**266**
France	1,013	1,180	17	951	949	-0.2	296	357	**21**	184	502	**173**
Germany	923	1,093	18	716	871	**22**	336	464	**38**	252	417	**65**
UK	1,225	989	-19	766	900	18	504	389	**-23**	243	441	**81.5**
USA	1,010	995	-1.5	627	798	**27**	296	357	**21**	276	701	**154**

Source: Constructed with data from FAOSTAT 2015.
Note: Bold indicates change greater than 20 percent (+ or –).

calories per capita per day) contribution of the same four generic food sources—animal products, cereals, sugars, and vegetable oils. If we consider that changes of 20 percent or higher are significant, as indicated in bold numbers, we get some interesting patterns and some anomalies. First, there was a general increase or stagnation in Canada in animal product consumption but a large decline in the United Kingdom. In cereals we see a general increase of 17 to 27 percent in all countries except France. With regard to sugar, all countries except Canada experienced significant changes, and only Canada and the UK had decreases in sugar consumption. Finally, all the countries in my small sample experienced a quite significant increase in the consumption of vegetable oils, from a 65 percent rise in Germany to a 266 percent surge in Canada. The world average narrowed the gap with rich nations, especially in animal products and vegetable oils.

Specific to my focus on the United States, it is important to consider how this dietary transition has disproportionately affected the low- to middle-income classes. Since the 1970s the United States has been experiencing an increase in its Gini coefficient, which measures the level of income inequality (OECD 2011). Other measures of inequality refer to income concentration by population percentile. *The Economist* (2012) reports that the proportion of income going to the top 1 percent of the US population declined from almost 20 percent in 1923 to a low of 7.5 percent in 1973. This low came after the Fordist era of mass production and mass consumption, combined with the growth of the welfare state that started in the Franklin D. Roosevelt presidency. The crisis of Fordism that began at the end of the 1960s, however, was ultimately resolved by cutting wages through outsourcing and other means and the social policies of the welfare state. After the neoliberal reforms (Harvey 2005; Peck 2010), the percentage of wealth captured by the top 1 percent returned to almost 20 percent again by 2010 (*The Economist* 2012) and to 21 percent by 2014 (Kenworthy 2017:2). If the wealthiest have captured so much of the nation's income, proportionally less income is available for lower- and middle-income classes. How has the inequality affected diets in the United States?

My general proposition is that in today's world, even in developed countries, lack of access to food continues to be a menace for some; in 2004, for instance, 88 percent of US households were food secure, but 12 percent were not (Nord, Andrews, and Carlson 2004). And yet the recent food security risk is in having access to too much energy-dense food and insufficient access to nutritious food, primarily for economic reasons related to inequality. Families in the United States spent on average 23.4 percent of disposable personal income on food in 1929 and 25.2 percent in 1933, at the height of the Great Depression; the figure fell below 10 percent by 2000, dropped to a low of 9.5 percent in 2008, then rose slightly to 9.8 percent in 2011. But these averages must be disaggregated to capture the impact of inequality.

FOOD AND INEQUALITY IN THE UNITED STATES

I offer here a statistical analysis of how inequality differentially affects the ability of US households to consume a variety of foods depending on class status. I base this analysis on data from the Consumer Expenditure Surveys for 1972–1973, 1984, 1994, and 2004, and 2014 conducted by the US Bureau of Labor Statistics (BLS). The BLS divided its data of US households into income quintiles of 20 percent each, from the lowest (poorest) to the highest (richest) income level. The quintiles are "categories of income reporters, ranked in ascending order of income and divided into five equal groups" (BLS 2007:7). Evidently, income quintiles are not equivalent to social classes, but they are proxies that give us a good idea about class inequality.

Figure 3.2 offers information on annual average household food expenditures in various years. The most surprising revelation is that inequality among households remained essentially unchanged from 1984 to 2014. The total dollars spent by the richest households stayed around three times as much as the expenditures of households in the poorest income quintile. And yet, that absolute amount of money spent by households in the richest quin-

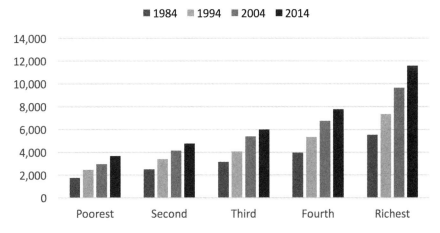

Figure 3.2. US average annual household food expenditures ($), 1984–2014, by income quintile. *Source*: BLS 2017b.

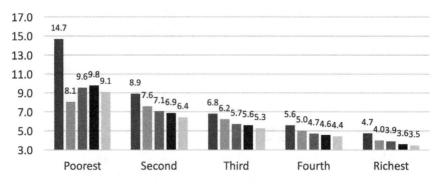

Figure 3.3. US average per capita food share of total household expenditures (%),
1973–2014, by income quintile. *Source*: BLS 2017b.

tile represents a much lower proportion of their total incomes, as reflected
in figure 3.3. By 2014 households in the poorest income quintile spent 9.1
percent of their total after-tax incomes on food, while the richest spent only
3.5 percent.

The figures underscore the big difference in the percentage of household
income devoted to food depending on the income quintile in which a household happens to fall. The calculations are made on a per capita basis by dividing household expenditures in food in each quintile by the average number
of people within households. The lower the share of the family budget that
is spent on food, the more funds are left for other necessities or luxuries. But
the percentages are calculated with respect to each quintile's respective income, so they are not a fair image of inequality.

Given the large differences of expenditures by quintile, I analyze how
such differences translate into household expenditures on specific foods depending on level of income. To highlight how inequality plays out, I equate
the expenditures of the richest quintile to 100 percent, as in all cases its households tend to spend more on all kinds of food than the other four quintiles
spend. This analysis highlights the effects of inequality on food accessibility.
Figure 3.4 presents calculations of the percentage, in rounded figures, that
each of the four lower quintiles spent as a proportion of those made by the
richest income quintile for selected years. Each of the four lower quintiles
had slightly decreasing proportions of food expenditures than the richest
quintile after 1973, with a slight 2 percent recovery for the poorest quintile in
2014. With very restricted budgets, however, households in the poorest quintile must have made sacrifices in other necessities. Caloric intake remained

similar across quintiles, and indeed the average increased, but food quality must have varied considerably depending on income levels for each quintile.

Next I examine the percentage that households in each income quintile spent on food away from home and on selected types of foods. Figure 3.5 depicts each quintile's share of the household food budget spent away from home in relation to its total food expenditures. Food expenditures away from home increased across the board from 1973 to 2014. Much of this expenditure appears to be at fast food restaurants, especially for all but the highest income quintile.

Let us now explore how households in different income quintiles spent their food budgets on a variety of foods, contrasting what I call "luxury" foods like meats, fruits, and vegetables with "basic" foods like cereals, sugars, and fats. Meats can in general be regarded as a luxury, but in the United States they have become generalized fare, with type of meat (such as beef versus chicken) becoming the more salient factor. Even beef is internally differentiated; hamburger meat is much more accessible than, say, ribeye steak. Figure 3.6 shows US meat production trends since 1961, revealing patterns of which type of meat became more or less accessible to consumers.

Beef consumption remained mostly flat after peaking in 1976, then de-

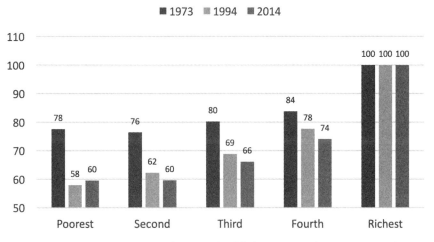

Figure 3.4. US per capita expenditures in food (%), 1973–2014, by income quintile (richest = 100). For this figure, household expenditures in food by each quintile were divided by the average number of persons per household in the quintile in each given year. The measurement does not consider the ages of household members, but the average household size varies considerably among quintiles (1.7 people in the poorest quintile versus 3.2 in the richest, as of 2014). *Source*: BLS 2017b.

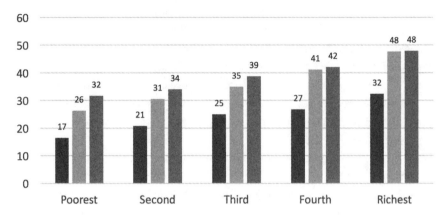

Figure 3.5. US food expenditures away from home (%), 1973–2014, by income quintile. *Source*: BLS 2017b.

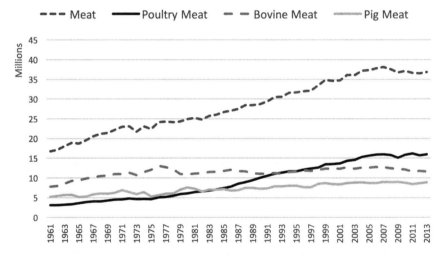

Figure 3.6. US meat consumption (metric tons), 1961–2013. *Source*: FAOSTAT 2017d.

clined slightly after the 2007–2008 financial crisis. Working-class families were the most likely to cut down on beef consumption. In contrast, poultry meat consumption has been on the rise since the mid-1980s, growing from 3.13 million metric tons in 1961 to a high point of 16 metric tons in 2013, with a slight dip after the crisis and recovering growth after 2009. Pig meat consumption remained mostly flat throughout the period, with an upward trend from about 5.24 million metric tons in 1961 to 8.85 in 2013.

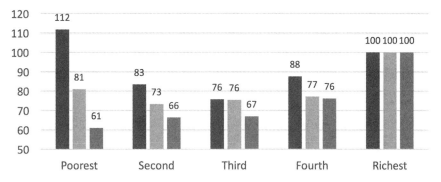

Figure 3.7. US per capita fresh fruit expenditures (%), 1973–2014, by income quintile (richest = 100). Absolute dollar household expenditures in fruit by each quintile were first divided by the average number of persons per household in each given year. These dollar figures were then divided by expenditures made in fruit by the richest quintile, which were equated to 100 percent. The same procedure is followed in tables 3.8 to 3.12 for each food item. *Source*: BLS 2017b.

By designating meat a luxury food, I am not implying that it is also more or less healthful. The main point about the basic/luxury dichotomy is economic access; basic foods are the most accessible, and luxury foods are the most expensive. It so happens, though, that fruits and vegetables, having been traditional foods in Mexico for centuries, have become luxury food items since the country's insertion into the global economy. Also, meats have become diversified in Mexico, with some qualifying as luxury meats and others as basic. Because of the greater economic accessibility of chicken, I would designate it a basic food and beef a luxury food. Chicken has become so widespread in North America (Schwartzman 2013) that I could call it "the neoliberal meat."

As shown in figure 3.7, fresh fruit expenditures for all but the top quintile declined from 1973 to 2014. The pattern is quite similar for expenditures in fresh vegetables, only in the case of fruits the drop in expenditures for the lowest two quintiles was more dramatic. If I restricted my analysis to how within-quintile shares of the budget spent on fruits in US households changed through the years, we would conclude that they all spent similar amounts; fruit expenditures within each income quintile were less than 4 percent of the household budget in 2014. Figure 3.7 puts this impression of similarity regarding fruit expenditures into perspective, though. The poorest quintile was spending proportionally more on fruit than the richest quintile in 1974; that proportion dropped to a mere 61 percent by 2014. All four lower

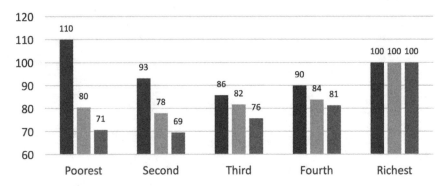

Figure 3.8. US per capita expenditures in fresh vegetables (%), 1973–2014, by income quintile (richest = 100). The procedure is the same as described for figure 3.7.
Source: BLS 2017b.

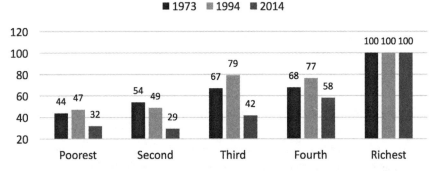

Figure 3.9. US per capita alcohol expenditures (%), 1973–2014, by quintile (richest = 100). Expenditures in alcoholic beverages by households in each quintile were divided by the respective average number of persons per household in each given year.
Source: BLS 2017b.

quintiles spent a smaller share on fresh fruits and fresh vegetables (figure 3.8) than the richest in 1994 and 2014. The difference was not just a result of the 2008 crisis. Rather, such decline is more likely a symptom of inequality combined with the more affordable elements of the neoliberal diet.

For comparative purposes with another luxury food, let us consider alcoholic beverages, in which we see a similar trend occurring. Households in the three lowest quintiles could make larger expenditures in alcoholic beverages from 1974 to 1994, yet all but those in the top quintile saw their per capita expenditures in alcohol decline by 2014 (figure 3.9). The steepest declines were experienced by households in the second and third quintiles.

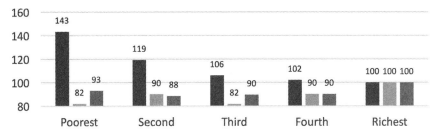

Figure 3.10. US per capita expenditures in cereals and cereal products (%), 1973–2014, by income quintile (richest = 100). Expenditures in cereals and cereal products by households in each quintile were divided by the respective average number of persons per household in each given year. *Source*: BLS 2017b.

Shifting the focus to basic foods, we can see a contrasting picture to that of luxury foods, although not exactly as I expected; the richest quintile simply spent larger sums of money on all types of food than other quintiles did. My expectation was that poorer quintiles would spend larger absolute amounts of money on the most energy-dense foods, such as cereals, sugars, and vegetable oils. That was the case until the early 1970s, but the trends changed. Figure 3.10 presents per capita household expenditures in cereals and cereal products other than bakery products. The most notable trend is that households in the four lower quintiles spent proportionally more on cereals and cereal products such as bread in 1973 than did the rich, who surely ate more of the luxury fare with more nutritious content. Although household expenditures on cereals in the four lower quintiles declined in relation to those of the richest quintile, they did not decline nearly as much as expenditures on luxury fare did.

If we look at bakery products in figure 3.11, it appears that these are basic foods that are more dear, leaning toward luxury foods, perhaps not so much for the high or low energy density but for their higher prices. Households in the four lower quintiles generally decreased their expenditures in bakery products after 1973, although the pattern is not entirely uniform among them after 1994. The pattern of expenditures in fats and vegetable oils shown in figure 3.12 roughly replicates that for cereals and cereal products.

The preceding analysis reveals significant dietary inequality in the United States, reflected in class-differentiated food consumption patterns. Moreover, in a high-income country such as the United States, inequality has far less to do with the amount of food consumed, whether it is sufficient or not. It has far more to do with the quality of that food, whether it is the more

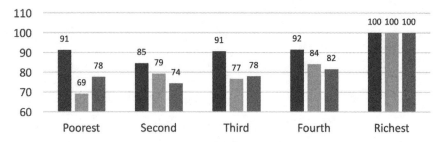

Figure 3.11. US per capita expenditures in bakery products (%), 1973–2014, by income quintile (richest = 100). Expenditures in bakery products by households in each quintile were divided by the respective average number of persons per household in each given year. *Source*: BLS 2017b.

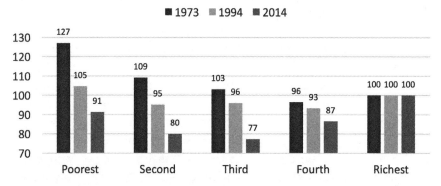

Figure 3.12. US per capita expenditures in fats and oils (%), 1973–2014, by income quintile (richest = 100). Expenditures in fats and oils by households in each quintile were divided by the respective average number of persons per household in each given year. *Source*: BLS 2017b.

nutritionally rich and diverse fresh fruits and vegetables or the cheapest, high-calorie, nutritionally poor, processed offerings of the neoliberal diet. Contrary to my expectations, by 2014 households in the richest quintile were making larger expenditures in all kinds of foods, including energy-dense foods. They were spending much more on fresh fruits and vegetables than households in other quintiles but also spending more on cereals, sugars, and fats and oils.

CONCLUSION

Data substantiate the historical transition to an energy-dense or high-fat and highly refined carbohydrate diet in the United States suggested by many others. We also can see that greater inequality in the United States results in a greater risk of exposure to the energy-dense portion of the neoliberal diet for low- to middle-income people, with all its extensive health consequences. It has become clear, though, that households in all income quintiles are consuming larger amounts of food, though average per capita consumption has declined somewhat since the start of the recession in 2008. While the richest quintile consumes more fresh fruits and vegetables, it also consumes more cereals, sugars, and vegetable oils than the other income quintiles on a per capita basis. When we consider these objective trends in the context of critical food debates, I see much reason to put forth the idea that disparities in dietary consumption are rooted in structural conditions. State policies that neglect the structural nature of the food system's problems and, notably, the structural inequalities that are inherent in it will fall far off the mark of food-system reform for social benefit.

While this discussion is limited to the United States, the trends are not exclusive to it; we can see them replicated globally to a greater or lesser extent, with some national differentiation. How the United States addresses the proliferation of obesity of its own making is of particular interest, as its agribusiness multinational firms have also been central actors in disseminating the neoliberal diet around the world. Winson has noted that the dietary changes could be called an "American" diet, given how powerful the American food industry has been in shaping it (2013:3).

Guthman argues that resolving the problems goes beyond farm and food policies (2011:196). Nonetheless, directly addressing those policies from a justice perspective would go a long way as first steps in addressing the health implications of the neoliberal diet. Scholarly understanding of the relation between socioeconomic factors and diet seems to support Drewnowski and Darmon's position that "encouraging low-income families to consume healthier but more costly foods to prevent future disease can be construed as an elitist approach to public health" (2005:265S). Notably, with the structural inequality around nutrition, the suggestion that unhealthful foods should be taxed as a way of providing an incentive to purchase better food is indeed regressive, as asserted by a representative of "Big Soda" (in O'Connor and Sanger-Katz 2016). Food taxes are "on their own, a simple solution to a complex problem" (Caraher and Cowburn 2005:1248). Despite strong opposition through lobbying and campaign funding, by 2016 seven US cities passed referenda to tax sweetened soft drinks (O'Connor and Sanger-Katz 2016). There is little doubt that the taxes are regressive, affecting primarily low-income people (Darmon and Drewnowski 2015). It is possible that subsidies of healthful foods (in the manner of subsidies to the sugar and fast food industries) could be a more progressive means to the same goal, although these are likely insufficient on their own, as they are also focused on consumption rather than production.

Working out the policy corrections for neoliberal diet production is not going to be self-evident; however, an important first step entails gaining a broader understanding of how states affect food production and how, in turn, inequality affects the types and quality of food to which people have access. The second step is having a concerted intention to make the structural changes in food production necessary for a healthful diet. In view of the close alignment between government and industry, it is promising that some are not waiting for policy corrections but are acting on their increased awareness through various alternative food and food system social movements. They include those advocating organic, fair trade, slow food, local provisioning, GMO-free, and other anti-ABM means of food provisioning. Rather than targeting the better-off "foodies," inequality-reducing policies could make the more healthful food at the center of these initiatives widely available for all.

Now that we have a picture of how the neoliberal diet emerged and developed in the United States, let us move into the larger North American region. It is here that we will gain some insight into how the industrial, American, or Western diet is becoming globalized.

CHAPTER 4

Class Diets in the NAFTA Region

DIVERGENCE OR CONVERGENCE?

I t was Carlos Salinas de Gortari, Mexico's president from 1988 to 1994, who proposed NAFTA in 1990. One of the main questions in the ensuing debate was whether such an association of two advanced capitalist countries, Canada and the United States, with a developing country like Mexico would lead to convergence or divergence in development outcomes. Would the three new partners converge downward to Mexico's level or upward toward that of the United States? Or would they take different paths depending on their levels of development? My focus in this chapter is on the NAFTA region as a microcosm of globalization- and neoliberalism-related dynamics. This is an important region in the global political economy of agrifood, as Canada and the United States have long been agro-exporting powerhouses in the world economy; the United States is the dominant producer of agricultural technologies and a robust proponent of trade liberalization, through which the country's dietary patterns are being globally disseminated. For its part, Mexico may be an example of the most radical adoption of the neoliberal doctrine, of which trade liberalization is a key component, particularly in agriculture. Thus, while increasing agricultural trade is a global phenomenon to varying depths, NAFTA provides a good illustration of the changes that occur because of neoliberal globalization and its contrasting impacts on countries with differing levels of socioeconomic development and state power.

In addressing the NAFTA debate, I argue that rather than an all-out convergence or divergence in agricultural trade, diet, and development outcomes, what has resulted in the region is a process of class-differentiated convergence. Agricultural trade has increased more than fivefold among the three nations but not symmetrically; clear patterns show the United States as the dominant player. Consumption patterns also show class-differentiated convergence, with consumption of meat, particularly of chicken, increasing in all three countries; however, beef consumption increased in Mexico while decreasing in Canada and the United States. I contextualize the neoregulatory stance in the NAFTA region in food regime literature and examine trade and consumption patterns as they relate to convergence and divergence in agriculture and development in the NAFTA region.

NAFTA AS REGIONAL FOOD REGIME

In NAFTA's early days, proponents touted its benefits for all three nations. Then US trade representative Mickey Kantor states that "the whole idea of NAFTA is to make all of North America more competitive and that will create jobs" (in Fagan 1994). This perspective was touted not only by American interests. The Mexican trade secretary Jaime Serra Puche is reported to have insisted "that new access for Mexican companies to Canada and the United States will accelerate Mexican economic growth in all parts of the country" (Fagan 1994). Indeed, neoclassical economic theory would anticipate enhanced trade among nations to lead toward their complementarity and convergence. The actual experience of economic integration of the three NAFTA partners, however, has been one of divergence in socioeconomic development outcomes between Mexico and its two wealthier neighbors.

NAFTA'S explicit economic goals of increased trade and foreign investment have been met in a differentiated way; trade increased sixfold between 1994 and 2014, that is, beyond expectations, but foreign direct investment rose much more in the two wealthier nations than in Mexico. Furthermore, socioeconomic development goals in Mexico have fallen quite short as the number and proportion of poor people have increased and inequality has deepened (Acosta Córdova 2014). Regarding agriculture, even the most enthusiastic neoliberal cheerleaders must acknowledge the adverse effects in Mexico. Neoliberalism's impacts were far more pronounced in Mexico because it had the largest number of people dependent on agriculture and the United States continued to support its farm sector through hefty subsidies. I see evidence of a resulting divergence in agricultural industrialization that has led to significant social consequences while increasing the Mexican people's food vulnerability. Trade liberalization has not resulted in consistent divergence, though. Most importantly, convergence is evidenced in dietary patterns, specifically through the globalization of the American diet.

To what extent does the neoliberal food regime dictate a particular dietary regime? Winson has made some effort to tackle this question. He argues that dietary regimes are complementary yet differentiated from food regimes, as they have "their own emphases and temporal demarcations" (2013:18). The first dietary regime does overlap somewhat with the first food regime, dating from 1870 to 1914 although Winson (2013) characterizes it as lasting nearly thirty years longer. Notably, it resulted from taking to industrial scale such technological developments as canning and flour milling; that allowed for the development of a range of new, increasingly processed products. The products were launched with ample mass marketing, which has become a central feature of the long process of transitioning from "whole foods," with many essential nutrients, to highly processed "industrial foods" that lack them (131).

Another similarity we can see between food regimes and dietary regimes is that the characteristics of one regime lay the groundwork for succeeding ones. Processing, mass marketing, and degraded diets are prominent features of successive regimes. In fact, their consistency is part of the distinction that Winson makes between food regimes and dietary regimes. He argues that the second food regime does not correlate with a transformation of diets; rather it corresponds to an intensification of the diet that formed in the previous regime (2013:28–29). This diet is one that perpetuated the nutritional degradation of food. It is composed of highly processed, high-fat, high-sugar, energy-dense food with low nutritional value (Drewnowski and Specter 2004). It is the neoliberal diet. An important feature of it is a notable class differentiation (Darmon and Drewnowski 2008; Dixon 2009; H. Lee 2011).

Winson argues that a third industrial dietary regime emerged post-1980. Its most distinguishing characteristic is the global expansion of the American diet such that it entails a "dramatic qualitative change in eating experiences, and subsequent health outcomes, of whole new populations across the globe" (2013:35). The change is so extensive that in the late 1990s it was called a "nutrition transition"; the regime's advance was greatly facilitated by a rise in cheap vegetable oils, the use of which is ubiquitous in the processing and fast food industries. Even in Asian countries where the consumption of animal fats was never as high as that of vegetable oils, consumption increased dramatically, particularly since the late 1970s. Data from FAOSTAT indicate that China's average per capita daily consumption of vegetable oils went from 64 calories in 1979 to a peak of 216 calories in 2009 and Japan's from 226 to 361 calories, increases of 238 percent and 60 percent, respectively (FAOSTAT 2017a).

There is significant evidence that with the globalization of the neoliberal diet has come an associated export of its health consequences already common in the United States. Mexico's adult obesity rate in 2013 was 32.8 percent, even higher than the 31.8 percent in the United States (Althaus 2013). Dietary inequities in the United States are sure to be replicated in the diet's exported manifestation, although the class demarcation is more complex in developing countries. Many of the cheap processed goods will be prohibitively expensive for those countries' lowest economic classes, so the consumers at greatest risk are likely to be in the middle-income classes.

DIET AND TRADE IN THE NAFTA REGION: CONVERGENCE AND DIVERGENCE

If the only goals of NAFTA were to increase trade and foreign investments, then it succeeded, although modestly in investment in Mexico. Indisputably Mexico's overall trade increased dramatically; by 2012 its total import and export flows were 5.3 times more than those in 1994. Exports multiplied by 6.1 and imports by 4.7, expanding Mexico's export power and providing many Mexicans—but not the majority—access to higher-quality products and services at lower prices. That is not the case for such basic goods as food, clothing, and public services (Acosta Córdova 2014:17). Mexico's total trade with the United States grew by 4.4 times during that period, with exports growing by 5.6 times and imports 3.4. Much of the growth in Mexico's exporting ability has directly benefited the United States. The US trade representative who negotiated NAFTA, Carla Hills, reports that "for each dollar Mexico gains in exports, it spends 50 cents in U.S. products" (in Acosta Córdova 2014:20). From the US perspective, imports from Mexico were 13 percent of the total, with 16 percent of US exports going to Mexico by 2016. US imports from Canada were 13 percent, the same as for Mexico, but its exports to Canada were 19 percent of total US exports. Much of NAFTA trade across the three partners involves cars and vehicle parts (Gambrell 2016:18). The vehicle and parts sector involves over tenfold the trade in agrifood; in autos and parts, Mexico holds a surplus.

Economic development measurements are made for the size of GDP and

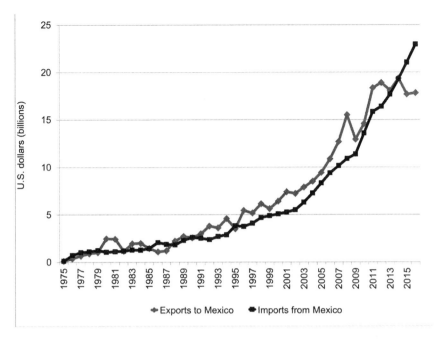

Figure 4.1. Mexico-US agricultural trade, 1991–2012. *Source*: USDA 2017c.

GDP per capita for each nation. From 1994 to 2012 Canada declined in world economic (GDP size) rank from seventh to eleventh, and Mexico declined from tenth to fourteenth, while the United States retained first place. The picture is different in terms of per capita income in each country during the same period. In per capita income, Canada went from twenty-first in world ranking to ninth, the United States dropped from ninth to tenth, and Mexico fell from fifty-third to sixty-first (Acosta Córdova 2014).

Specific to agriculture, we have seen both imports and exports increase in all three countries, but the patterns of trade in each pair are considerably different. The United States has developed strong mutual agricultural trade relations with each of its two neighbors (figures 4.1 and 4.2). Trade between Canada and Mexico has remained comparatively minor. Mexico's main agricultural trade relation is with the United States. Mexico has had an agricultural trade deficit since the early 1990s except after the 1994 peso devaluation crisis that forced it to decrease all its imports. A decline in Mexican food imports showed up again in 2014–2015, after the fall of oil exports and a concomitant decline of about 30 percent in the value of the peso. Conversely, the United States had its first food trade deficit with Mexico since the late 1980s, given its poorer neighbor's inability to import food, while US consumers had

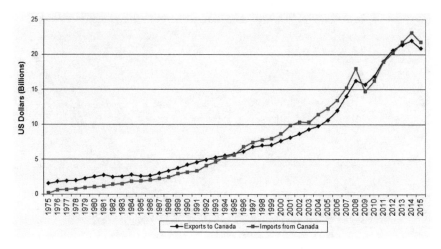

Figure 4.2. Canada-US agricultural trade, 1991–2012. *Source*: USDA 2017b.

no need to decrease their food imports from Mexico with a much stronger dollar. Interestingly, the global food crisis of 2007–2008 was not reflected in declining US imports from Mexico but prompted a large dip in Mexico's imports from the United States.

These differentiated trends likely have to do with two distinct but combined issues. First, Mexico's imports from the United States are primarily basic foods that make up more than 40 percent of total caloric intake and disproportionally affect the lower-income population. Second, US imports from Mexico are primarily fruits and vegetables that make up only about 2 percent of total caloric intake; these foods are consumed mainly by middle- and upper-income people who are least affected by food price inflation, given the relatively minor share of their total expenses on food. Sharp differences in inequality in the neighboring countries compound the effects of the combined issues; the official poverty rate, which is related to food insecurity, is less than 15 percent in the United States but 45.5 percent in Mexico. Food insecurity in this context means that each 1 percent rise in food prices corresponds to a 0.75 percent decrease in food expenditures (von Braun 2007).

The agricultural trade relation between Canada and the United States also strengthened after NAFTA took effect. In contrast to the US relation with Mexico, however, Canada's relation with the United States marginally shifted from a deficit in the early 1990s to a surplus. US-Canada trade relations replicate but invert the relation the United States has with Mexico; the United States exports luxury foods to Canada and imports basic foods from it. Another contrast is that US imports from Canada sharply declined during the 2007–2008 food crisis, indicating that these were primarily basic foods, but Canada's imports from the United States were hardly disrupted because they were primarily fruits and vegetables sold to higher-income consumers. If I use affordability of continued access to luxury foods as a criterion of good living standards, Canada appears to have benefited the most from NAFTA. This benefit is supported by its higher world ranking in per capita income.

If we look at the nature of agricultural imports and exports in the three countries more generally, not limited to NAFTA trade, we again find that by dollar value, the top agrifood imports in the United States were still largely luxury goods—in this case, alcoholic beverages, beef and veal meat, coffee, and crude or raw materials for processing. In Canada the pattern was similar, with top agrifood imports by dollar value captured by alcoholic beverages, crude materials, chocolate preparations, and pet food (Pechlaner and Otero 2010). In Mexico, however, the greatest increase in food import dependency has been in basic foods including grains and cereals (Otero, Pechlaner, and Gürcan 2013). But Mexico has also developed dependency on the import of some luxury foods like meats, especially chicken, and wine.

I should clarify that "luxury" foods change across time and are not necessarily more or less healthful than other foods. Sugar was a luxury food for the British aristocracy in earlier centuries but became a food for the working classes in the early 1800s (Mintz 1985). Meat was mostly a luxury item but then became a staple of the US diet by the 1940s. Since the 1970s, however, chicken has displaced beef as the most accessible meat for working classes, including middle-income wage workers. I can thus say that chicken is the neoliberal meat. Beer, in contrast with wine, could be said to be the neoliberal alcoholic drink. Not only has it become more prevalent among the working classes, but its market has become more concentrated and globalized; by 2013 the top four companies controlled well over 50 percent of world beer trade (P. Howard 2014).

Finally, basic foods also have varied across time. A single ingredient like wheat flour can have different incarnations; whole wheat used to be the main type of flour, but after its refining it became a specialty product for foodies (Johnston and Baumann 2010). In the twenty-first century, the more foods are processed, the more accessible—and basic—they become, if not necessarily the most nutritious. The contrary is more likely the case. In Mexico corn tortillas and beans have continued to be roughly accessible, albeit less so (Appendini 2014). The problem is that basic foods are being replaced by the neoliberal diet at an accelerated pace.

Import dependency in the context of food security pushes the importing country to internalize the world price for a commodity. For countries like Canada and the United States with long-standing traditions of agricultural exports, this issue by itself does not cause major concerns about domestic prices for two main reasons. These nations have long been articulated to agricultural world markets and have exercised protectionist or other support policies for their farm sectors, such as sugar in the United States and the dairy sector in Canada. They also tend to be price fixers rather than takers. But new food import dependency for Mexico, which had long protected its consumers and producers from volatile world prices, has introduced considerable food vulnerability for its population by subjecting it to world prices. When this dependency is in a basic food item, the impacts can be profound on those with the lowest incomes, who spend a greater proportion of their incomes on food. In the NAFTA region, this population is disproportionately in Mexico.

I propose that imports over 20 percent of domestic production in any food product represent import dependency status. I have investigated the top five food sources for each country and assessed their dependency levels before and after the neoliberal turn by comparing 1985 and 2007 figures (Otero, Pechlaner, and Gürcan 2013). In table 4.1 I refine my analysis, showing changing import dependencies based on the crops that make up 80 percent of each country's diet. The crops highlighted in bold indicate those that make up 50 percent of a country's diet, starting with the highest caloric contributor.

The first thing we can notice in table 4.1 is the greater diversity in the Canadian diet as compared to that in the diets of Mexico and the United States. That diversity decreased marginally between 1985 and 2007 but was still significant. We can also see at a glance that dependency did not increase significantly in Canada in the number of crops, although there is a fair amount of dependency in both periods. Of those crops that made up 80 percent of Canada's food supply, the country was import-dependent on twelve in 1985 and fourteen in 2007. It should be noted that imported raw sugar plays a very particular role in Canada, which processes and refines it, and thus it has been excluded from our list of food sources on which the country is dependent. One could say that importing raw sugar in Canada parallels what occurred in early manufacturing countries that imported raw materials for their industrial transformation, in this case into refined sugar.

Most of the crops were not highly significant to the Canadian diet, although they were more important in 2007 than in 1985. In 1985 none of the foods on which the country was dependent amounted to even 2 percent of total food supply, and many amounted to much less. By 2007 we do see slightly greater import dependency in important foods, but even then only three of them contributed more than 3 percent to the total food supply (rapeseed and mustard oil at 9.75 percent, soybean oil at 3.34 percent, and maize at 3.32 percent). If I calculate what percentage of the food supply is made up by all the foods in which the country is dependent, we see some change between 1985 and 2007. Overall, Canada had greater than 20 percent import dependency in about 11 percent of the country's food supply in 1985. Import dependency jumped to about 32 percent by 2007, a noticeable increase. Still, Canada's food import dependency was widely spread among many products, each of which made up a small contribution to the total average food intake. Given Canada's long-standing engagement with trade, such food dependency does not seem to have affected its food security. On the contrary, it increased Canadians' access to a diverse diet. Besides, Canada has a considerable agrifood trade surplus.

Diets in the United States have been consistently less diverse than in Canada, with a far smaller number of crops accounting for 50 percent and even 80 percent of the US diet. US dependency increased between 1985 and 2007 by only one crop. The United States remained consistently dependent in sugar, and in 2007 the country was also dependent in rice, importing 25 percent of the domestic supply. Again, looking at the overall change in dependency on imports for the food supply as a whole, we see that the United States was more than 20 percent dependent for 8.5 percent of the food supply in 1985 (for sugar), and that increased to 11.2 percent by 2007 with the addition of rice, comprising an import dependency increase of only 2.7 percentage points in the period 1985–2007. It should be clarified that sugar has been an imported item in industrial nations for centuries and undergoes further processing in the importing nations. Sugar thus fits the traditional pattern of a developing country exporting a primary good and a developed country industrializing it. Since the first food regime led by the British, sugar has come to represent a significant share in caloric intake because of its relative abundance in world markets. Given its massive consumption, sugar can be counted as a basic food although it is empty of nutritive qualities.

Mexico has a less diverse diet than the United States has, but we can see that dietary diversity in Mexico has increased since NAFTA. That trend is more consistent with expectations about trade liberalization in agriculture than we see in the United States. Food import dependency increased more in Mexico than in the other two countries. In 1985 Mexico was dependent in only two of the crops that made up 80 percent of its food supply; by 2007 it was dependent in seven of them. This increase in dependency is notable,

TABLE 4.1. NAFTA partners' dependency levels in top 80 percent of food supply (kcal/capita/day), 1985 and 2007, by imports/domestic supply

COUNTRY	1985		2007	
	TOP FOODS	IMPORTS > 20%	TOP FOODS	IMPORTS > 20%
Canada	**Wheat; milk; rape and mustard oil; fats, animals, raw; pig meat; potatoes; bovine meat**; beer; poultry meat; soybean oil; butter; ghee; vegetables, other; eggs; rice (milled equivalent); groundnuts; maize germ oil; apples; cream; oranges, mandarins; maize; tree nuts; fruits, other; bananas; grapes; oats; sweeteners, other; tomatoes; beverages, fermented	Tree nuts, 104%; rice (milled equivalent), 100%; groundnuts, 100%; oranges, mandarins, 100%; bananas, 100%; other fruits, 81%; grapes, 79%; vegetables, other, 47%; apples, 40%; maize germ oil, 34%; tomatoes, 33%	**Wheat; rape and mustard oil; milk, excluding butter; poultry meat; fats, animals, raw; pig meat; soybean oil; maize**; potatoes; bovine meat; rice (milled equivalent); sweeteners, other; beer; vegetables, other; butter, ghee; pulses, other; cream; eggs; groundnuts; maize germ oil; fruits, other; tree nuts; olive oil; apples; bananas	Rice (milled equivalent), 141%; groundnuts, 120%; tree nuts, 104%; olive oil, 103%; fruits, other, 102%; sweeteners, other, 100%; bananas, 100%; vegetables, other, 68%; apples, 53%; maize germ oil, 40%; **soybean oil, 35%;** rape and mustard oil, 25%; bovine meat, 21%; **maize, 20%**

Mexico	**Maize; sugar (raw equivalent)**; wheat; milk; pig meat; beans; sunflower seed oil; soybean oil	Milk, excluding butter, 24%; sunflower seed oil, 21%	**Maize; sugar (raw equivalent); wheat;** milk, excluding butter (total); pig meat; soybean oil, poultry meat; beans (total); rice (milled equivalent), bovine meat; palm oil	Palm oil, 86%; rice (milled equivalent), 76%; **wheat, 58%**; soybean oil, 33%; pig meat, 29%; **maize, 28%**; milk, excluding butter, 22%
United States	**Wheat; soybean oil; milk; sugar (raw equivalent);** sweeteners, other; bovine meat; pig meat; poultry meat; beer; fats, animals, raw; potatoes; maize	**Sugar (raw equivalent), 36%**	**Wheat; soybean oil; milk; sugar (raw equivalent); sweeteners, other;** poultry meat; pig meat; bovine meat; beer; maize; potatoes; rice (milled equivalent); fats, animals, raw	Rice (milled equivalent), 25%; **sugar (raw equivalent), 22%**

Source: FAOSTAT 2013.

Note: Top foods are ordered by ranking in each country. The food sources in bold account for 48 to 50 percent of the total food supply and might be regarded as the most basic food sources by consumption volume. Imports over 100 percent indicate that the crops are processed and re-exported.

and the country's profound descent into food dependency is highlighted in summary statistics for dependency in the food supply. The two crops in which Mexico had import dependency in 1985 made up only 8.49 percent of the country's total food supply. In contrast, by 2007 the seven foods in which it was dependent amounted to a whopping 56.29 percent of the country's average daily diet (table 4.1). We can see that trade liberalization has had marginal to modest effects on Canada and the United States but a profound impact on Mexico in terms of food dependency. Given the greater impact that food price inflation has on lower-income populations, dependency on world food prices has a disproportionately adverse effect on this developing country and particularly on its poorest people.

THE NEOLIBERAL DIET IN THE NAFTA REGION

The following data analysis shows how the neoliberal diet has evolved in the three member countries of NAFTA. My assumption is that the neoliberal diet emanated primarily from the United States and became hegemonic in the neoliberal era; my goal here is to determine how it has been expressed in each of the three NAFTA countries. I start with a basic assessment of per capita food consumption in these regions using "food supply" (existing stocks plus domestic production plus imports minus exports) as a proxy for consumption.

The first major point to be shown is that the least developed country in the association, Mexico, experienced the greatest increase in per capita food consumption *prior* to joining NAFTA. By the late 1970s and early 1980s, Mexico's per capita food intake was greater than Canada's, almost reaching the level of the United States in 1981. After the neoliberal turn in Mexico, its food consumption declined or flattened (figures 4.3 and 4.4), while its developed neighbors experienced substantial increases in average per capita food consumption. On average, at least, Mexico has never reached the level of food caloric intake that it did in its peak year of 1981, after the government implemented the Sistema Alimentario Mexicano (Mexican Food System), an agricultural support program for attaining self-sufficiency. In contrast, Canada and the United States experienced an upward convergence in food consumption after NAFTA; consumption peaked around 2005, declined after the global food price crisis through 2011, then picked up again after that. After 1981, Mexico's food consumption remained mostly flat; it picked up in 2000, declined after 2007, and picked up slightly in 2011 but did not reach the 1981 peak.

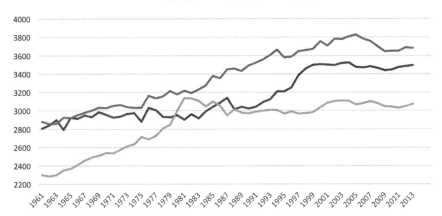

Figure 4.3. NAFTA countries' total food supplies (kcal/capita/day), 1961–2013. *Source*: FAOSTAT 2017c.

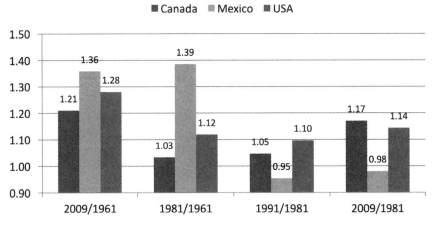

Figure 4.4. NAFTA countries' ratios of total food supply increases or decreases, 1961–2009. *Source*: FAOSTAT 2017c.

Figure 4.4 shows how the increase or decrease in per capita food consumption has evolved in different periods between 1961 and 2009. I divided this long period in order to differentiate 1961–1981, the era prior to the start of the neoliberal turn, from the time after that. The earlier era was marked by food production that was based primarily on the domestic market, with very little agricultural trade. Food trade became very important in later times, particularly after the start of NAFTA in 1994. In the calculation of food consumption data I must take into account that Mexico's per capita caloric intake was much lower at the start of the period, in 1961, than that for its northern neighbors, which had similar consumption rates. So, Mexico's overall increase in food consumption between 1961 and 2009 was relatively larger than increases in Canada and the United States. But the main point here is that Mexico's greatest gains were achieved prior to the neoliberal turn of the mid-1980s and prior to NAFTA in 1994. I show this in figure 4.4 simply by calculating the ratios of food intake increase in the specified periods by dividing the later year's average per capita daily food intake by that of the earlier year. The resulting ratio of food intake change indicates how much food consumption grew or declined from one period to the other. Mexico's caloric intake actually decreased in the two periods 1991/1981 and 2009/1981, while those for Canada and the United States increased.

Per capita food consumption is only one aspect of the neoliberal diet. Another is the increasing role of meat and the somewhat more complex role of fruits and vegetables, which is complicated both by the industrialization of diets and the increasing class dynamics of consuming fresh produce. Indeed, I find that the components of the neoliberal diet change differentially depending on which economic classes have primary access to any particular food type. Changes in consumption patterns of luxury foods such as meat, fresh fruits, and wine differ from changes in the patterns of consumption of basic foods such as grains. Beef provides an illustration.

A general trend in Canada and the United States is that the per capita consumption of beef has declined, especially after the crisis of Fordism in the late 1970s. One interpretation of this trend is that while middle-income and perhaps lower-income people used to have access to beef prior to the crisis in the two countries, lower-income people had greater difficulties buying it after 1976. At around the same time, health concerns made the consumption of red meat less desirable in Canada and the United States, so many people switched to chicken, also a cheaper meat. The chicken industry became sharply concentrated during the neoliberal era of capitalism and involved much more precarious working relations with mostly Latino and Latina workers (Schwartzman 2012; Striffler 2005).

In Mexico, however, the middle- to upper-income classes were the primary adopters of a US diet based on milk, meat, and wheat (Pechlaner and Otero 2008). Therefore, as figure 4.5 indicates, Canada and the United States experienced increasing consumption of beef prior to 1976, after which beef consumption mostly declined. Mexico started from a considerably lower base than its two northern neighbors and experienced substantial increases in beef consumption after 1975, with a few blips, but a decline after 2008.

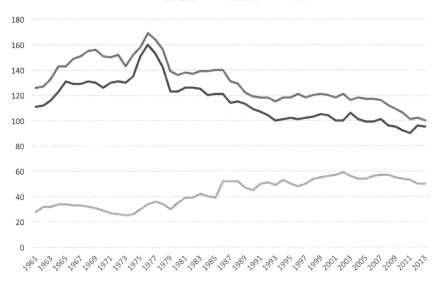

Figure 4.5. NAFTA countries' beef supplies (kcal/capita/day), 1961–2013.
Source: FAOSTAT 2017d.

Its absolute levels of per capita consumption remained well below the averages of its more developed neighbors, likely indicating that beef was consumed primarily by middle- to upper-income classes. By 2013 Mexico's average per capita caloric intake from beef was just fifty calories per day, while Canada's was ninety-five and the United States' was one hundred. Considering Mexico's deeper class inequalities, primarily middle- and upper-income classes have had steady access to beef, so their per capita levels of its consumption likely equal or surpass those of equivalent classes in Canada and the United States.

Many people in NAFTA countries have turned to chicken meat, which appears in a growing number of industrialized food preparations such as chicken nuggets. Pollan (2006) notes that chicken piles corn upon corn, the main subsidized crop in the United States. Since the 1970s the dramatic increase in chicken production has been largely based in the United States. Production has also been increasing in Mexico since the 1990s, although it is still far below that in the United States. As noted, in addition to cost concerns, by the 1980s health concerns about red meat in the United States further facilitated the chicken revolution. The change of diet has taken place, Winson notes, although poultry raised in the confined animal feeding system has sufficient saturated fat to cast doubt on this "purportedly healthier

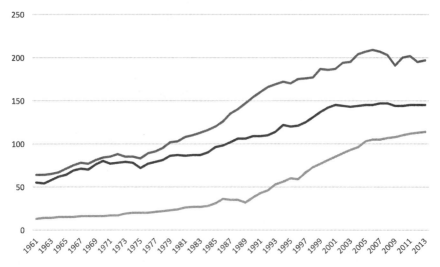

Figure 4.6. NAFTA countries' poultry meat supplies (kcal/capita/day), 1961–2013.
Source: FAOSTAT 2017d.

meat" (2013:145). Still, as figure 4.6 illustrates, all NAFTA countries experienced substantial per capita increases in the consumption of poultry meat, but the increases are higher in the more developed countries because of the greater purchasing power of their working and middle classes.

As also evident from figure 4.6, despite the lower price of chicken, its per capita consumption nonetheless declined in the United States and less so in Canada after the 2007–2008 food inflation crisis through 2009 but continued to grow slightly in Mexico. My class interpretation of these trends is that chicken consumption had been widely adopted by lower- to middle-income working classes in Canada and the United States that then had to reduce their consumption with the crisis. Conversely, in Mexico it was mostly middle- to upper-income people who had greater access to chicken meat and did not have an economic need to reduce their intake, as food expenditures for these classes make up a smaller proportion of family budgets. By the time of the crisis, in fact, Mexico's supply of chicken meat had increased substantially through imports from the United States and domestic production using imported US corn as feed (Martínez-Gómez et al. 2013; Schwartzman 2012). In contrast to beef, one could say that chicken became the main neoliberal meat, as its consumption increased throughout the period since 1961 but most dramatically after 1990. Mexico's rate of growth in chicken consumption was faster, but it started from a much lower basis. By 2013, average daily per capita caloric intake from chicken meat was as follows: United States, 197; Canada, 145; and Mexico, 114.

Another frequently articulated aspect of the changing international division of labor in agriculture has been the production and export of fresh fruits and vegetables by developing countries for wealthy consumers in developed countries. Nagatada (2006) conducted an extensive investigation of global trade flows in fruits and vegetables to conclude that their trade indeed expanded to form the "most significant part of the global agro-food systems under the third food regime" (38). At the same time, however, he argues that North-South differentiation is actually more nuanced and could even be characterized as multipolar, as economic growth in developing countries fueled their importation of fresh fruits and vegetables. Nonetheless, Nagatada documents a significant amount of reciprocal "NAFTA flow" of vegetables between the three partner countries (39).

Somewhat surprisingly, average per capita fresh vegetable consumption in Mexico has increased since the 1970s and particularly since NAFTA, as we can see in figure 4.7. There have been only modest changes in the United States and Canada but always with much higher starting points than in Mexico. In another calculation, as a percentage of total caloric intake, Mexico's intake from vegetable consumption started at just above 0.5 percent in 1961 and moved up to about 1.3 percent of total food intake in 2009. The figures for its northern neighbors were around 2 percent of total food intake throughout the period, with Canada surpassing the United States in

Figure 4.7. NAFTA countries' vegetable supplies (kcal/capita/day), 1961–2013.
Source: FAOSTAT 2017c.

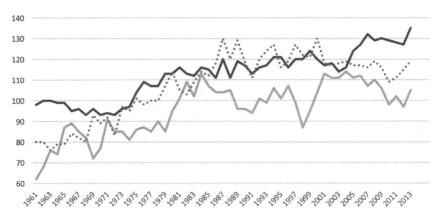

Figure 4.8. NAFTA countries' fruit supplies (kcal/capita/day), 1961–2013.
Source: FAOSTAT 2017c.

1972. While converging upward, then, Mexico remained far below the other
two in vegetable consumption. These long-term trends are related to changing class diets in the three countries, of increased fruit and vegetable consumption in higher-income classes and flat or declining consumption among
the working classes.

Looking at fruit in figure 4.8, we see that in the mid-1960s, early 1970s,
and early 1980s, Mexico's per capita fruit consumption was actually greater
than that of the United States but lower than that in Canada except for 1984.
In the latter part of the 1961–2013 period, following the food-price crisis of
2007, fruit consumption declined in all three countries, recovering slightly
after 2011, when Canada took a clear lead. Mexico's average fruit consumption
fluctuated widely and rarely exceeded the pre-NAFTA high mark in 1984,
barely surpassing it in 2001 and 2003. I suspect that Mexico's modest increases
in fruit consumption in the latter part of the period were due mainly to the
purchasing power of higher-income groups. Humberto González (2013) has
shown that increased exports of fruits and vegetables from Mexico made
them more expensive in the domestic market, thus reducing their earlier affordability. We can surmise that the increased consumption we see in figure
4.8 is indicative of increased consumption by the wealthier classes.

INEQUALITY IN FOOD CONSUMPTION: THE CASE OF MEXICO

In general, advanced capitalist countries have lower levels of inequality than
developing countries have, but the neoliberal turn in the 1980s made most

countries less equitable. In particular, many social scientists have expressed grave concern for increased wealth concentration in the top 1 percent of the population (Stiglitz 2014). In order to demonstrate class inequality in food consumption, the next analysis focuses on the case of Mexico. I disaggregate Mexican consumers into five income quintiles and examine how much of the household budget was devoted to food consumption and different food sources in each case. Each quintile represents 20 percent of the population by income, from poorest to richest. Mexico's Instituto Nacional de Estadística, Geografía e Informática (INEGI) actually presents the data in deciles, or ten segments of 10 percent each. I merged pairs of deciles for ease of presentation in graphic form and better comparison with the United States. The analysis is meant to disaggregate the previous presentation of average per capita daily food supply for Mexico. Quintiles are not social classes, but they provide a proxy that helps us ascertain the extent to which inequality shapes food intake across income groups.

Figure 4.9 presents total expenditures in food and beverages by households as a percent of their respective total incomes in 1984, 2006, and 2012. This comparison across time allows for an interesting analysis of how Mexico's household expenditures in food changed from before the neoliberal turn to just before the global food crisis and a few years later. In 1984 households in the richest quintile spent 24 percent of their incomes on food, while those in the poorest quintile spent almost double that share of their budgets on food, at 45 percent. Food inequality subsequently widened considerably. The richest quintile devoted a decreasing share of its budget to food expenditures by the 2000s, reflecting increasing incomes, while the poorest quintile decreased its food expenditures prior to the crisis but fared

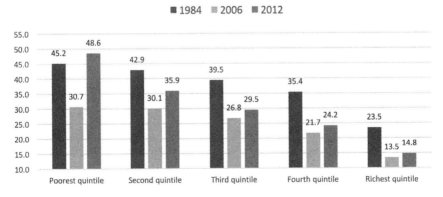

Figure 4.9. Mexico household food expenditures (% of current income), 1984–2012, by income quintile. *Source*: INEGI 1985, 2007, 2013.

far worse afterward. By 2012 the poorest households were spending almost half of their incomes, 49 percent, on food, contrasted against 15 percent for the richest. Still, all quintiles had to spend larger shares of their budgets on food in 2012 than in 2006, reflecting the higher prices and relative inelasticity of demand.

In figure 4.10 I put inequality between income quintiles into perspective to get an idea of the orders of magnitude spent on food by each quintile. I calculated food expenditures by the lower four quintiles as a percentage of those by the richest. In other words, food expenditures by the richest quintile were turned into 100 percent. The differences are staggering. The four lower quintiles had to spend increasing proportions of income on food. One exception is for the third quintile when its food expenditures dropped slightly, from 55 percent to 54 percent, from 2006 to 2012.

Here I explore how inequality translates into the ways households in the different income quintiles can afford or not afford basic and luxury foods. As expected, poorer quintiles spent lower percentages on luxury foods like meats and fruits than the richest did, but most spent higher percentages of their budgets on basic foods like corn tortillas and sugar. Expenditures by poorer quintiles on basic foods were well over 100 percent of those in the highest-income quintile, who spent a much lower budget share on food to begin with.

The contrast between fresh fruits and vegetables is like that between beef and poultry (not presented in my figures); fruits, as with beef, are more a luxury than vegetables, and their consumption is more inequitable across income quintiles. Figure 4.11 depicts the trends for fruit consumption.

Differences in basic food expenditures are astounding; lower quintiles spent more of their incomes than the richest quintile did, representing consumption of cheap calories. Corn is the most basic of cereals in Mexico, and tortillas are its main form. Figure 4.12 clearly indicates that people from the second to the fourth quintiles, lowest to highest, spent larger absolute shares of income on corn tortillas, but those in the lowest quintile were too poor to spend as much as those in the richest one.

A similar but even more dramatic picture emerges in figure 4.13 on sugar, which is high in calories but nutritionally empty. In this case, the poorer the income quintile, the higher its relative expenditures on sugar, likely because sugar is less expensive than other foods; it is consumed in sweetened soft drinks, candy, and sweet bread. Sugar intake may be the main factor behind Mexico's overweight and obesity issue, as suggested by nutritionists (Pérez Escamilla et al. 2014).

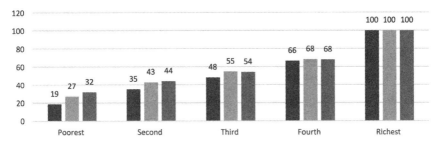

Figure 4.10. Mexico household food expenditures (% of richest), 1984–2012, by income quintile. *Source*: INEGI 1985, 2007, 2013.

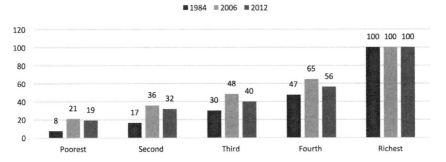

Figure 4.11. Mexico household fruit expenditures (% of richest), 1984–2012, by income quintile. *Source*: INEGI 1985, 2007, 2013.

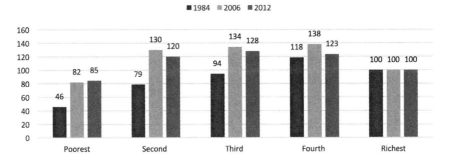

Figure 4.12. Mexico household corn tortilla expenditures (% of richest), 1984–2012, by income quintile. *Source*: INEGI 1985, 2007, 2013.

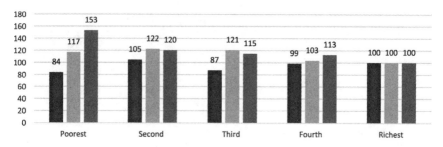

Figure 4.13. Mexico household expenditures in sugars (% of richest), 1984–2012, by income quintile. *Source*: INEGI 1985, 2007, 2013.

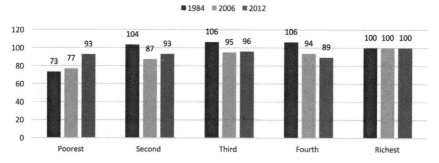

Figure 4.14. Mexico household expenditures in fats and oils (% of richest), 1984–2012, by income quintile. *Source*: INEGI 1985, 2007, 2013.

Figure 4.14 reveals the high rates of consumption of vegetable oils and animal fats across income quintiles. We could assume that all income categories increased their oil consumption with the proliferation of the neoliberal diet. Then, given the increased importance of vegetable oils in this diet, demand by all income categories remained relatively high, that is, with low price elasticity, despite price increases in the 1990s. But those in the poorest quintile had to shift more of their expenditures to oils to keep them as a basic category or simply because oils became integrated into processed foods; they spent almost as much as the richest group. The point here is similar to that of corn tortillas; there is high consumption across income levels, but the richest quintile spent slightly more than the poorest on oils and fats by 2012.

CONCLUSION

Because of NAFTA, agricultural trade in all three partner countries grew significantly, a predicted result of trade liberalization. But there is also a marked divergence in the nature of agricultural trade between NAFTA countries, most notably from the perspective of import dependency of the least developed partner. The social consequences of this dependency are profound when prices rise, as was evidenced by the 2007–2008 world food price crisis. All indications are that this vulnerability will have increasingly dramatic consequences in the future as extreme weather, population pressures, and land shortages consistently push food prices upward. Already we see that since 2011 the FAO's world food price index has not dipped below what it was during the crisis; indeed, for many years it was considerably higher—201.4 in the 2008 crisis, 229.9 for 2011, 213.3 for 2012, and 209.8 for 2013 (FAOSTAT 2017d). We have seen the predicted convergence in trade flows and dietary patterns in all three NAFTA countries, but if we consider this trade from the perspective of human well-being, there has been significant divergence in the experiences of Mexico and its wealthier neighbors. Such divergence is class-differentiated too, as shown in the analysis of different food consumption patterns by income quintile.

In dietary content we see a convergence toward US dietary patterns. While there are still significant differences between NAFTA countries—predictably, given the development differences between Mexico and the other two—there is also evidence of increasing class-differentiated convergence, most notably in meat and fruit consumption. In short, NAFTA has largely produced divergence in socioeconomic development indicators but also has facilitated dietary, if class-differentiated, convergence. Given that this socioeconomic divergence has adverse consequences on social inequality and food security and that dietary convergence has harmful effects on health, this case study strongly suggests that less-developed countries may experience a double-barreled impact from trade liberalization.

CHAPTER 5

NAFTA, Agriculture, and Work

MEXICO'S LOSS OF FOOD AND LABOR SOVEREIGNTY

I cannot analyze Mexico's economic development since the 1980s without referring to its growing integration with its wealthier neighbors well before the start of NAFTA. Thus I begin by exploring how the US economy faced the crisis of the Fordist stage of capitalism since the 1970s by focusing on a cheap labor strategy to restore profitability for US firms. By endorsing NAFTA, US officials ensured access to an abundant supply of labor south of the border and, perhaps as an unintended consequence, inside the United States, namely in agriculture.

For their part, Mexico's political technocrats placed their bet for economic growth on the comparative advantage of cheap labor. This has been a losing bet for the workers of both countries; neoliberalism and Mexico's integration into the North American economy—without free labor mobility—have had a detrimental impact on workers, particularly in Mexico. The counterpart of its loss of food self-sufficiency by growing dependency on US grain imports has been the loss of labor sovereignty. Defined as a nation's ability to offer gainful employment to a majority of its workforce (Bartra 2004), labor sovereignty has been a casualty of Mexico's economic integration with its northern neighbors. The most visible results of this loss have been growth in the informal sector of the economy to upward of 60 percent of the labor force and substantially higher outmigration rates as vast numbers of displaced Mexican workers flowed into the United States to search for work, most of them unauthorized or undocumented. Because of the economic slowdown in the United States after the recession that started in 2008, migration flows between the two countries became neutral, with similar numbers of people moving north and south, or even reversed in 2011, with more people moving from the United States to Mexico than the other way around.

In this chapter I explore the relation between food self-sufficiency and labor sovereignty amid Mexico's integration to its northern neighbors, especially to the US economy. I compare food self-sufficiency in the three NAFTA countries around production for the domestic market, per capita calorie consumption, and overall food trade. The main proposition is that food self-sufficiency is a necessary condition for a country to enjoy labor sovereignty. Of the three NAFTA nations, Mexico is the least self-sufficient and hence the one that has economically expelled the largest proportion of migrants. While Mexican migration was cyclical for decades, since the 1990s the US government has invoked much tougher policies, which have prompted many migrants to stay for years in the United States. It is important to also describe work conditions for Mexican farmworkers across the three NAFTA countries, with special focus on the United States and Canada, as these are mostly the Mexican workers, often from indigenous regions, who lost their peasant economies at home.

While Mexico's exports of fruits and vegetables to the United States and Canada increased substantially as of the late 1980s, that sector did not generate nearly enough employment to absorb bankrupted peasants. Therefore, Mexico became dependent on the importation of basic subsistence grains that used to be produced by smallholder peasant farmers. Many peasants became redundant in the Mexican economy, and their only way out, literally, often has been to migrate to the United States or Canada. Although most migrants to Canada, a small minority, enter that country as part of state-sponsored guest worker programs (Preibisch and Otero 2014), the great majority of migrants to the United States do so as undocumented or unauthorized workers (Schwartzman 2012).

The presence of large masses of supposedly low-skilled workers in the United States, more properly called "manually skilled workers" (Runsten, Mines, and Nichols 2013), authorized or not, raises serious issues of labor rights, discrimination, and exclusion. An inverse relation has been documented between their numbers and rights (Ruhs and Martin 2008); the more migrant workers there are in rich countries, the fewer their rights are.

Employer demand for workers is "negatively sloped" with respect to labor costs, which means that more rights for migrants typically means higher costs (Ruhs and Martin 2008). The United States tends to have much higher numbers than rights, whereas Canada tries to fit the Scandinavian model of fewer numbers and more rights. But numbers of guest workers coming into Canada started to outpace the numbers of immigrant newcomers as permanent residents or citizens as of 2006 (Preibisch and Otero 2014). The Canadian trend has raised the question of whether both of NAFTA's rich countries are converging toward the numbers side of the equation to the detriment of workers' rights. When the Liberal Party regained the national leadership in Canada in 2015, it moved to reverse the trend back in favor of increasing the number of immigrant workers with permanent residence that leads to eventual citizenship; such a policy sets the conditions for all workers to have equal rights.

One question about the numbers/rights trade-off is what human and labor rights policy makers and activists can envision in addressing it. Answers to this question will depend on the perspective one takes in the migration debates. Although I briefly address this concern, I am mainly interested in examining the root causes of Mexico's outmigration: its growing food dependency and consequent loss of labor sovereignty. Consistent with this focus, the structural solutions to workers' rights lie in Mexico's agrarian structure more than in migration policy, because migration is a symptom. While the issue persists, nevertheless, the human and labor rights consequences for migrants must be addressed in the United States and Canada.

NEOLIBERAL GLOBALIZATION AND NAFTA

The crisis of Fordism in the late 1960s and early 1970s was expressed as a crisis of profitability that resulted from an excess productive capacity in relation to effective demand. The productivity of US workers was growing at a slower pace than in Germany, Japan, and some other countries. This productivity-growth differential was eventually expressed in growing and unsustainable trade deficits between the United States and Japan, for example, during the 1980s. Hence US multinational firms sought to relocate their manufacturing plants to the less-unionized US South first and then, increasingly, to cheap-wage countries like Mexico.

The flow of manufacturing investments into Mexico, however, reproduced and expanded the capital-intensive technologies that were necessary to compete internationally in the emerging global economy. Linkages between these investments and the rest of the Mexican economy were scarce (Sklair 1989). That meant locally sourced components were few, if any, as most raw materials were imported from the United States or elsewhere. Similarly, the only market for Mexican-produced manufactures by multinational corporations lay mostly in the United States. In the end, the main goal of restoring profitability for US firms was based on the exploitation of cheap labor (Cypher and Delgado-Wise 2010).

Overall, the US-Mexico trade balance has been positive for Mexico since NAFTA. Total trade in goods between the two countries was estimated at $523.8 billion in 2016. US exports to Mexico were $229.7 billion, and US imports from Mexico were $294.1 billion, resulting in a US trade deficit of $64.4 billion (US Census Bureau 2017). The US deficit was compensated in part by US surplus in sales of services of $7.6 billion in 2016. Furthermore, the sales of services in Mexico by US-owned affiliates was $45.9 billion in 2014, while the sale of services in the United States by Mexican-owned affiliates in 2014 was $8.5 billion (USTR 2017). In 2015, US foreign direct investment in Mexico was $92.8 billion, while Mexico's foreign direct investment in the United States was $16.6 billion. With these figures, Mexico represented the second export market for the United States, after Canada, highlighting the tight market integration between the three NAFTA countries. It should be clear, though, that although each of the two US neighbors is indeed very tightly integrated and dependent on the United States, the reverse is far from true. Over 80 percent of Mexico's trade is with the United States, as is about 75 percent of Canada's trade. But the share of US trade with Canada is 16.1 percent and with Mexico is 12.9 percent.

The relative sizes of the economies and mutual dependencies of the three NAFTA partners should be borne in mind, especially when we consider the agriculture and food sectors, in which Mexico has had substantial trade deficits from the start. Centrally, Mexico's agriculture absorbed 19 percent of the labor force in 1994, and this figure collapsed to 13.4 percent by 2011. With a labor force estimated at 53 million in 2015 out of a total population of 123 million, compared with 93.5 million total in 1994 (CIA 2016), these percentages represent sizable numbers of people.

The internationalization of production led to what came to be known as "globalization." Its peculiar character since the 1980s, it must be emphasized, was neoliberal, the attempt to give free rein to private investments in the market while keeping the bearers of labor power—workers—rooted in their national states. An exception is highly skilled workers, for whom special legal provisions have been made to allow for freer but not unrestrained mobility. The process of globalization, once China joined the World Trade Organization in 2001, has signified the quadrupling of the world's labor force since 1980. Reporting on a study by the International Monetary Fund (IMF), *The Economist* (2007) puts it thus: "Weighting each country's workforce by its ratio of exports to GDP, the IMF estimates that global labor supply has in effect risen fourfold since 1980 as China, India and once-communist countries have opened up." Therefore, by the sheer strength of market forces, workers of the world have lost considerable bargaining power to capital. This interpretation is confirmed by Piketty (2014); in the United States it has manifested as an important driver of the weakening of unions, seen in the decline of union membership in the private sector from 34 percent in 1973 to 6 percent in 2007 (Western and Rosenfeld 2011:513). One macroeconomic result even in the ten wealthiest countries has been that the share of wages over GDP declined by several percentage points. In the United States, the incomes of a large majority of the population have stagnated or declined, giving rise to serious concerns about inequality (Piketty 2014; Stiglitz 2012, 2014).

The neoliberal model shifted Fordism's focus on capital accumulation in national states to its accumulation on a global scale. An initial reshaping of globalization took the form of building large regional economic blocs like the European Union and NAFTA. At first it was not clear whether such regional arrangements would result in new regional protectionist fortresses beyond the nation-state or in new regional conduits to neoliberal globalization. In the case of North America, it has been argued that NAFTA is an agreement through which the partner states tried to regulate the silent but ongoing process of economic integration that started de facto in the 1980s (Castillo 1996). Through the WTO, multinational capitalists have tried to ensure that regional blocs would not become protectionist fortresses but rather facilitate the globalization of trade and investment (Robinson 2008; Sklair 2002). And yet, the WTO has failed to break the protectionist barriers that the richer countries maintain around their agriculture industries. Mexico, however, unilaterally opened its economy even ahead of NAFTA starting in the late 1980s. The ravages of neoliberalism have been deeply felt in Mexico and the United States.

Both countries have experienced a tremendous process of socioeconomic polarization resulting from the disarticulation of their economies. For migrant farmworkers, disarticulated economies mean a separation between the point of production in the United States and reproduction of their families in Mexico. Mexican migrants produce food in the United States or Canada and send remittances back to Mexico so their families can survive; production happens in one place, social reproduction in another. Similarly, most of the manufacturing products that used to be produced in the United States are now produced in Mexico, China, or other low-wage countries. The US population has been able to expand consumption even while income remains stagnant or declines in real terms, thanks to cheap manufactured imports. One expression of the ravages of neoliberalism and how it has contributed to the disarticulation of Mexico's economy is its food sector.

NAFTA'S FOOD DIVISION OF LABOR

The profile of food imports by Canada and the United States from Mexico consists predominantly of luxury items like fruits and vegetables. In contrast, Mexico's agrifood import profile consists mostly of basic foods. There is no doubt that Mexico is far more food vulnerable than the other two NAFTA partners. Of the three NAFTA countries, only Mexico has seen food prices rise significantly during the global food crisis starting in late 2007 and spiking again in 2011 and 2012. Canada actually experienced a 0.6 percent food deflation in 2012, likely caused by the appreciation of its currency by about 30 percent between 2002 and 2012; the Canadian currency was down by 34 percent in 2016 after the collapse in oil prices in 2014. For the most part, however, Canada is also substantially self-sufficient and has had a consistent food export surplus, as has the United States for decades.

World Bank President Robert Zoellick says in a 2011 *Bloomberg Business-Week* article about the food price crisis, "The price hike is already pushing millions of people into poverty and putting stress on the most vulnerable, who spend more than half of their income on food" (in Pooley and Revzin 2011:8). The FAO (2016) considers Mexico a middle-income country where households spent close to 35 percent of their incomes on food. Still, any price increases have a much more serious impact in Mexico than they do in either Canada (FAO 2017a) or the United States (FAO 2017b), where households spent on average 9 percent to 12 percent of their budgets on food. I focus on how Mexico has fared in the NAFTA-defined food division of labor.

Although Mexico unilaterally opened its borders for most agricultural products in the late 1980s in preparation for NAFTA, the agreement contained some selective protection and phase-out periods for various crops. Corn, beans, sugar, and milk were given the longest phase-out period of protection, fourteen years, ending in 2008. However, in 2003, eight years after the start of NAFTA, most agricultural products became liberalized, and that contributed to stirring up a peasant protest movement (Bartra and Otero 2009). Even the London-based conservative newsweekly *The Economist* (2002), an enthusiastic supporter of free market policies, and *BusinessWeek*'s correspondent in Mexico City (Smith 2002), covered the Mexican government's meager support for its agricultural sector; the concern was not about globalization per se but about doing it without protecting the most vulnerable sectors of society. The articles highlight the international context of widespread agricultural subsidies throughout advanced capitalist countries. The authors of a USDA report find that in the NAFTA countries, "relative to the value of national agricultural production, budgetary expenditures on farm payments during 1999–2001 equaled 15 percent in the United States, 10 percent in Canada, and 7 percent in Mexico" (Zahniser, Young, and Wainio 2005:2).

Agricultural trade liberalization in Mexico caused a big shift in food production to higher-priced fruits and vegetables for export over lower-priced grains for the domestic market; Mexico largely imported these basic foods from heavily subsidized US farmers. Between 1997 and 2005, large-scale animal feed companies in Mexico imported maize that was priced 19 percent below its production costs (Echánove Huacuja 2013:62; Appendini 2014). Because of such a division of labor, by 2003 Mexico had become dependent on the United States for some of its most critical foodstuffs, including maize, milk, soybeans, and meat, four of its leading agricultural imports. Significant amounts of corn were first imported from the United States in 1989, a tendency that grew to the point that 23 percent of Mexico's corn supply was imported by 2007. Once completely liberalized, corn imports in January 2007 were nineteen times higher than in the same month of the previous year.

It should be clarified that Mexico imports yellow corn to produce animal feed, high-fructose corn syrup, and ethanol; it continues to be self-sufficient in the production of white corn for human consumption, mainly in the form of tortillas. White and yellow corn should properly be considered two different products, but the reality is that the usually lower import prices of yellow corn have also caused prices for white corn to fall for producers. Imported corn and soybeans are used primarily in the livestock production sector, especially for chickens (Martínez-Gómez, Aboites-Manrique, and Constance 2013; Schwartzman 2013). Since the 1990s, state policy has shifted from supporting small farmers producing grain to open imports and offer social assistance programs for those producers. With the 2007 food price crisis, the policy shifted toward supporting large producers of feed grains. Yet, Flavia Echánove Huacuja finds, the "principal beneficiaries of the commercialization subsidies for grains are agribusiness, marketing firms, and medium and large-scale producers" (2013:79).

Trade liberalization rendered Mexico highly vulnerable to price fluctuations originating in other countries. A dramatic example of this is the corn crisis triggered in 2006 when US President George W. Bush introduced a subsidy to produce corn-based ethanol to reduce US dependency on Middle Eastern oil imports. It was a time when the United States imported over 60 percent of its oil. Although the ethanol policy may well benefit US and Canadian farmers, tortilla prices in Mexico suffered a 60 percent rise in early 2007 due to increased dependency on maize imports (Roig-Franzia 2007). Price increases were also seen in wheat and its derivative products such as bread and pasta as many farmers abandoned wheat production in favor of corn to benefit from its higher price. By 2008, subsidies and bad weather in several grain-producing countries generated the highest food prices in decades or centuries, Jason Moore reports (2010). Articles in the daily news warned of popular uprisings in about forty nations around the world; a Mexico City news site raised concerns of a food shortage in that country (*Reforma* 2008).

A review of Mexico's agricultural trade data from FAOSTAT confirms the conclusions of other studies of its food dependency and vulnerability; Mexico's trade balance in agricultural production was in deficit before the start of NAFTA but increased considerably after 1994 (Ita 2007; González Chávez and Macías Macías 2007). I agree with the definition of "food vulnerability" given by Humberto González Chávez and Alejandro Macías Macías as "the situation that characterizes countries, social sectors, groups and individuals who are exposed or are susceptible to suffer from hunger, malnutrition or illness from not having physical, economic, and sustainable access to sufficient, nutritious and culturally-acceptable food, or for eating unsafe or contaminated products" (2007:48). Although their definition builds on the main elements of that of the FAO, the proposed concept gives a more precise definition of food vulnerability. Mexico used to be food self-sufficient and even export surpluses; NAFTA and neoliberalism turned it into a food import-dependent nation. By 2005 rice imports made up 72 percent of domestic consumption; wheat imports were 59 percent, maize 23 percent, and beans 9 percent (González 2013:35). Figure 5.1 shows how dramatically Mexico's food import index increased after the unilateral market opening that started in 1989 and greatly expanded after NAFTA's inauguration in 1994, with a brief drop in 1995 because of an abrupt devaluation in Mexico's peso in December 1994.

Placed in the context of Mexico's overall integration into the North

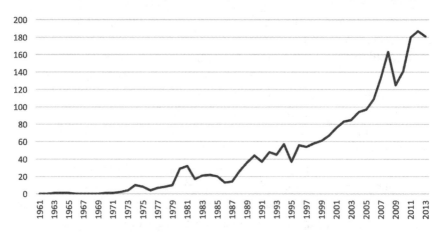

Figure 5.1. Value index of Mexico's total food imports (%) excluding fish, 1961–2013 (2006 = 100). *Source*: FAOSTAT 2017g.

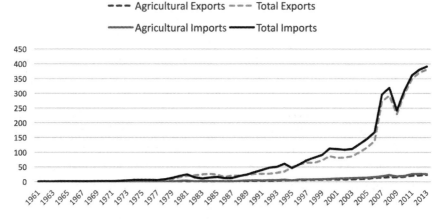

Figure 5.2. Mexico's agricultural and total merchandise trade ($ billion), 1961–2013. *Source*: FAOSTAT 2017b.

American economy, agricultural trade is dwarfed when compared to total merchandise trade. Prior to the mid-1970s, agricultural trade accounted for nearly all merchandise trade. Yet, as depicted in figure 5.2, by the 1980s non-agricultural trade took off and by the 2000s was well above ten times larger than agricultural trade.

In the context of this larger integration into the global economy and particularly into the US economy, Mexico became highly dependent on the importation of food of all categories. More specifically to its basic food imports dependency, figure 5.3 depicts three-year average calculations of Mexico's

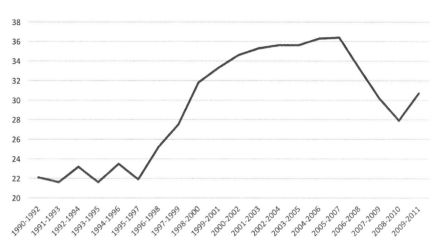

Figure 5.3. Mexico's cereal import dependency ratio (%), 1990–2011, by three-year average. *Source*: FAOSTAT 2017f.

dependency on cereals imports. Every three-year period after NAFTA began, Mexico's cereal import dependency was well over the FAO's 15 percent threshold to define dependency and above my 20 percent threshold, which is stricter to strengthen the analysis. The apparent decline in cereal import dependency noticed in the 2005–2007 period has nothing to do with Mexico gaining more agricultural independence. Rather, it is due to the global food price inflation that rendered Mexico less capable of keeping up with its prior level of imports, increasing its food vulnerability.

Mexico's agricultural trade deficit with the United States is unreciprocated in that the US market for its exports and the sources for its imports are much more diversified (USDA 2017c). Overall, 84 percent of Mexican exports were destined to the United States from NAFTA's onset to 2007; they reached a peak of 89 percent in 2005 (González Chávez and Macías Macías 2007:58). The greatest grain imports to Mexico are maize, wheat, barley, and rice in addition to signficant imports of soybeans and sorghum. The main Mexican exports to the United States are vegetables — notably tomatoes, followed by green chilies and peppers, in volumes that have grown remarkably since the start of NAFTA — as well as barley beer and fruits such as avocados, lemons, limes, and grapes. Mexican agricultural exports have indeed grown considerably, and Mexico is the number one supplier of fresh and processed fruits and fresh vegetables to the United States. Overall, Canada was the main food supplier to the United States, with more than $22 billion in exports in 2014, followed closely by Mexico with $19.2 billion. These figures represent a sizable share of total US food imports, at 18.5 percent and 16.1 percent, respectively (USDA 2017e). The next major exporters of food to the United States are relatively new, China and India, accounting for a distant 4.8 percent and 3.5 percent of the total, respectively (USDA 2017e). Of all of these US food import figures, though, Mexico still accounted in 2014 for the lion's share of imports of fresh fruits, at almost 40 percent, and vegetables, at almost 69 percent (USDA 2017e). This may explain why there are so few linkages between agriculture and domestic industry in Mexico.

It might be expected that Mexican producers have benefited massively from the increased agricultural exports, but only 20,000 of its seven million agricultural producers are the most dynamic. In a 2007 report, of 32,000 firms in the Mexican food industry, only 1,692 engaged in exports and 300 firms, less than 1 percent of the total, accounted for 80 percent of all exports (González Chávez and Macías Macías 2007:58). Another possible beneficiary of Mexico's increased imports of cheaper food are consumers, but as suggested, consumer food prices doubled from 1993 to 2007 (up 733 percent for tortillas and 736 percent for white bread) in relation to general price inflation (up 357 percent) since NAFTA's implementation. The minimum wage deteriorated by 21 percent in real terms during the same period (González Chávez and Macías Macías 2007:67–68). Unlike their counterparts in Canada, Mexican consumers have not benefited from trade liberalization.

Though Mexico's employed labor force increased by 9.8 percent between 1998 and 2007, it decreased in agriculture by 23.9 percent, from 7.5 million people to 5.7 million (González Chávez and Macías Macías 2007:68). Other sectors of the Mexican economy have not produced the expected employment opportunities to absorb the surplus labor, as new manufacturing and service investments are marked by capital-intensive or labor-saving technologies required for global competition. Consequently, Mexico became the main contributor to international labor migration in the world; between 2000 and 2005, more than two million people left the country; most of them went to the United States (Corona and Tuirán 2006). The outward migration phenomenon for twenty-first-century Mexico has several consequences. Dollar remittances sent by migrants — $23 billion in 2006 — became the second-largest infusion of foreign currency into the economy after oil revenues; remittances began to flatten in 2007 but spiked again by 2016. After NAFTA's implementation, Mexico also lost its labor sovereignty. Rural unemployment resulted in a worsening of inequality as measured by the Gini coefficient. Trends also include decreasing per capita consumption of proteins and calories by the Mexican population.

In sum, the invasion of US grains led to the bankruptcy of a huge number of Mexican peasants, and the increase in vegetable and fruit exports from Mexico has not been enough to generate employment for peasants who became redundant. Unfortunately, Mexico's bid to use these "liberated" workers to attract foreign direct investment failed; in the US slowdown of 2001, Mexico lost 600,000 jobs during the first six months of that year as dozens of maquiladoras fled to even cheaper labor havens including China, which joined the WTO on 1 December 2001. The pattern was repeated much more dramatically with the deeper US recession of 2008–2010. In short, the only beneficiaries of the export bonanza have been the more capitalized agricultural entrepreneurs and US firms and consumers. Agricultural liberalization has provoked the greatest population exodus from Mexico's countryside in its history. Thus, far from having achieved better living standards for Mexicans, NAFTA increased the country's food vulnerability and dependency, a point not lost on NAFTA's detractors. It is this very confluence of detrimental impacts that sparked the widespread peasant resistance movement and may yet influence the future direction of neoliberal globalization in North America.

MIGRATION DEBATES ON HUMAN AND LABOR RIGHTS

The economic and demographic factors behind international migration are well established. Advanced capitalist countries, mainly in the geographic North, have low or negative natural population growth, so to keep economic growth at a stable pace they must rely on migrant or immigrant workers. This demographic characteristic leads to a growing thirst for labor in the North, where its own citizen workers no longer want to perform harsh and/ or low-paid menial work; they become powerful magnets for migrants from less-developed countries. Developing countries tend to have proportions of younger people and rates of economic growth that are not high enough to absorb workers productively and at living wages. The result is an almost inexhaustible supply of potential migrants from developing countries, given the wide gap between them and wealthier countries (Castels and Miller 2003; Portes and DeWind 2004). Migrant social networks become self-sustaining, even after initial economic motivations, further bypassing official efforts to channel or suppress migrant flows (Portes and DeWind 2004:831).

Furthermore, the sending countries' governments have no incentive to stem migration flows that serve as a safety valve to alleviate political pressure and contribute financial resources through remittances. Ultimately, there is also an ambivalence of states and policies in the receiving countries; though native populations are generally hostile toward migrants, this is not universal, and hostility tends to be diffuse and unorganized, in contrast with the highly focused efforts of migrants and their employers. Yet states are not impotent; they are the key institutional actors, but their policies can have paradoxical consequences. For instance, "get tough" policies implemented in the United States after the Clinton administration of 1992–2000 led to minimizing of circular migration so that migrants tended to stay and bring their families; in turn, networks were consolidated that enhanced future migration (Hellman 2008; Portes and DeWind 2004). The liberal paradox consists in receiving countries being democracies in which civil society organizations can pit their judiciary systems, which defend human rights for all, against their executive branches that may try to summarily violate migrants' human rights.

Advanced capitalist countries require more workers than their populations can provide to maintain similar rates of economic growth, but considerable ambivalence remains in their populations about accepting immigrants or guest workers. The question in terms of labor and human rights is whether these workers are incorporated into destination societies on a parity with the rest of their citizens or are at a disadvantage, with fewer rights. Before addressing this question, let us first establish perspectives on the effects of outmigration on sending countries.

MIGRATION SEEN FROM SENDING COUNTRIES

There are three main positions in assessing the impacts of migration on the development of sending countries: the neoclassical modernization and development approach of generally regarding the effects favorably; a social democratic approach that considers problems and promises for sending countries; and a critical approach primarily viewing the development impacts of outmigration as detrimental. Studies in the first camp range from assessing the micro scale, the motivations of individual migrants, to collective motivations and utility for the migrants' communities and countries (Stark and Bloom 1985). For his part, Edward Taylor (1999) has attempted to infuse some optimism to migration and development studies, starting from the observation that in 1995, international migrant remittances exceeded $70 billion worldwide. He asks, "How have these remittances shaped development in migrant sending countries?" (63). His assumption is that "migration and remittances should have a positive effect on local production" (76). Presumably this would result from migrant households being able to overcome credit and risk constraints for engaging in production (76). Later studies show, however, that development effects of remittances are negligible (Ellerman 2005), and most funds are spent on simple reproduction needs rather than on expanded reproduction or capital accumulation (Cypher and Delgado-Wise 2010). In other words, remittances are spent by the families of migrants primarily on their own maintenance and survival including, in the best of cases, building family houses.

The social democratic position also views some positive impacts from migration in sending countries while also clearly acknowledging disparities (Portes 2009:19); some call for a joint development policy from sending and receiving countries to maximize beneficial development outcomes. Alejandro Portes (2009), for instance, seeks to reconcile opposing views on the matter between those who argue that migration can be beneficial and those who believe that "migration is not only a symptom of underdevelopment, but a cause of it" (6). From Portes's perspective, migration can have positive development impacts, but he differentiates between cyclical and permanent migration, with the former being the preferred mode. Portes points out that the "positive developmental potential of settled professional communities abroad depends, as in the case of cyclical migration, on the existence of an infrastructure capable of absorbing technological innovations and investments" (17). He distinguishes between manual labor and high human capital migration. With regard to manual labor, he explains, scholars who contend that migration has a beneficial developmental impact on the sending country might be right when the migration occurs in cyclical flows, but he contends that "permanent out-migrations tend to have the opposite effects" (8). If migration maintains a cyclical nature, the benefits for the development of the home country can be significant (13–17). Moreover, Portes argues that a "world system" approach can be used to expand the scope of the analysis (14). He explains that cyclical flows in which workers return to their homelands provide the most benefit for the sending countries (19). Portes argues that the policies between the United States and Mexico were unbalanced and needed to be revised to be mutually supportive for the development of both nations (19).

The critical perspective considers that sending countries are losing valuable workers and thereby decimating their basis for sustainable development. Raúl Delgado-Wise and James Cypher argue that NAFTA is based on a "cheap labor export led model" (2007:120). For them, NAFTA primarily benefits transnational corporations, as the agreement has driven down wages and benefits in both sending and receiving countries (122). The authors explain that the maquiladoras imported 77 percent of production inputs from the United States in 2007, thus limiting Mexico's ability to develop backward and forward linkages with the rest of its domestic market (126, 129). Cypher and Delgado-Wise (2010) argue that NAFTA and the neoliberal economic model adopted by Mexico intensified the exportation of its labor force. They point not only to the vast and direct physical emigration of Mexicans across borders, especially to the United States, but also to the exportation of labor in its "disembodied form." Whether through the maquila sector, the disguised maquila sector, or direct migration, "the only Mexican-made value/input in this complex transnational process is cheap labor" (121). Maquiladoras are assembly plants typically located along the US-Mexico border, while disguised maquiladoras are those located in the interior but with a majority of their production destined for exports. The prime examples of disguised maquiladoras are those that predominate in the auto and auto parts industry. The lack of local inputs other than cheap labor largely has to do with Mexico's importation of machinery, technology, and partly assembled inputs. The alternative would be that such inputs could be produced in Mexico and in turn help create new industries and employment through backward linkages to the local economy, the main ingredient for sustainable development suggested by Celso Furtado (1976) and Leslie Sklair (1989).

AGRICULTURE AND WORK IN NORTH AMERICA

For David Ellerman (2005), migration becomes a developmental trap for the sending countries. In this relation, the sending countries forgo self-development in favor of being long-range bedroom communities to supply labor in a semipermanent "3 D's deal" of dirty, dangerous, and difficult jobs in the North or receiving countries. Mexican workers have become inserted into US and Canadian agriculture in ways that unfortunately fit that description.

Analysis here is based on ethnographic studies about working conditions in US agriculture, including livestock processing factories, as well as interviews and a survey on farmworkers' health and safety conditions in British Columbia, Canada, that Kerry Preibisch and I conducted between 2007 and 2009 and have discussed in earlier works (Otero and Preibisch 2010; Preibisch and Otero 2014). We find that while peasant agriculture was largely bankrupted by the neoliberal turn in Mexico, some former peasants have been able to reappear as farmworkers in the countryside of its northern neighbors. It is often said that in the United States most workers in agriculture and animal processing plants are Latinos. The majority are Mexican, most often unauthorized or undocumented, but there are growing numbers of Central Americans. Vanesa Ribas (2016) describes the ethnic mix in a hog processing plant as migrants from ten Latin American countries and with varying legal status. But she also found African Americans who stayed in North Carolina after returning from New York as well as Native Americans. Most exotically, Ribas says, there were even a few white workers (5).

Work in Farming and Food Processing in the United States

The most salient feature of agricultural work in North America is its precarious nature, as dirty, difficult, and dangerous labor. Ribas observes that workers who got sick feared losing their jobs: "They were convinced that seeking medical attention would get them fired, especially if they were unauthorized workers" (2016:xiv). At the pig processing plant in North Carolina she describes, workers spent most of their waking time in a single location, between twelve and fifteen hours a day, five to six days a week (9). Angela Stuesse (2016) finds that repetitive-motion injuries are common in the livestock processing industry and can permanently cripple workers (139). It is relatively easy to avert this outcome simply by rotating workers to different work stations. But regulations do not compel employers to do so, despite workers' requests. Stuesse quotes a worker in a chicken processing plant on this point: "A lot of people is asking for rotation. Rotate these people out if that's what it's going to take to get them well! Don't treat them like dogs! This is not slavery days anymore!" (140).

Exploring the US poultry industry, Kathleen Schwartzman (2012) argues that it confronted a dual crisis in the 1980s of overproduction and declining profits after the introduction of Taylorist production techniques along with heightened worker militancy. In response to the crisis, industry managers opted to displace African American women workers with Hispanics. Managers actively recruited Mexican workers even if they were undocumented. Schwartzman focuses on five southeastern states and presents three strong pieces of evidence: there was a sharp rise of Hispanic population in the five states, where Hispanics were largely absent prior to 1980; many workers were undocumented; and by 2000 Hispanics had replaced African Americans. After a unionization drive in the US South, employers brought in Mexican workers with false documents. To prevent them from accessing union rights, migrants were generally fired after ninety days and rehired the same day under different names. The issue was not that African American workers no longer wanted the dirty, dangerous, difficult, and underpaid jobs in poultry production. Schwartzman shows that although they continued to apply for these jobs, their access to new industry jobs was limited. They consequently experienced higher levels of unemployment and poverty. Tragically for the workers, poultry industry managers used labor strikes as an excuse to get rid of an increasingly combative labor force.

Having long favored the poultry industry through policies such as feed grain subsidies, the American state stepped in to address the issue of overproduction. In response to the increasing lobby power of this concentrated industry, the US government subsidized exports to promote foreign markets. On the side of labor, Schwartzman asserts, organizing proved to be difficult "because the national office often supported local CIO officers whose position was antiblack and anti-Communist" (2012:71). While a vigorous union movement eventually emerged, the capitalist response was fierce, triggering anti-union legislation in the 1980s.

Within this industry-friendly political milieu, poultry companies systematically engaged in illegal behavior such as underpaying migrant workers and underreporting injuries and accidents. Lawsuits against Tyson Foods resulted in acquittals or light consequences. The active hiring of undocumented migrants led to declining unionism. By the 1990s, the United Food and Commercial Workers Union shifted from an antimigrant position toward trying to organize migrants, at least the legal guest workers. But employers still preferred vulnerable undocumented migrants to either white or black US citizens who could more readily organize. Ethnic succession, then, was in fact intentional ethnic displacement.

The chicken processing industry has one of the highest injury rates in the United States. Adding insult to injury, workers have faced abuse from superiors in Mississippi, "injuring the spirit, threatening workers' sense of dignity, self-worth, and justice" (Stuesse 2016:127). Other forms of abuse include wage theft by underpayment of overtime or unwarranted deductions, denial of bathroom breaks, and jobs that push workers beyond their physical limits.

A key feature in attracting capital to southern states has been their low rate of unionization, which can leave workers more vulnerable to exploitation. At the North Carolina pig plant that Ribas investigated, workers often complained that the company cared more about the *marranos* (pigs) than the workers (2016:48). Stuesse (2016) describes working conditions in southern chicken processing factories as "plantation capitalism" with a neoliberal twist; most employers were white men and employees were working-class people of color controlled "through bodily discipline; employers wield power that treats workers' bodies as exploitable, expendable machines" (127). The neoliberal twist is that labor control is driven by new technologies, while production also is facilitated by "the influx of 'hardworking' immigrants—workers the Black community is presumed to have been incapable of producing" (127).

Neoliberal plantation capitalism in the South was thus built on race, ethnicity, gender, and citizenship as the bases of workers' identities. Yet, as documented by Seth Holmes (2013), racism extends also to the states of Washington and California, where much fresh fruit is produced. Holmes, a physician and anthropologist who conducted fieldwork in those two states, describes a hierarchy of suffering along ethnic lines: "The more Mexican and the more 'indigenous' one is perceived to be, the more psychologically stressful, physically strenuous, and dangerous one's job" (95). A severe tendonitis suffered by a Triqui (an ethnicity from Mexico's Oaxaca state) worker, argues Holmes, had a social and political genesis: "His pain was caused unequivocally by the fact that he, as an undocumented Triqui man, had been excluded by both international market inequities and local discriminatory practices from all but one narrow and particularly traumatic labor position" (94). The further down the line one is situated in the hierarchy of suffering, "the more degrading the treatment by supervisors, the more physically taxing the work, the more exposure to weather and pesticides, the more fear of the government, the less comfortable one's housing, and the less control over one's own time" (95). While the workers also suffer from risks of heart disease and many cancers, their greatest concerns are about pesticide poisoning, musculoskeletal injury, and chronic pain. In this context, Holmes finds, Triqui pickers bear an unequal share of sickness and pain (96), although they are mostly young workers, at an average age of twenty-nine and with very few over sixty (100).

Even bodily position reflects hierarchy in farmwork. Those occupations that require one to be seated tend to be associated with the mind, so they are more prestigious. But jobs executed standing up or walking have a clear association with bodily work and are less esteemed. Holmes observes, "The jobs at the bottom of the hierarchy that require bodies to kneel in the dirt or bend over in the bushes are the least respected. Like animals, these workers are seen 'on all fours'" and often derided by supervisors as *perros* (dogs) and burros. Berry pickers were thus treated as subhuman and their bodies subjected to work conditions that inevitably led to deterioration (174–175). This perception is confirmed by Sarah Bronwen Horton (2016) based on her prolonged fieldwork in California tomato harvests. One research participant said, "Everyone was there on their knees in the dirt, scrabbling for tomatoes and throwing them onto the band. It was just gross (*cochino*)! And the *mayor-domo* [foreman] was standing over them, yelling insults at them; he wouldn't let them rest one second" (60). For that worker, who previously did landscaping jobs, the experience of tomato harvesting highlighted the relative dignity of landscaping, which not only was clean but allowed laborers to stand upright and avoid verbal abuse.

The few white workers who got jobs in US agriculture ended up quitting quickly, Horton notes. Their US citizenship and English skills made it less likely for them "to remain in an industry that profits from the vulnerability of foreign-born migrants" (2016:70). In the United States deaths at work declined nationwide from 2000 to 2016, Horton reports, but the rate of fatalities doubled in agriculture, almost entirely among foreign-born workers (71). One of the chief policy factors behind such statistics is that since the New Deal in the 1930s, agriculture has been a sector of exceptions to overtime, child labor, and workers' compensation laws; these exceptions were justified as necessary to guarantee the food supply, in fact subsidizing the cost of food for the rest of the working class. "The embodied effects of farmworkers' exceptional status are exceptionally inhumane," says Horton (177); she highlights the need to rectify such policies as a step toward guaranteeing human and labor rights for all.

Immigrant and Migrant Farmworkers in Canada

In 2011 Canada welcomed a historically high number of migrants on temporary employment authorization, marking a significant policy shift for a nation with a strong immigration tradition. Unlike the United States, where unauthorized immigrants added some 8.3 million workers to the labor force by 2007 (Passel and Cohn 2009), or the European Union, where the common labor market resulted in significant movement from eastern to western member states following the 2004 enlargement (Holland 2012), Canada had large increases in labor migration largely through its suite of temporary migration programs. A rise in temporary migration has been most pronounced in western Canada, where temporary worker entries began outpacing those of permanent residents by 2007 in Alberta and by 2008 in British Columbia (Citizenship and Immigration Canada 2012).

The increase in temporary worker entries has been opposed by the general public (Tomlinson 2013) as well as by anti-immigrant campaigners. It should be noted that the language on migrants is slightly different between Canada and the United States. In Canada, an immigrant is someone who enters the country with permanent resident status that leads to citizenship in a few years. A migrant is someone who comes to Canada as a guest worker with a view to going back home. It is the latter category that is most opposed by the Canadian public, as it is seen as a category of workers with precarious positions that debilitate the overall fight for workers' rights.

A growing social movement identifies a range of practices that exploit migrants who are excluded from the rights and entitlements granted to citizens and permanent residents (Justicia for Migrant Workers 2013; Migrant Workers Alliance for Change 2013). At the heart of this movement is the demand to grant migrant workers permanent resident status on arrival, that is, to remove conditions on their right to remain in Canada. "If I'm good to work, I'm good to stay" goes the slogan of Justicia for Migrant Workers. At least legally, this policy change to grant permanent residency on arrival would place migrant workers on a level playing field in having the same labor rights as other workers in this mostly immigrant society.

Agriculture in Canada relies on a combination of recent immigrant workers with permanent residency and thus a path to citizenship and temporary guest workers, but health and safety conditions for farmworkers can still be described as precarious. A comparative study of workplace health and safety among temporary migrant guest workers and immigrants in Canada shows how precarious legal status or racialization circumscribes differential inclusion in the agricultural labor market and affects workers' lives (Preibisch and Otero 2014). The research with South Asian immigrant and Mexican migrant farmworkers examined employment practices, working conditions, and health care access. Both groups, including immigrant workers with citizenship, engaged in precarious work with consequences for their health and safety. Nevertheless, migrant guest workers were subject to more coercive forms of labor discipline and a narrower range of social protection than immigrants. While formal citizenship can mitigate some dimensions of precarity for racialized farmworkers, a safer and more just food system will require broader policies to improve employer compliance and address legislative shortcomings that only weakly protect agricultural laborers.

The principal occupational risks for farmworkers in Canada have been identified as exposure to agrochemicals, plants, soil, insects, sun, and climatic extremes; machines, vehicles, and confined spaces; and repetitive and stressful ergonomic positions (Hennebry, Preibisch, and McLaughlin 2010; J. McLaughlin 2009). Repetitive motion and accidents are among the principal occupational exposures in agriculture that can cause acute problems and long-term disabilities (Hennebry 2008). Some farmworkers perform tasks that entail constantly breathing in particles or working in poorly ventilated, enclosed spaces. In 2008, three workers at a mushroom farm in British Columbia were killed and another two left with severe brain damage after being overcome by toxic gas in a composting shed (CBC News 2012).

Unsafe transportation also presents a significant occupational health hazard, particularly for farmworkers hired by contractors known to use unsafe vehicles and careless, tired, untrained, or unlicensed drivers (Fairey et al. 2008). A report on a traffic accident in which three greenhouse workers were killed found that the fifteen-passenger van had faulty brakes and poor tires, was overloaded, and was equipped with only two seatbelts (CBC News 2009). In an accident in 2012 that killed ten farmworkers (nine of them Peruvian migrants) and the driver of the other vehicle, police found that the driver transporting the farmworkers was not properly licensed (Ontario Provincial Police 2012).

Poor living conditions constitute a further principal health risk. Rural housing is often low quality, poorly maintained, and crowded. Chemical overspraying or drift poses hazards for those who live on or near their worksites. Poor hygiene and sanitary conditions at the workplace and in farmworker housing have also been identified as hazards; among such conditions are compromised access to adequate drinking water and hand-washing, toilet, and laundry facilities (Hennebry, Preibisch, and McLaughlin 2010).

The social contours of the survey participants corroborated existing descriptions of the workforce (Otero and Preibisch 2010). On average, South Asian immigrant farmworkers were older, married women who came from India as family-class immigrants and held Canadian citizenship (65 percent) or permanent residency (35 percent). Most had very little formal education; more than a fifth lacked primary school education. Mexican migrants were most often young, married men and had completed at least junior high school. The majority were from the more populous and poorest central and southern states of Mexico; more than half spoke an indigenous language, a strong indicator of indigeneity. While South Asian survey participants included mixed numbers of newcomers and longer-settled immigrants, most Mexican migrants (84 percent) had just begun their labor trajectories in Canada, and more than 75 percent had worked only in British Columbia.

The research found a labor regime in agriculture characterized by coercive employment practices in a weak regulatory environment, with serious consequences for workplace health and safety, even for those who had achieved formal citizenship. To begin, a principal finding was that farmworkers' fear of losing hours or jeopardizing their current or future employment led both groups to accept work or transportation they perceived as unsafe, to work long hours, to work while ill or injured, and in the case of migrants, to acquiesce to poor housing. A common perception among Mexican migrants was that questioning their employers, let alone refusing work or long hours, would risk their current and long-term employment in the Seasonal Agricultural Workers Program (SAWP) through unfavorable evaluation, failure to be recalled, or premature dismissal or deportation (Preibisch and Otero 2014). A Mexican migrant's response illustrates migrants' reticence to raise concerns: "The tractors don't have signal lights and the brakes are failing. Sometimes you have to drive on the highway when you're going from one field to another, and this worries me. But if [the employer] says the signal lights or brakes are working, I'm not going to contradict him" (185). South Asian immigrants similarly feared that speaking out could result in losing income and their jobs. A former farmworker turned advocate explains, "Today if I speak something against the contractor, the next day I'm not going to be picked up. He'll say, 'Fine, stay at home. You'll come to know'" (185).

Fear of losing hours or jeopardizing future employment led immigrants (79 percent) and migrants (69 percent) to work when ill or injured and/or avoid reporting health concerns. Migrant interviewees responded with statements such as "We tolerate the pain and don't say anything" and "There are people who have injured themselves horribly, and even so they keep working" (Preibisch and Otero 2014:185).

Besides short-term economic motivations such as losing hours for working while ill or injured was a general fear of employer reprisals. When respondents were asked to agree or disagree with the statement "On my farm there are coworkers who work when they are ill because they are afraid to tell the boss," 48 percent of Mexican migrants responded affirmatively, as did 44 percent of South Asian immigrants (Preibisch and Otero 2014:185–186). Three responses illustrate this view, two from Mexican migrants and the third from a South Asian immigrant:

You don't want to stop working because you think maybe they [employers] won't ask for me [next year] if they see me complain and because I'm hurt.

I'm still in pain, but I've decided not to say anything because I'm ashamed [and] afraid the boss will send me back to Mexico.

I have felt sick a few times at work, but I was afraid that the owner may get angry at me if I asked for a holiday. (Preibisch and Otero 2014:186).

Farmworker advocates state that a common employer response to illness or injury among migrants is firing the individual and arranging his or her deportation. This practice has been widely documented in eastern Canada (Basok 2002; J. McLaughlin 2009; United Food and Commercial Workers Canada and Agriculture Workers Alliance 2011).

Fear was fostered also through degrading treatment. Study participants reported enduring verbal aggression such as yelling, insults, and racist remarks and even physical violence (Preibisch and Otero 2014:186). When asked to rate activities they carried out on the job in terms of the perceived risk to their health and safety, on a risk scale of 1 to 10 in which 1 indicated very low risk and 10 indicated very high risk, 44 percent of the Mexican migrants and 22 percent of the South Asian immigrants rated "working with an aggressive boss or supervisor" as high risk, at least a 7. Thus while both groups perceived aggressive management as a risk, it was of considerably greater concern to Mexican migrants (186).

Fear of jeopardizing their employment likewise induced both groups to acquiesce to long shifts. Mexican migrants, however, worked significantly longer shifts than their South Asian counterparts. During high production, Mexican migrants worked an average of 12 hours on weekdays and 8 hours on Saturdays and Sundays, while South Asian respondents averaged 9 hours on weekdays and 5 hours on Saturdays and Sundays. The trend for Mexican migrants to work longer hours held up in low production periods, when they reported an average of 9 hours on weekdays and 5 on Saturdays and Sundays, while South Asians worked an average of 6 hours Monday through Friday, 3 on Saturday, and 2.5 on Sunday. Thus even low production periods meant 55-hour work weeks for Mexicans, substantially higher than the 30.5-hour work weeks for South Asians. While both groups perceived long hours as risky, they were more concerning to South Asian immigrants who were, on average, older than the Mexican migrants. Among South Asian respondents, 43 percent rated "working long hours" as a high-risk activity, compared to 28 percent of Mexican respondents. A South Asian participant said, "The hours worked [are] a risk. During the rush season, I'd work 11- to 12-hour shifts for two straight weeks. My body would be sore, but I knew I'd have to get up and gut it out" (in Preibisch and Otero 2014:186). Some individuals in both groups worked even extraordinarily longer days, up to twenty hours in a continuous shift. Mexican migrants reported working for two weeks straight before having a day off. Although the workers were motivated to work as many hours as possible during their work permits and while separated from their families, they could jeopardize their employment if they refused to work extremely long shifts.

Study participants perceived that unreasonable productivity targets, piece-rate wage systems, and pressure from management intensified the production process to an extent that increased their risk of workplace injury. A Mexican migrant responded, "Since we use very sharp knives and they ask us to cut very quickly, there's always a risk. They ask us to cut 13 boxes of [green peppers] per hour per person, so you have to work very fast, and I've cut myself twice" (Preibisch and Otero 2014:188). A South Asian immigrant responded, "To make work safer, I feel that we should receive three breaks per day and not get pushed so hard by our contractor to work faster" (188).

Employers also used ethnic or national competition as a disciplinary tactic to increase productivity or gain acquiescence, and they intimidated South Asian farmworkers with their potential substitution by Mexican migrants and vice versa. With the spectacular growth of the SAWP, such threats needed little reinforcement among South Asians. However, labor replacement also constitutes a threat for Mexican migrants. The year after a group of Mexicans became the first migrant agricultural workers to unionize in British Columbia, their employer rehired only a dozen migrants out of the original thirty-eight and complemented the workforce with twenty-eight Canadians (Sandborn 2009).

Housing was also a specific concern for migrant workers in the study (Preibisch and Otero 2014). Among Mexican survey respondents, 37 percent disagreed with "The state of my housing does not present any risk to my health" and reported shortcomings in facilities such as inadequate sanitation, with some dwellings lacking indoor plumbing and potable water (189). Farmworker and advocate interviewees emphasized concerns of overcrowding as well as insufficient facilities. An advocate pointed out, "People are living nine, ten, eleven to a house with access to one bathroom; without even a stove but three or four electric hotplates for nine people. No washer, no dryer. There are houses that . . . are not even adequate for human abode" (189–190).

SAWP guidelines state that a laundry facility should be provided for every fifteen occupants, yet 19 percent of migrants in the study had no washing machine and 25 percent had no tumble dryer (Preibisch and Otero 2014:190). That is a significant concern, considering the importance of washing clothes to mitigate pesticide exposure. Further, inadequate refrigeration space was troubling, as migrants' access to supermarkets was generally limited to one day per week. The risks of gastrointestinal problems were increased by insufficient cooking appliances that impeded migrants' ability to heat meals adequately if at all. The poor housing conditions indicate inconsistent employer compliance with the SAWP agreement and regulatory deficiencies in monitoring and enforcement.

Throughout high-income countries such as Canada and the United States, noncitizen migrants are a growing or still substantial component of the labor market supporting food systems. The debate about sustainable agriculture and sustainable food systems has not focused enough, if at all, on the issue of sustainable and safe employment for agricultural workers (Preibisch and Otero 2014; Weiler, Otero, and Wittman 2016). It must be emphasized that social sustainability—including respect for workers' labor and human rights—is just as important in this context as environmental sustainability, and a food system that depends on precarious working conditions cannot be viewed as sustainable.

CONCLUSION

There are two quite different ways of addressing the issue of human and labor rights for Mexican migrants in the United States. One is building a North American union similar to the European Union, with free labor mobility across NAFTA partners; this approach would make it viable for the United States to continue using the Mexican labor force without infringing on workers' human and labor rights. The other is for Mexico to rearticulate its economy and enhance its food self-sufficiency by strengthening smaller-scale agriculture and the countryside; doing so would have the added benefit of enhancing biodiversity. Short of constituting a North American union, the second alternative would focus on promoting sustained economic development in Mexico to make it possible for citizens to stay home, make living wages, and strengthen their families and communities. Both approaches would take considerable social mobilization to implement; given the sharp divisions on migration issues in the United States and the 2016 US presidential election results, the North American union alternative may lie in a distant future at best. I conclude that Mexican politicians and activists should bank on the second alternative.

As Mexico is a less than democratic nation, the way its ruling class and government technocracy bought into neoliberalism had little to do with how broader sectors of the nation perceived this development model. Although the trends have proven dire, massive protests by peasant groups and their supporters are sufficient to question whether neoliberal globalization and the international division of labor in food will be sustainable in Mexico. One could say that the 2016 electoral results in the United States, apparently favoring a nationalist and protectionist stance, are the result of ravages on the working class caused by NAFTA. But it is Mexico, the least-developed NAFTA partner, that has suffered the harshest repercussions from neoliberal restructuring; consequently, it faces the most resistance from the ground.

It is ultimately at the level of the nation-state that neoliberal regulation takes hold. Pedro Magaña Guerrero, a Mexican peasant whose organization is a member of Vía Campesina, puts it this way after praising militancy at the global level: "The consolidation of alternatives rests completely on what is happening at the local level, it depends on the development of organizations in their regions, in their countries" (in Desmarais 2007:135). Looking within nation-states will allow for studying how and whether their internal socio-political dynamics may become independent factors that could alter dominant trends in the world economy from the bottom up.

CHAPTER 6

Globalizing the Neoliberal Diet

FOOD SECURITY AND TRADE

T rade liberalization has been a hallmark of the neoliberal reformation of capitalism since the 1980s. Agricultural trade was liberal during the first food regime, from the late nineteenth century to World War I; agriculture was oriented toward national markets in the second food regime, from the aftermath of World War II to the late 1970s. By the 1980s, agriculture had become the most inward-looking sector of national economies, and producers were highly protected. One of the leading discursive tools to liberalize agriculture in the 1980s was the idea of food security, which was supposed to be better achieved through trade rather than national self-sufficiency.

In looking beyond the NAFTA region I offer a critique of the notion of food security through trade, as promoted centrally by suprastate organizations like the FAO, World Bank, and WTO. The empirical question that emerges is to what extent food import dependency enhances or worsens food security in developing countries compared with that in advanced capitalist countries. As defined by the FAO (2008, 2012), food security is the availability of food for everybody's sustenance, in spite of price fluctuations, as well as the physical and economic access to food for an active and healthy life. My hypothesis on this is simple: the more that developing countries become dependent on food imports and exports, the more they will be importing the world food price for the relevant commodities. The world price is the price of goods or services in all countries other than one's own. It influences international trade to the extent that the world price is net of any export or import taxes and subsidies. Internalizing the world price for food crops means that domestic food prices will be affected by global trends in the international food market. On one hand, food price deflation will affect those countries most linked to world markets. On the other, and this has been the more salient issue since 2007, food price inflation will more adversely affect their working classes, which spend larger shares of their household budgets on food. I offer tentative corroboration of this hypothesis by an analysis of how food price inflation has affected the seven countries studied here between 1985 and 2007. The impact was much lower in Canada and the United States, but it was severe in all developing countries.

My empirical focus is emerging nations — Brazil, China, India, Mexico, and Turkey — in comparison with two long-standing agricultural exporting powerhouses, the United States and Canada. I contrast food consumption and trade in large countries with varying locations in the world economy and agricultural exporting strengths. I use FAO data comparatively for two periods, 1985 and 2007. These two years allow for an analysis that contrasts the time before the neoliberal reformation of agricultural trade rules (1985) and after it but just before the global food price crisis (2007).

McMichael (2009a:287) has argued that what he calls the "corporate" food regime has led to "deepening food dependency in both directions," that is, in the North and South. Using longitudinal data from the FAOSTAT database, I add nuance and specificity to the neoliberal food regime and show that its food security can best be characterized as uneven and combined dependency. This is a modification of Leon Trotsky's (1934) term "unequal and combined development" about capitalism in Russia; in the present context, the dependency indicates that states' insertion into and adaptation of this regime are based on their different stages of development. That is, I wish to show that emerging food dependencies under neoliberal capitalism are not parallel between advanced capitalist countries and emerging economies. Rather, the former display mild levels of dependency on the importation of luxury foods that invariably make small contributions to total food caloric intake, while the latter generate varying degrees of dependency on the importation of basic foods; they have uneven types of dependency. Wealthier countries are importing higher-priced and mostly higher-quality foods, while they are exporting mass and industrially produced grains and cereals, often the product of biotechnology such as maize and vegetable oils.

In addition to this very uneven dependency I see an increasing trend to homogenize food consumption patterns across the world; the dominant economic actors are large agribusiness multinational corporations orchestrating global food production and dissemination. The most significant ABMs are based in the United States. Although they participate heavily in the international economy, the United States remains their most significant locale and the country where they most influence state policy (Panitch and Gindin 2012).

The rules of the game seem to have fundamentally changed the role of state intervention and opened the door for ABMs to operate relatively freely in a variety of national markets. This process coincides with the technical revolution in agriculture represented by biotechnology, which I see as an enabling technology that was taken over by large ABMs. In their hands, biotechnology has become the central technological form of the neoliberal food regime, extending the modern agricultural paradigm that originated with hybrid corn in the United States in the 1930s (Kloppenburg 1988; Otero 2008). Centered on transgenic crops that were engineered to resist the effects of herbicides aimed at weeds or to insert *Bacillus thuringiensis* (Bt) as a biological pesticide into cotton or corn, biotechnology has made modern farmers around the world dependent on inputs purchased from ABMs. In the case of corn, the herbicide-resistant variety was initially more successful than Bt corn, but eventually over 90 percent of the land surface devoted to corn was planted with "stacked" corn, genetically modified for herbicide resistance and having the Bt pesticide. With soybeans, from the start only the herbicide-resistant variety succeeded in gaining farmers' adoption (USDA 2017a). Transgenic soybeans and corn have become two of the most traded agricultural commodities in the world; since the mid-2000s much of the corn surplus has been absorbed in the United States to produce subsidized ethanol (Bjerga and Thomasson 2017:14). Thus, the uneven food dependencies between North and South are at the same time combined in the pattern of capital accumulation across the world economy.

How are we to characterize the food regime emerging from the new regulatory configuration that places trade at center stage in achieving food security? Any theoretical characterization of the emergent food regime would have to fulfill at least two analytical requirements: it must contribute to enhancing knowledge and understanding of reality and point toward a progressive direction to reduce or eliminate food vulnerability and ensure true food security. To characterize the food regime, we need to first decipher its main dynamic factors in order to then identify its foremost antagonisms and transformative elements. The food regime argument takes a worldwide perspective on capital accumulation in food and agriculture, a view of systematic divisions and dependency between North and South; I explore the data for two advanced capitalist countries in comparison with five developing, emerging countries. The point is to make it as hard as possible to falsify the dependency assumptions of the world systems theory. If even these emerging markets are indeed dependent on the North, then a much direr outcome can be expected for smaller developing countries.

Rather than peripheral in the world economy, the emerging countries in my sample may be regarded as semiperipheral in the sense that they may be best placed to buck any dependency trends in a world economy with enhanced trade. If, however, dependency between North and South varies significantly across countries, we need a more nuanced analysis than that allowed by McMichael's perspective. In fact, I argue that we need a meso-level analysis of the food regime that accounts for specific national-level variations in food dependency. For operational purposes, I define food dependency as resulting from imports of one or more food sources that exceed 20 percent of domestic supply. This definition varies from the FAO's 15 percent as a measure to strengthen my analysis. If my points can be sustained with a more conservative, stricter threshold, then my conclusions about dependency should be stronger.

FOOD SECURITY AND TRADE

In the post–World War II period, agriculture remained the exception for trade liberalization, outside of all multilateral agreements. Agriculture in most countries, especially larger ones with greater agrobiological diversity, focused primarily on self-sufficiency for domestic markets and trade of surpluses. The state intervened vigorously in most cases with several kinds of farm supports, from direct subsidies and cheap loans to technical assistance for production and organizational help to market farm products nationally and even internationally. Support also included concessional sales of surplus production to export markets, compensation to control supply through set-aside land schemes, and use of sanitary and phytosanitary regulations to protect home markets (Thomson and Metz 1998).

Such an exceptional situation for agriculture started to change slowly but surely after the Uruguay Round of GATT. Negotiations for the round started in 1987 and concluded only in 1993, to take effect starting in 1995 in the brand-new WTO, which absorbed the GATT and its more limited mandate.

The United States dominated the food regime after World War II that has involved a central double standard ever since: the United States promoted free trade around the world while practicing protectionism and subsidies for its agricultural sector. This position was adopted by the European Union, Japan, and Canada as well and prevented any advancement in the talks at the WTO's Doha Development Round, which were begun in November 2001 specifically to address agricultural trade liberalization. The double standard of advanced capitalist countries has faced strong resistance from governments of developing countries; resistance by social movements from below has also been key to blocking agricultural trade liberalization.

The concept of food security has been central to the neoliberal pitch for opening national agricultures. The latest incarnation of the concept, which has evolved over time, is as follows: "Food security exists when all people, at all times, have physical, social and economic access to sufficient, safe and nutritious food which meets their dietary needs and food preferences for an active and healthy life" (FAO 2012). The official view distinguishes four dimensions of food security: physical availability of food, economic and physical access to food, food utilization, and stability of the other three dimensions over time. Food security is achieved once all four dimensions are simultaneously fulfilled (FAO 2008:1).

The idea of food security can be traced back to the 1948 UN Declaration of Human Rights, which included the right to food. The term "food security" as such, however, was not articulated until 1974, and food security did not come to dominate official discourse in suprastate organizations until the mid-1980s, once the neoliberal reformation of capitalism was in full swing (Jarosz 2011). From then on, food security became irrevocably linked to trade and aid as ways to make food available. The official view justified the neoliberal shift from a supply-led to a free trade-oriented food security paradigm, which relies on the ideas of "balancing supply and demand," "differentiating between food self-sufficiency and food security," and "comparative advantages" (FAO 2006:1).

Following the FAO's reconceptualization of food security, an influential 1986 World Bank report on poverty and hunger drew a close link between food insecurity, high levels of structural poverty, and low levels of income (Reutlinger and van Holst Pellekaan 1986). The FAO has since identified poverty and low incomes as hindrances to the demand side of food security (FAO 2006:1). The 1986 World Bank report further states that "there is no necessary link between self-sufficiency and food security" (Reutlinger and van Holst Pellekaan 1986:31). Prior to the 1986 report, the World Bank had already drawn attention to the need for identifying cost-effective ways to improve food security (Reutlinger and van Holst Pellekaan 1985:6–7), labeling food self-sufficiency as a costly and inefficient solution and arguing for a free trade model (3, 18). Similarly, a 1997 World Bank document on rural well-being advises that "only with stable, integrated long-term access to world markets can countries comfortably refrain from costly food self-sufficiency policies" (Serageldin and Steeds 1997:16). A World Bank report in 2001 firmly insists that "the overall benefits of liberalization will always outweigh the costs," even though it might lead to undesirable outcomes in the short run in certain cases (World Bank 2001:2).

According to an FAO training manual on food security policies (Thomson and Metz 1998), food self-sufficiency can be viewed as an expression of an autocentric development approach that should be replaced by an outward-looking view of development incorporating international specialization and comparative advantage. In the 2000s the FAO continued to argue for an import-driven, outward-looking model of food trade based on comparative advantages, recognizing food imports as a fundamental means for achieving food security (FAO 2000, 2003, 2005).

Nonetheless, the FAO (2003) has cautioned that the benefits of *comparative* advantage could be reversed once large multinational corporations gain *competitive* advantage to the detriment of small producers' and states' ability to derive gains from international free trade. Comparative advantage ensures—at least in theory—a positive-sum game by enabling all players to specialize in the branch where they can be most efficient; competitive advantage entails the monopoly over profits derived from a monopoly over specific products in a given branch, mostly thanks to the big players' technological superiority (FAO 2003; Lara 2007). In agriculture, the situation is embodied in corporate control of biotechnology production in contract farming, supermarket control of purchasing, and multinationals' control over the distribution chain between production and final sale (FAO 2003).

The most significant social movement that has challenged trade liberalization in agriculture has been Vía Campesina, a transnational organization of peasants and farmers (Desmarais 2007). While not opposing trade as such, Vía Campesina's central proposal to ensure food security revolves around the program of food sovereignty to be based on small-scale farmers and agroecological, sustainable production. The food sovereignty movement aims to make sure that states have the right to protect markets, exert democratic control of the food system, and revalue peasant production. Once food sovereignty is achieved, surpluses can be traded. One could argue that the political struggle of Vía Campesina centers on defending the value of peasants' and small-scale farmers' labor power. More broadly, the movement defends the ability of small-scale commodity producers in agriculture to guarantee food security if they are not made to deal or compete directly with large ABMs.

Some researchers assert that food sovereignty emerged as a counterframe to the neoliberal conception of food security, which champions keeping the markets free of government intervention, further liberalizing food and agriculture, and increasing productivity through high-tech approaches such as the adoption of genetically modified seeds. Rejecting the neoliberal approach to food as a regular commodity and to peasants as individuals, food sovereignty highlights peasant solidarity, collective rights, and ownership of resources by also putting a finger on the power dimensions inherent in food and agriculture (Fairbairn 2010; Wittman, Desmarais, and Weibe 2010). In their introduction to *Food Sovereignty: Reconnecting Food, Nature, and Community*, the editors define food sovereignty as "the right of nations and peoples to control their own food systems, including their own markets, production modes, food cultures and environments" (Wittman, Desmarais, and Weibe 2010:2).

Efe Can Gürcan (2011) has argued that food sovereignty points to the importance of state and social movement partnership in achieving food security. Such a partnership rests on a four-pillar strategy, of land collectivization through radical agrarian reforms with a strong emphasis on cooperative organizing; socialization of participatory urban agricultural practices, considering urban growth rates in the developing countries; support for local agricultural markets that would promote local access to food; and transnational peasant alliances that would empower peasant movements vis-à-vis the state. So, how can we adjudicate whether food security can be achieved through trade liberalization or a food sovereignty program? Let me turn to a comparative analysis of several emerging economies for possible answers.

FOOD SECURITY OR UNEQUAL AND COMBINED DEPENDENCY?

Rather than deeply examine the historical specifics of certain emerging nations, I attempt to broaden the understanding of food security by taking a sampling of countries. Yet, I also seek to differentiate more specifically the agricultural dependencies of various countries to introduce more nuance than the broad framework of a world system or dependency theory argument might do. McMichael, for example, cites Mexico's increased exports of fruits and vegetables and imports of corn to argue that they amount to an asymmetrical form of "corporate 'food security,' based in a dialectic of Northern 'overconsumption' and Southern 'underconsumption'" (2009a:288). Mexico, however, has actually increased its importation and domestic production of meats based on subsidized US grain. It is primarily Mexico's middle and ruling classes that consume meat, making it a value-added or luxury food if not necessarily a more healthful one. The working classes have had to face escalating prices for imported basic foods and higher prices for the fruits and vegetables that Mexico has increasingly exported. In other words, fruits and vegetables formerly produced primarily for the domestic market have become more expensive for Mexico's consumers with the internalization of their world prices.

When once-traditional foods such as fruits and vegetables become a major component of a country's agrifood exports, they assume the going world prices. During food inflationary times like those that have prevailed since 2007, world prices become internalized into the domestic market; they are higher than when those foods were traditional and produced for the domestic market. In spite of higher prices for fruits and vegetables, Mexico's consumption of fruits and vegetables increased, particularly since the start of NAFTA in 1994. But that is just an average. An analysis by income quintile reveals how inequitable such consumption has been by class as higher-income groups in Mexico expanded their access to and consumption of meat.

Asymmetry is not between countries as such. It is not countries per se that overconsume or underconsume; analysis needs to account for differential class diets. Thus, there is theoretical and empirical importance to introducing some nuances into the dependency style of analysis to distinguish between basic and luxury food imports and exports. As advanced capitalist countries, the United States and Canada have become dependent on imports of such luxury goods as fruits, vegetables, and alcoholic beverages, although they much more than offset these imports with strong agricultural surpluses. They are net food exporters. Luxury foods in advanced capitalist countries do not amount to much more than 2 to 3 percent each of average daily per capita caloric intake. By comparison, cereals like maize and wheat constitute over 40 percent of caloric intake in Mexico. These are examples of what I mean by uneven and combined dependency.

All the emerging countries I compare here have become more vulnerable to food price fluctuations, but Mexico has become decidedly dependent on the importation of most top basic foods and some luxury foods. I focus on main food source flows and food security. Through this empirical analysis, I strive to tease out actual historical developments in agrifood trade and illuminate the threads that weave the food regime together.

All data were constructed using the FAOSTAT database of each country's official statistics and the FAO's estimates. I conducted an inductive study comparing food dependency levels in 1985 and 2007. The general proposition is that emerging countries that have resisted all-out neoliberal reform since the 1980s have retained significant levels of food self-sufficiency because state policies made it a priority to safeguard the countries' farmers and agricultural sectors without shunning trade. In other words, a self-sufficiency policy is not incompatible with globalization and trade.

One of the main challenges of empirically assessing food security is that its definition refers to individuals rather than nations. The data I analyze refer to nations and averages of daily food intake per person, and thus I must define some indirect parameters to assess whether the countries' overall positions in food security have benefited or deteriorated by joining the neoliberal food regime. In line with the food sovereignty literature and program, I assume that food self-sufficiency is a better guarantor of food security, as has been the case with Brazil. Jennifer Clapp (2014) has rightly suggested that this discussion should not be dichotomous as either food sovereignty or food security. The overall goal must be food security, but the policy question must include the place of food self-sufficiency in each country and the means to achieve it—ideally without resorting to antitrade or protectionist measures. Trade can enhance complementarities in diets, so any surpluses should be available for export, which can just as well finance needed food imports.

My assumption is that losing self-sufficiency is a condition that may lead to a country's loss of food security or at least increase its vulnerability to price fluctuations in food. Further, increased dependency in agricultural exports necessarily internalizes world prices for the relevant crops to the domestic economy. Price fluctuations disproportionately affect the lower-income groups in any country. These groups tend to spend larger shares of their household budgets on food, which aggravates any conjuncture of food price inflation. Food price elasticity is much greater in developing countries than in developed ones (von Braun 2007).

Food self-sufficiency is operationally defined as a country's ability to provide basic food for its people without relying on imports that exceed 20 percent of a given crop's domestic supply. Domestic supply is made up by the sum of existing stocks plus domestic production plus imports, all of this minus exports. Given the cultural specificity of basic foods, I tailor my food vulnerability assessments to each country through its consumption data by inductively selecting crops that make up 50 percent or higher of national daily caloric intake. In some countries this is made up of a limited number of crops, and in others the diet is more diversified. With the determination of each country's basic crops, I assess the level of dependency in each of these crops. Table 6.1 presents data on dependency levels in the top five foods

TABLE 6.1. Emerging and North American countries' dependency levels in top five foods (% = imports/domestic supply), 1985 and 2007

COUNTRY	1985		2007	
	TOP CROPS	IMPORTS >20%	TOP CROPS	IMPORTS >20%
Brazil	Cereals; sugars; rice; wheat; maize; starchy roots	Wheat, 51%	Cereals; sugars; wheat; meats; rice; maize	Wheat, 69%
Canada	Cereals; wheat; sugars; meats; milk butter; pork	Sugars, 101%	Cereals, wheat, oils, sugars, meats, milk	Oils, 45%; sugars, 103%
China	Cereals; rice; wheat; meats; sweet potatoes; sugars	Sugars, 26%	Cereals; rice; wheat; meats; pork; oils	Oils, 39%
India	Cereals; rice; wheat; sugars; oils; pulses	Vegetable oils, 27%	Cereals; rice; wheat; oils; sugars; pulses	Oils, 42%
Mexico	Cereals; maize; sugars; wheat; meats; milk	Milk, 24%	Cereals; oils; maize; sugars; meats; wheat; milk– exc. butter	Cereals, 39%; oils, 44%; maize, 28%; meats, 21%; wheat, 58%; milk, 22%
Turkey	Cereals; wheat; oils; sugars; fruits, excluding wine; milk, excluding butter; vegetables	Oils, 38%	Cereals; wheat; oils; sugars; milk- exc. butter; maize	Oils, 44%; maize, 25%
United States	Cereals, excluding beer; wheat; sugars; milk, excluding butter; meats; alcoholic beverages	Sugars, 20%	Cereals, excluding beer; wheat; oils; sugars; wheat; meats; milk, excluding butter	Oils, 24%

Source: FAOSTAT 2012b.

Note: "Sugars" in plural indicates that sources are sugarcane, sugar beets, and/or high-fructose corn syrup.

for the seven countries in 1985 and 2007. A country with dependency levels reaching 20 percent or more of its domestic supply in a majority of its basic crops is considered to have lost its food self-sufficiency. This condition increases the country's vulnerability to price fluctuations in food. Some overlaps appear in the food categories in table 6.1, such as "cereals" and "corn," but they were not counted twice in the calculations.

FOOD SOURCES, DIVERSITY, AND DEPENDENCY

To determine the basic foods for each country's domestic consumption—the top crops that made up at least 50 percent of each nation's daily caloric intake—I began by investigating the twenty-five crops that contributed most to average daily per capita caloric food intake in each country. I took these from the more than one hundred food categories recorded by the FAO, including milk as well as crops. Somewhat surprisingly, the top five food sources made up at least 59 percent of caloric intake in all the sample countries and as much as 78 percent. From the twenty-five main food crops in each country I identified those food sources with high dependency levels, that is, with imports higher than 20 percent of the domestic supply. Given that the top five food sources accounted for over 50 percent of caloric intake, I conducted my dependency assessments on these, as compiled in table 6.1.

One general pattern for all the countries is that cereals made up the largest percentage of food sources. But the proportions varied considerably from one country to another, in terms of both the composition of cereals and their contribution to total food supply. For instance, Canada and the United States consumed about half as much food in the form of cereals (around 23–25 percent) as Mexico did (around 43 percent), indicating that Mexico's cereal import dependency was all the more acute. Figure 6.1 depicts each country's dependency level on cereals, measured as the relation between imports and domestic production. This is a less conservative measure of dependency than the one used in table 6.1, which is the relation of imports over domestic supply (domestic production plus imports minus exports).

Vegetable oils had also become increasingly important by 2007, reflecting a global shift in diets away from roots and tubers and toward livestock products and vegetable oils (WHO/FAO 2003: section 3.2). In a basic reading of table 6.1, we can see some increases in dependency. Mexico demonstrated the most dramatic shift to dependency in basic foods, having more than 20 percent imports for four of its top five basic foods. Turkey developed significant dependencies in two of five top crops. A few other countries, among them

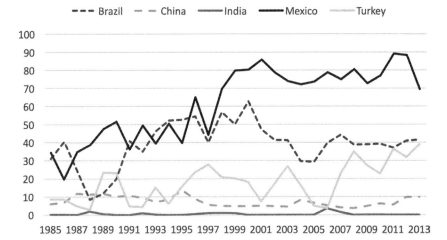

Figure 6.1. Cereal import dependency in five countries (import quantity over domestic supply × 100), 1985–2013. *Source*: FAOSTAT 2017c, domestic supply; FAOSTAT 2017b, imports.

Brazil and India, had higher levels of import dependency in crops on which they were already dependent.

In discussing the data on a country-by-country basis I begin the food import dependency analysis with Brazil and proceed through the rest in alphabetical order. With the exception of a few years in the late 1980s, Brazil was dependent in well over 20 percent of its domestic cereal supply, with a value of 41 percent in 2013. Save for wheat, no other main crop met the dependency level in Brazil, and wheat's share of total food intake actually declined from 14 percent in 1985 to 12 percent in 2007. The most remarkable trend, however, is that wheat became the third major source of food, displacing rice, which moved to fifth place, after meat, by 2007. Given the climatic requirements of wheat, this is likely a crop that is difficult to grow in Brazil, and Brazil continued to import this temperate-weather crop.

In terms of dependency, the story of sugars is quite peculiar to Canada. As mentioned earlier, the country has been a free trader in this crop for many decades; it imports raw sugar from the free market, that is, the market beyond about 80 percent of this crop's world product committed in several regional trade agreements (Otero and Flora 2009). In 2007 Canada imported 103 percent of its domestic supply of sugar, which is explained by the processing of raw into refined sugar for Canada's domestic and export markets. In other words, given the abundance of sugar production in the world and despite its price fluctuations, Canada cannot be deemed to have a compromised food supply based on its raw sugar imports dependency. The ranking of sugars in the top five food sources for Canada moved from second in 1985 to third place in 2007, and its contribution to total food intake declined from 15 percent to 14 percent. This is a relatively marginal but welcome trend nutritionally.

Vegetable oils, however, became the second source of caloric intake in Canada by 2007, even though they did not even appear in the top five sources in 1985. The imports of vegetable oils represented 45 percent of domestic supply for this caloric source in 2007. Their price was an important component of the food price inflation crisis that started in 2007 (McMichael 2009a). In the case of meats of all types, their contribution to total caloric intake declined both in ranking (third to fourth place) and in proportion (12 percent to 11 percent), while their import level almost reached my dependency threshold by increasing from 12 percent in 1985 to 19 percent of the domestic meat supply by 2007. By 2012 some observers were sounding alarm bells (McKenna 2012). Overall, though, Canada continued to be an agricultural exporting powerhouse, with a hefty agricultural trade surplus that more than made up for all its food imports.

India's composition of main food sources shifted a bit, with a 4 percent decline between 1985 and 2007 in the overall contribution by cereals to average daily per capita caloric intake. Further, the contribution of rice declined from 33 percent to 30 percent, while that of wheat increased from 19 percent to 22 percent in the same period. An important shift in food composition was that of vegetable oil; its contribution increased by 50 percent, from 6 percent to 9 percent of total food intake. Vegetable oils' rank increased from fourth to third place, and its dependency levels increased from 27 percent to 42 percent. The increase explains why the 2007 global food price inflation crisis had a considerable impact in India, along with its importation of the world price for rice, still the major contributor to India's total caloric intake. In 2007, one estimate indicated that up to half of all of India's children were undernourished (Sen 2011). India became the world's main rice exporter in the 1990s, but the government set up export restrictions in 2007 to guarantee domestic supply during the global food price crisis. It regained its top exporting place again in 2011, displacing Thailand and Vietnam, by eliminating export floors (Mukherjee 2012; USDA 2012).

In India, pulses, consisting of dry, yearly, high-protein grains like lentils and beans, also underwent a slight shift; from 6 percent of total food intake in 1985, they declined to 5 percent, yet their import level increased from 3 percent to 17 percent of domestic supply, almost reaching my dependency threshold. Sugars also declined in total contribution to food, from 10 percent to 8 percent, but their import level disappeared, from 10 percent of domestic supply in 1985 to zero in 2007. Overall, then, India is a largely self-sufficient producer of food. Still, the disproportionate food price inflation it has suffered since 2007 must be related to its increased dependency on vegetable oil imports and internalization of the world prices for both rice and wheat.

For Mexico in 1985, only four of the top twenty-five crops met my dependency criterion: milk, with 24 percent imported; sorghum, 33 percent; oil crops, 46 percent; and soybeans, 63 percent. By 2007, however, the number of imported crops that met my criterion of dependency, 20 percent of domestic supply, ballooned to eleven of the main twenty-five food sources: cereals (total, excluding beer), 39 percent; maize alone, 28 percent; milk, 22 percent; sorghum, 23 percent; oil crops, 78 percent; meats, 21 percent; wheat, 58 percent; cereals (other), 100 percent; soybeans, 98 percent; starchy roots (total), 21 percent; and potatoes, 22 percent. Some of the categories are subsets of larger categories, such as cereals (wheat and maize), oil crops, and starchy roots (potatoes). Both soybeans and sorghum are used as animal feed crops, underscoring the larger role of meat, especially from poultry, in Mexico's diet (Martínez-Gómez, Aboites-Manrique, and Constance 2013). Of the seven countries, Mexico is the one whose dependency levels on basic food imports became the most acute. Overall, Mexico became dependent for well over 56 percent of its total food sources by 2007, without counting the importation of animal feeds. It should not be surprising, then, that as of 2014, Mexico's food inflation was three to four times higher than that of its NAFTA neighbors, Canada and the United States (figure 6.2). As a result, domestically, food prices increased at twice the pace of general inflation from 2007 to 2011, and minimum wages declined in real terms by 24 percent (CONEVAL 2012).

A 2015 study by CONEVAL, Mexico's Consejo National de Evaluación de la Política de Desarrollo Social (National Social Policy Evaluation Council) finds that food security continued to deteriorate from 2010 to 2014. Based on nationally representative samples, the proportion of households with food expenditures below the cost of the basic food basket increased from 68.3 percent in 2010 to 69 percent in 2012 to 72.1 percent by 2014. This measurement is adjusted by scale economies and use of adult-equivalent scales (CONEVAL 2015). With these staggering figures in mind, it may be easier to understand that without offering poor households cheaper alternatives to acquire food calories, taxing sweetened soft drinks since 2014 was likely to have regressive effects. What this means is that the tax further polarized people's access to calories.

Turkey's main food sources changed toward a much greater empha-

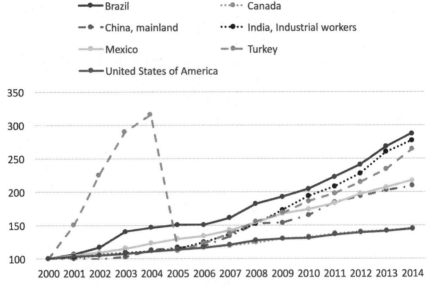

Figure 6.2. Food price indices in seven countries, 2000–2014 (2000 = 100).
Source: FAOSTAT 2017a.

sis on vegetable oils for cooking and a decline in the ranking of fruits and
vegetables as top foods. In 1985 vegetable oils were already the second food
source, with a 38 percent import dependency level. By 2007 vegetable oils
accounted for 15 percent of total average daily per capita food intake. Wheat
accounted for 41 percent, down from 47 percent in 1985. Sugars declined
in their total caloric contribution from 8 percent to 7 percent in the same
period but remained in third rank. Fruits — excluding wine — and vegetables
fell in rank by one spot, each contributing 4 percent to total food intake.
Although lower in rank by 2007, this proportion is considerably higher than
the role played by fruits and vegetables in the other countries of comparison.
Food trade dependency was present for vegetable oils in 1985, but by 2007
two of the top five food categories had high import dependency levels, at
44 percent of vegetable oils and 25 percent of maize. The maize apparently
was used primarily for livestock feed, as imported meats, at 4 percent in
1985, were no longer imported in 2007 even though meats continued to offer
3 percent of total food intake. This is a much lower percentage than those of
meats in most other countries in 2007, such as Brazil (12 percent), Canada
(10 percent), China (14 percent), Mexico (9 percent), and the United States
(12 percent). India, however, consumed even less meat than Turkey; meats
ranked as the thirty-sixth source of food in India in 2007.

The United States imported larger proportions of foods in 2007 than in 1985, but the country still did not meet my threshold of food dependency except for sugars in 1985 and vegetable oils in 2007, although the country exported almost as much in vegetable oils as it imported. By 2007 several top twenty-five crops met my dependency criterion but cannot be regarded as food dependency for two reasons: the foods are part of what may be regarded as luxury rather than basic foods, and they make up a proportion of total food intake that is less than 5 percent. Of all food sources that were not among the top five, only fruits, excluding wine, met my dependency criterion of over 20 percent imports; they went from 37 percent imports in 1985 to 52 percent in 2007. But fruits constituted only 3 percent of total food intake in both years. All in all, then, the United States was even less dependent than Canada in fruits and primarily in luxury foods.

In sum, my analysis introduces some nuance into McMichael's assertion that the neoliberal food regime generates a mutual dependency for North and South in the world economy. Only by conducting a disaggregated analysis of food import dependency at the national level can we effectively assess the specific nature of such mutual dependency. What we have is an uneven and combined dependency in which advanced capitalist countries have increased their imports of fruits and vegetables as well as wine and alcoholic beverages, but neither group is a basic food and both make up minor percentages of total food intake. Conversely, Mexico, which has taken up the neoliberal reforms most wholeheartedly of all the developing countries analyzed, became dependent on the importation of basic foods. Although its exports of fruits and vegetables to the north increased considerably, they did not offset the even larger inflow of basic food imports. This makes Mexico a net food importer, while Canada and the United States are net food exporters. The other emerging but developing countries have retained their self-sufficiency to a much greater degree than Mexico. Yet their food source profiles are becoming more Westernized in the sense that the countries now rely more heavily on wheat, vegetable oils, and meats, each a product of the global food regimes that started around 1870.

How have uneven and combined dependencies affected food inflation? As figure 6.2 indicates, there is a sharp disparity in food inflation rates between developed and developing countries. Figure 6.2 depicts an inflation index constructed on the basis of making prices in 2000 equal to 100. Any price increases after that year are recorded as percent increases in relation to prices in 2000. Figure 6.2 orders each country from high to low according to the latest inflation index. Brazil appears at the top, with the highest food inflation rate in 2014, and Canada and the United States at the bottom, with the lowest. Canada and the United States had accumulated inflation rates since 2000 of about 45 percent, while all the developing countries had rates four to eight times higher.

Somewhat surprisingly, Brazil's inflation was greater than Mexico's, likely due to its strong export orientation, which contributed to importing the world price for the relevant crops. While Brazil had a heavy net food trade surplus, as did Canada and the United States, it was among the developing countries that continued to score a medium food security risk by 2011. The rest of the emerging nations also had a medium risk except India, which had a high risk (Carrington 2011). India continued to have about 250 million undernourished people, including half of its children (Sen 2011). So, why is it that Canada and the United States, which, like Brazil, had large food trade surpluses, did not face the same level of food inflation as Brazil? At least part of the answer is twofold: the United States and Canada have engaged in agrifood trade, particularly in wheat, for more than a century, and their production vastly exceeded their domestic needs; and food expenditures constitute a relatively small share of total household expenditures.

CONCLUSION

I started this chapter with a discussion of how suprastate institutions promoted the idea of food security as achievable through trade or aid. I thus start the concluding remarks with official assessments by these institutions of the historical record of the extent to which trade liberalization in agriculture since the 1980s has resulted in food security. The self-criticisms are quite sharp, even if neoliberal policies have not changed. The markets, as it turns out, "for many temperate-zone products and basic food commodities are substantially distorted by government subsidies and protection, particularly in Organisation for Economic Co-operation and Development (OECD) countries" (FAO 2005:vii). Furthermore, trade liberalization "benefited countries competitive in the export market, but discouraged farmers where agriculture was not competitive. They now rely even more on food imports than before and are more susceptible to food price increases on the global market" (POED 2012:7). Finally, "the claim that [trade liberalization] will bring net gains to the least developed countries as a whole is at best questionable and at worst outright wrong" (FAO 2003:38).

In other words, the free trade pitch made in the 1980s turned out to be mostly ideological rhetoric based on the comparative advantages paradigm. But the realities of strong competitive advantages held by countries that traditionally exported agricultural products prevailed. This reality has not meant a mutual dependency in food between North and South. Rather, given the specificities of each country and the way the states decided to incorporate their nations into the world economy, dependencies have become uneven and combined. While my data are still exploratory and need further refinements and additional national case studies, I can see that there are important differences in dependency patterns. Only the developing nation that wholeheartedly adopted neoliberalism, Mexico, became import-dependent in basic foods. For the rest of the developing countries analyzed, to the extent that they became incorporated into agricultural free trade, they also imported world prices for certain foods. The result has been increased food security risk, expressed in price inflation rates much higher than those in advanced capitalist countries.

From my broader assessment of import and export data it is clear that Canada and the United States increased their imports of fruits and vegetables, which may be regarded as luxury foods. At the same time, the contributions of fruits and vegetables to total food intake was quite modest, on the order of 2 to 3 percent each. My sample of developing countries, in contrast, demonstrates an expansion of some degree of dependency on basic foods; Mexico became decidedly dependent on most of the foods that make up more than 50 percent of its average daily caloric intake. Here the empirical support for dependency being uneven and combined is strongest. It suggests a glaring need for supplementing traditional nation-based dependency analyses with more nuanced analysis of intranational class diets like those presented earlier for Mexico and the United States.

CHAPTER 7

Food Security, Obesity, and Inequality

MEASURING THE RISK OF EXPOSURE TO THE NEOLIBERAL DIET

*Refusing to deal with numbers rarely
serves the interests of the least well-off.*

THOMAS PIKETTY, *CAPITAL IN THE
TWENTY-FIRST CENTURY*

My goal in this chapter is to advance in the understanding of the global shift to the neoliberal diet. I offer a quantification of the risk of exposure to the energy-dense components of this diet for the low- to middle-income working classes. The neoliberal diet risk index that I generate allows us to compare a country's food performance across time and with other nations. The NDR index is a composite of five indices that capture increased food import dependence, income inequality, disruption of agrifood systems in the form of urbanization rates, female labor force participation, and economic globalization. I calculate the geometric mean of these indices to determine the NDR.

The neoliberal diet is the industrial diet as it becomes globalized and accessed primarily by the poor to middle classes, but it also encompasses the more newly available higher-quality foods for the rich who can afford fresh fruits and vegetables from world markets. The neoliberal diet is thus differentiated by class into basic and luxury foods. Which specific foods make up basic and luxury categories in each country have changed historically as food provisioning has moved from peasants, communities, and regional markets to appropriation and control by capital. Mexico's neoliberalization since the mid-1980s and ultimate incorporation of its economy into NAFTA in 1994 not only eradicated the peasant sector and many *tortillerías* (small manufacturers of corn tortillas) but also forced people in those enterprises to migrate to urban centers and the United States (Lind and Barham 2004). This particular dependency relation becomes a mirror in which other emerging nations can see themselves as neoliberal globalization advances. How did substitute, processed ingredients become cheaper than fruits and vegetables? In the early 1980s fruits and vegetables represented nontraditional exports promoted by the World Bank and the IMF to generate the foreign exchange needed to pay the foreign debts of developing countries (Barndt 1999; Friedmann 1999; Robinson 2008; Wilkinson 2009). Those foods became organized by capital, and domestic purchasers had to compete with rich consumers at home and abroad (González 2013).

The prevalence of sweetened soft drinks, based since the 1980s on high-fructose corn syrup in North America, has been facilitated in large part by US supply management policy (price supports for corn) along with the industrialization of corn. Food regimes have reshaped diets since the 1870s (Dixon 2009; Friedmann and McMichael 1989), often in deleterious directions such as promoting sugar, refined wheat, and as of the 1980s, high-fructose corn syrup and vegetable oils. So, diets change in tandem with changes in agricultural production (to export-oriented production of cocoa, coffee, or wheat) or land tenure (from communal to plantation), often leading to famines in the earlier eras of capitalism (Davies 2001).

Since the 1950s, meat has been at the center of the US diet; it has become more central to the neoliberal food regime since the mid-1980s. Using data from FAOSTAT, we see that yearly average per capita meat consumption in the United States was 88.7 kilograms in 1961 (the first year for which global data are available), compared with a world average of 23.1 kilograms. The United States reached its peak average meat consumption just prior to the world food price crisis in 2007 at 126.1 kilograms per capita, compared with the world average of 40.8 that year. Thus, on average, the world's per capita meat consumption rose from 26 percent of that in the United States in 1961 to 32 percent in 2007. After the 2007 crisis, US meat consumption declined to a per capita yearly average of 117.6 kilograms in 2011, compared to a growing world average of 42.4 kilograms. In absolute terms, though, world consumption of all meats (beef, pork, poultry, and other) was 4.2 times that consumed in the United States in 1961. By 1985 this multiple rose to 5.7, which represents a 35 percent rate of increase from 1961. By 2011 the world was consuming meat at a multiple of 7.8 compared to US consumption, representing a 38 percent rate of increase between 1985 and 2011. During this period, however, the US population declined from representing 6.2 percent of the world's total population in 1961 to 4.5 percent in 2011. In fact, the world's population grew by the equivalent of another 22.4 United States of Americas from 1961 to 2011. Clearly, then, growth in meat consumption has not been proportional to population growth in the world. Rather, it has been primarily the upper-middle- and upper-income classes of the world that have had greater access to meats. Hence I focus primarily on the energy-dense portions of the neoliberal diet.

Not only is the transition to the neoliberal diet with all its consequences a global phenomenon, but there are also strong indications that adoption of this diet is occurring far faster in developing countries. Obesity rates are rising faster in developing countries (Monteiro, Moura, et al. 2004:940), such that "the maximum mean BMI [body mass index] in more developed countries might be exceeded by those in less developed ones" (Bhurosy and Jeewon 2014:4). Globalization is indubitably key to this rise; by "radically altering the nature of agri-food systems, [it] is also altering the quantity, type, cost and desirability of foods available for consumption" (Hawkes 2006:2). One of the main problems with the way neoliberal globalization has been implemented is that a series of policies were adopted in a one-size-fits-all approach. Agrifood sector regulation has made industrial production and consumption patterns compatible with neoliberalism through "conventionalization," the imposition of certain market standards by mainstream players such as organized industrial producers and relevant state institutions (Guthman 2004).

FOOD SECURITY: QUANTITY AND QUALITY

Because food insecurity can be politically explosive, the 2007 global food price inflation crisis and its continued spikes into 2012 renewed governments' concerns about food security. Even in wealthy Canada and the United States more than 10 percent of the populations suffer from food insecurity (Taber 2014), and the rate has increased since 2006. Of the 870 million people in the world identified in a 2012 report of the FAO as suffering from food insecurity, 850 million—almost 98 percent—resided in developing countries. Food security is thus a central issue in a world that produces enough food for all but in which class inequality prevents many from having access to sufficient and healthful food.

While differential access to sufficient food itself is already a stark marker of class inequality, I focus here specifically on inequality in access to quality food. Consequences of the neoliberal diet are already apparent. According to the World Health Organization, "65% of the world's population live in a country where overweight and obesity kills more people than underweight" (WHO 2009:16). This happens through health impacts such as coronary heart disease, ischaemic heart disease, strokes, type-2 diabetes, and various cancers. The WHO report estimates that by 2005 a billion people suffered from overweight and 300 million from obesity (17). With the increased diffusion of the neoliberal diet, it is likely that millions more have been added to these statistics since 2005. Unfortunately, obesity has not supplanted straight food insecurity; rather, the paradoxical double-headed specter of famine and obesity are increasingly and simultaneously plaguing the world (Patel 2012).

The neoliberal diet is the logical consequence of the neoliberal food regime (Otero, Pechlaner, and Gürcan 2013; Pechlaner and Otero 2008, 2010), which transcended the nation-centric focus of agriculture through trade liberalization. The neoliberal food regime is characterized by trade liberalization and other state and suprastate regulatory structures and legal frameworks that favor large corporations such as the food processors and agribusiness multinationals that profit from the neoliberal diet's proliferation. Since the 1990s, agricultural biotechnologies have become the main technological form in agriculture; this change is another important component of the neoliberal diet, with its associated consolidation of agrifood corporate power (Clapp and Fuchs 2009; Pechlaner 2012a).

If the neoliberal food regime is the articulation of a set of regulations and institutions that allow for stable capital accumulation in agriculture, then the global food price crisis set off in 2007 represents its crisis, or at least its contradictions (Otero 2013). The inflation crisis arrived after well over a century of declining food prices (Moore 2010) that had made food, particularly the neoliberal diet, broadly accessible. The working classes, including people with middle incomes, have been the most adversely affected by food price inflation, which ironically served to further entrench their dependency on the nutrient-poor foods of the neoliberal diet. At the same time, the greatest beneficiaries of the crisis have been financial speculators, grain traders, agribusiness multinational corporations, and large supermarket chains (Baines 2015; Lean 2008; McMichael 2009b; Rosset 2009). Madeleine Fairbairn and colleagues contend (2014:657), "Retailers and traders, now beholden to financial backers, are finding new ways to produce shareholder value at the expense of the most vulnerable food system actors. In this way, food workers and small farmers find their positions further weakened in the drive for financial profits." What I turn to, then, is a class analysis of diets.

THE NEOLIBERAL DIET AND CLASS

What Anthony Winson (2013) calls "the industrial diet," based on the industrial processing of food, antedated the neoliberal turn of the 1980s by four decades. The industrial diet came to prevail primarily in advanced capitalist countries. As the neoliberal diet has gone global, it has consolidated the trend; it has been disseminated to emerging nations and has its own specificities. Importantly, significant components of the neoliberal diet are based on raw materials such as corn, canola, and soybeans, feed crops at the forefront of the biotechnology revolution (Otero 2008). Corn and soy, the raw materials for a wide range of processed food products, are heavily subsidized in the United States in part because, Pollan notes, they "are among nature's most efficient transformers of sunlight and chemical fertilizer into carbohydrate energy (in the case of corn) and fat and protein (in the case of soy)" (2008: 117). Most centrally, though, these crops are subsidized because powerful groups get huge profits from them (Baines 2015; Winders 2012). Thus agribusiness technology, agricultural policy, and agrifood processing are all inextricably linked in the industrial production of the foods ultimately made available in the neoliberal diet.

The neoliberal diet has high calorie content (is energy-dense) and low nutritional value, such as highly processed convenience foods and those available from fast food restaurants. That said, this diet is not just heavily supplemented with the chips, candy bars, and french fries traditionally associated with junk food. It has been transformed more broadly so that the staple foods not formerly associated with treats — everything from breakfast cereals to meats — have become so highly processed and nutritionally compromised that Winson (2013) calls them "pseudo foods" and Pollan (2008) calls them "fake foods." The three principal additives of these foods are fat, salt, and sugar (Moss 2013), and a factor in their predominance has been the concerted and effective effort by processed-food companies to privilege taste over nutrition. A host of labs and marketing strategies have been enlisted to successfully hook people on these foods (Moss 2013:37).

While the popular debate over obesity associates the so-called epidemic with the United States broadly speaking, it has not affected the country uniformly. Scholars have increasingly identified significant class differences in the adoption of the energy-dense foods of the neoliberal diet (Darmon and Drewnowski 2008; Drewnowski 2009; Drewnowski and Darmon 2005; Drewnowski and Specter 2004; Freeman 2007; Harrington et al. 2011; H. Lee 2011; McLaren 2007). Indeed, there is a notable consensus that "obesity in America is a largely economic issue" (Drewnowski and Darmon 2005:265S), especially if we include other aspects of socioeconomic status such as education, occupation, and even environmental factors such as those investigated by food desert scholars (Beaulac, Kristjansson, and Cummins 2009; Gordon et al. 2011; Guptill, Copelton, and Lucal 2013; Morland et al. 2002; Rose and Richards 2004; Shaw 2006; R. Walker, Keane, and Burke 2010).

One of the simplest reasons for the relation of socioeconomic status and obesity is that industrial food producers have made tremendous efforts to maximize the neoliberal diet's appeal and create products that are relatively low in cost. Neoliberal diet foods are significantly cheaper than more nutritious alternatives such as fresh fruits and vegetables, whole grains, and leaner, unprocessed meats. The substitution of real ingredients such as peaches with processed ones like peach flavor and the increased durability and shelf life of processed foods are main factors in the price reduction. These types of goods cost less per megajoule of dietary energy than their more perishable counterparts of fresh meats and produce, making them understandably very appealing to those in the lower- to middle-income classes (Drewnowski and Specter 2004:9).

US food desert literature suggests that environmental factors such as limited access to supermarkets and big-box chain stores reduce the ability of lower-income consumers to cheaply purchase nutritious foods. Supermarkets are more likely to have cheap, healthful, high-quality foods than convenience stores or small neighborhood stores have, but supermarkets are less likely to be situated in poor neighborhoods whose occupants are further hampered by transportation issues. Limited access forces the poor to purchase more of their food from small convenience stores that disproportionately stock processed foods. Winson (2013) calculates that pseudofoods make up over 70 percent of shelf space in convenience stores in the United States. Importantly, he has found even greater proportions in two case studies he conducted in Mexico and Argentina (205).

Far greater complexities in the class-diet relationship in the United States exist than can be elucidated here; they include factors such as gender, age, and race/ethnicity and dietary impacts such as those of fast food restaurants. Suffice it to say, particularities and causal features aside, the working-class basis of the so-called obesity epidemic is unambiguous in the United States (Otero, Pechlaner, and Gürcan 2015). Furthermore, the evidence is sufficiently strong to warrant the class-diet relation's characterization as a form of "food oppression" (Freeman 2007), as it has become another mechanism for deepening existing inequalities in the United States. My overall argument, though, is that class trumps both gender and racial/ethnic inequalities. This point is well highlighted by Guthman (2011), who finds that affluent women have the time and means to have gym memberships, buy organic foods, and eat at high-end chefs' restaurants, none of which is the case for poor women.

In the United States, a considerable and historical overlap between lower classes and nonwhites has led to a fruitful discussion of intersectionality, or how gender and racial/ethnic oppression exacerbates class exploitation. Thus, much of the discussion about how blacks or Hispanics have a higher propensity for overweight and obesity likely has more to do with the intersectionality of class with race or ethnicity. Empirically assessing this point would require a fine-tuned representative sample in which economic class can be held constant for different gender and racial/ethnic groups. Such a research agenda requires more refined data than are currently available. For the time being, let us turn to the cheapest energy-dense food components in the neoliberal food regime, as these shape the class determination of diets.

Figure 7.1 shows that vegetable oil consumption, as a percentage of total food intake, has increased in every country of my sample. If wheat and sugar have been prime energy-dense foods since the first food regime (1870s to 1914) or earlier, the neoliberal food regime has added vegetable oils. The composition or combination of oils in each country varies, but in most cases they are converging toward soybean oil. Turkey has the highest intake of vegetable oils among the BRICSTIM, a group of emerging countries comprised of Brazil, Russia, India, China, South Africa, Turkey, Indonesia, and Mexico. I join the acronym in this specific way as a play on words, suggesting the possibility that this TIM (or team?) could represent an emerging pole in the world economy, in building a multipolar world.

Like the wealthier countries, Turkey was consuming above 15 percent of its daily caloric intake from vegetable oils by 2011, consistent with the nutrition transition identified in the 1990s (Popkin 1998; Drewnowski and Popkin 1997). The nutrition transition is the global transformation of diets resulting from rising incomes and urbanization (Drewnowski and Popkin 1997:31). It consists of increased access to cheap fats and sugars and transforms traditionally low-fat diets as a result; cheap vegetable oils make "high-fat diets acces-

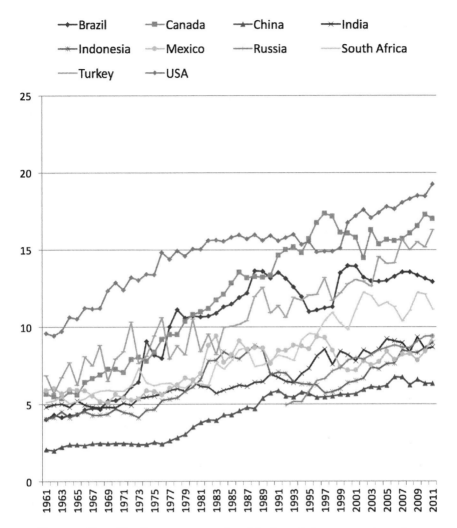

Figure 7.1. Vegetable oils as percentage of total food supply in ten countries, 1961–2011. *Source*: FAOSTAT 2017c.

sible even to low-income societies" (Drewnowski and Popkin 1997:40–41). Through their own societal changes and the lowered economic barrier to such consumption habits, developing countries can now more readily adopt the diet of wealthier nations—and its consequent health impacts.

Next are Brazil and South Africa, whose consumption of vegetable oils in 2011 lay between 10 and 15 percent of total food intake. The rest of the countries consumed up to 10 percent of calories from vegetable oils, topped by Mexico and Russia. China had the lowest consumption, at 6.3 percent. Considering that China started the period in 1961 consuming a mere 2.1 percent of food in vegetable oils (compared with 9.6 percent for the United States the same year), the ending number for China by 2011 does represent quite a dramatic increase, by a factor of three. As total food consumption increased across the board, the absolute amount of vegetable oil ingested by today's population is quite substantial.

It is not surprising that the nutrition transition to vegetable oils parallels what the WHO calls a "risk transition," how a country's level of development is associated with a shift in its population's diseases from primarily infectious to noncommunicable diseases. This risk transition may be linked to what Gyorgy Scrinis (2013) calls "nutritionism," a reductive focus on nutrients rather than the actual foods that contain them. For instance, saturated fats from animals were seen as unhealthful, and that led to a rise in vegetable oil consumption. An alternative approach could have been to suggest that we eat less meat and fewer processed sweets (Scrinis 2008). Jane Dixon calls this "nutritionalism," when diets are promoted solely on the criterion of their nutritional qualities (2009:323). Dietary guidelines introduced in the United States in the 1970s, with an increased focus on specific nutrients, provided justification for commercial exploitation by large corporations producing processed foods and dietary "supplements."

Top among noncommunicable diseases are cancers and heart diseases associated with overweight and obesity (WHO 2015). Developing countries are facing the impacts of these noncommunicable diseases at the same time as they still face infectious diseases related to insufficient nutrition, resulting in a double whammy of diet- and nutrition-related diseases. Thus in developing countries we see an "epidemiological transition" as health issues that used to be associated with affluence overlap with those coming from malnutrition (Maio 2014). Notably, these same countries are the ones with the least funding to deal with the mitigation and impact of such diseases.

FOOD TRADE DEPENDENCY

On intercountry inequalities, my hypothesis is that, far from improving food security, trade liberalization in agriculture has worsened it, at least in the form of a heightened risk of exposure to the neoliberal diet. That is to say, the more agricultural trade dependency grows, the more food insecurity grows in the form of enhanced risk of neoliberal diet exposure. Food import dependency does not directly translate into more imports. Rather, the degree of food dependency has a bearing on general food vulnerability and the extent to which masses of peasants are pushed out of smallholding agriculture into cities and have to buy more energy-dense foods; they move away from traditional food fare, which may become dearer. The level of dependency relates to food exports as well as imports. As mentioned, fruits and vegetables have become less accessible to Mexico's working classes since capitalized farmers started to rely more heavily on the export market. To the extent that food and agricultural trade depends heavily on capitalized farmers and processing firms with direct foreign investment, the neoliberal food regime has also involved a major shift in the overall agrifood system.

I distinguish between basic and luxury foods, as this is critical to understand the differentiated convergence of class diets with economic globalization. Basic foods are primarily cereals and sugars but also, increasingly, vegetable oils (figure 7.1). Luxury foods are fresh fruits and vegetables but also economically value-added foods like meats and wine. Meats in particular are absorbing an increasing share of grain production that could otherwise be consumed directly by humans. Weis (2013a) calls the phenomenon "meatification" and highlights its devastating ecological implications.

Increased trade was expected to enhance food security in all countries. But such expectation assumes that all countries involved in trade would capture the comparative advantages equally, as if they would all be set in a level playing field. The fact is, however, that the leading agribusiness corporations in buyer-driven or producer-driven global value chains have had competitive advantages that put them ahead of the game (J. Lee, Gereffi, and Beauvais 2012). The multinational corporations have considerable advantages in financing and marketing networks that put them well ahead of companies or producer groups in developing countries. Concentration in the agrifood industry happens to be sharper than in most other sectors.

One result of free trade with highly inequitable competition is that the world is increasingly adopting a US diet with a heavy basis of corn and vegetable oils that tend to be produced with transgenic seeds using genetic-engineering techniques like recombinant DNA and popularly called GMOs (Kloppenburg 2004; Otero 2008). The same type of seed goes into the production of feed for chickens, which have become the neoliberal meat for the low- to middle-income classes in North America (Schwartzman 2012; Martínez-Gómez, Aboites-Manrique, and Constance 2013). In China, pork consumption has increased the most among meats, with grave social and ecological impacts (Schneider 2011). Although pigs are omnivores that can eat a wide range of foods, corn and soybean meal are the main feed crops used by commercial pig farmers.

BASIC AND LUXURY FOODS

The distinction between basic and luxury foods has to do primarily with the cost per calorie, with basic foods being the most widely accessible to most people. Depending on each country's culture, fresh fruits and vegetables may well be part of the traditional basic diet, but this has changed as globalization has made them more widely accessible while also more expensive in domestic markets where they are exported. Cereals are the most basic foods in many countries, and more so in developing countries. I suggest that where the direct food consumption of cereals increases across time, it is broadening access to basic foods for its working classes. A decline in the consumption of basic foods, in contrast, could mean either a decline in the standard of living or a move toward substituting basic cereals for more vegetable oils and/or more costly foods like meats, fruits, and vegetables. For those reasons, it is useful to comparatively explore sample basic and luxury foods in tandem to interpret the overall food consumption trend in each country.

Tables 7.1 and 7.2 show how cereal supplies changed across three points in time: 1961, 1987, and 2013. One general trend of note is that the consumption of basic foods increased in the sample countries from 1961 to 1987. The exception to this trend is Russia, with data for the Union of Soviet Socialist Republics for those two years. But there were declines in six countries from 1987 to 2013. When such decline in the consumption of cereals is combined with an increase in the consumption of luxury foods like meats or fruit, one can say that the country likely gained a higher standard of living. From the tables it is clear that China has experienced the greatest transition from basic to luxury foods. In contrast, Mexico and Turkey had slight declines in basic foods and flat consumption of fruits during the neoliberal period. That could indicate a general decline in their standards of living; they happen to be the countries most integrated into the wealthiest economic blocs. In both cases, percent declines in basic food consumption from 1987 to 2013 are significant, of –8.4 percent in Mexico and –24.2 percent in Turkey and flat consumption of fruits. The trend toward flat consumption of fruits, in particular, must be causally related to the export dependency of these countries in the neoliberal era, as Humberto González Chávez (2013) has found to be the case in Mexico.

TABLE 7.1. Ten countries' cereal and fruit supplies (kcal/capita/day), 1961–2013

COUNTRY	CEREALS (BASIC)			FRUIT (LUXURY)		
	1961	1987	2013	1961	1987	2013
Brazil	835	947	969	88	107	113
Canada	628	664	909	98	120	135
China	814	1,607	1,416	6	17	104
India	1,265	1,423	1,361	30	35	70
Indonesia	1,030	1,637	1,751	30	37	74
Mexico	1,312	1,424	1,314	62	104	105
Russia[a]	1,528	1,265	1,154	27	66	85
S. Africa	1,521	1,543	1,537	30	45	42
Turkey	1,650	1,905	1,601	211	160	160
USA	627	742	801	80	130	119

Source: FAOSTAT 2017c.

Note: **Bold** = countries that experienced decline in basic and/or luxury foods intake from 1961 to 1987 and/or from 1987 to 2013.

[a]Data for 1961 and 1987 are those for the Union of Soviet Socialist Republics.

THE NEOLIBERAL DIET RISK INDEX

I have developed a neoliberal diet risk (NDR) index to estimate people's risk in having access predominantly to its energy-dense foods component. I find that the most affected are primarily the working classes, whose low to middle incomes shape their food availability and choices. I compare measures of food trade dependency and inequality that are likely to increase the risk of exposure to the neoliberal diet for the group of emerging nations that includes and amplifies the original BRIC nations—Brazil, Russia, India, and China—by adding South Africa, Turkey, Indonesia, and Mexico. Jim O'Neil of Goldman Sachs coined the "BRIC" acronym in 2001 as a grouping of countries for financial analysis. The BRIC countries represented some emerging markets attractive for new investment. By 2014 South Africa had

TABLE 7.2. Ten countries' rates of change in cereals and fruit supplies (%), 1961–2013

COUNTRY	CEREALS (BASIC)		FRUIT (LUXURY)	
	2013/1987 % CHANGE	1987/1961 % CHANGE	2013/1987 % CHANGE	1987/1961 % CHANGE
Brazil	13.4	2.3	21.6	5.3
Canada	5.7	27	22.4	11.1
China	97.4	–13.5	183.3	83.7
India	12.5	–4.6	16.7	50.0
Indonesia	58.9	6.5	23.3	50.0
Mexico	8.5	–8.4	67.7	1.0
Russia[a]	–17.2	–9.6	144.4	22.4
S. Africa	1.4	–0.4	50	–7.1
Turkey	15.5	–19	–24.2	0.0
USA	18.3	7.4	62.5	7.4

Source: Data from table 7.1, constructed with data from FAOSTAT 2017c.

[a]Data for 1961 and 1987 are for the Union of Soviet Socialist Republics.

joined the original nations to form BRICS as a set of countries intent on organizing a development bank as an alternative to the World Bank, which is largely controlled by the United States. I add Turkey, Indonesia, and Mexico to my analysis because they have requested membership in BRICS as a bloc of emerging nations; for brevity, as described, I call this larger group BRICSTIM. I include some data on two advanced capitalist countries that are also agro-exporting powerhouses—Canada and the United States—as people in these countries have been exposed to the industrial diet since the 1940s and yet the countries' levels of inequality are lower than in the BRICSTIM countries.

One common feature of the BRICSTIM nations is that they all have large enough populations and most have sufficient land and water resources to attempt a postneoliberal development model, potentially with a popular democratic character that includes a food sovereignty program. I realize that the food sovereignty program is still controversial in critical agrarian studies. Henry Bernstein (2014) has elaborated one of the more skeptical views, and indirectly so has Tom Brass (2014). I consider early statements of the program by Vía Campesina and scholarly defenses like those by Desmarais (2007), Edelman (2014), and van der Ploeg (2014) to be more convincing but subject to empirical testing by practical deployment. The main question is whether an agroecological orientation based on smallholder peasants can produce enough healthful food for all and be environmentally and economically sustainable.

Popular democratic development presumably would be oriented in large part to mitigate the ravages caused by neoliberal globalization. It would build the basis for sustainable, endogenous development. Some critical differences among BRICSTIM nations include their specific insertions in the world economy. Mexico and Turkey have integrated with their wealthier neighbors. As seen above, this association as well as their wholehearted adoption of neoliberalism—a state policy feature also shared by South Africa—has led to greater levels of food dependency, including food export dependency, and more exposure to the neoliberal diet, expressed in a higher NDR.

The United States was the leader in the overweight and obesity increase by 2008, with an average prevalence of those conditions in about 31.5 percent of all US males and females, but other countries have not taken long to follow the US lead. Mexico had an obesity prevalence in 2008 of 26.7 for males and 38.4 percent for females, well above the regional average reported by WHO (2009, 2015); the rate of overweight among adults over twenty years of age had grown fastest in the world since 1980, at a 31 percent increase. Next come Brazil and South Africa, each with a 26 percent increase in the rate of overweight adults, and then the United States, with a 24 percent increase (C. Howard 2012). As of 2008, the prevalence of obesity in Brazil was 16.5 for males and 22.1 for females ages twenty years or more; rates for South Africa were 23.2 for males and 42.8 for females. The question is how we can measure a population's risk of exposure to the neoliberal diet, which is so highly associated with overweight and obesity.

Overweight and obesity are phenomena caused by a multiplicity of factors. As mentioned earlier, they cannot be called an epidemic because they are not contagious medical conditions. They are, however, gateways to such illnesses as diabetes, hypertension, and several cancers. Leaving the biomedical causal factors aside, I will focus only on those socioeconomic determinants that contribute to overweight and obesity. In developing the NDR index I made several logical assumptions. First, upper classes in any country do not suffer from food insecurity or from unavoidable neoliberal diet risk; they have economic choice in what to eat, although they may well be highly tempted by the general availability and aggressive marketing of energy-dense foods. Second, scarce resources limit food choices for the poor and many with middle incomes. Neoliberal ideology blames the victim for presumably making the wrong food choices, but it is a myth that such choices even exist (Guthman 2011). My Mexico case study shows important evidence of the income determinant of diet composition. Third, urban families in which all or most adults must work are severely affected by the neoliberal diet risk. Urbanization also exacerbates the extent to which females join the labor force. I add female labor-force participation not because I believe that women should stay at home, as prescribed by patriarchal cultural patterns. Rather, their inclusion in the labor force has to do with the insufficiency of wages of former main breadwinners to cover the costs of reproduction of a family. Without compensating for women's time devoted to household activities (including maternity leave benefits and free quality child care), there will be less time for food preparation, even if household chores become more evenly distributed between men and women. Thus, besides other scarce resources, these households have little time to prepare good, healthful food. They are time poor. Increased urbanization also reflects the extent to which peasant economies have been expelled from the agrifood systems.

The NDR is made up of the geometric mean of five measurements, and the result is represented by an index that ranges from 1 to 100. The NDR is most effective as a comparative measure; it allows us to assess if a country's low- to middle-income classes' risk of exposure to the neoliberal diet increases or decreases across time and to compare its level between countries. The five components of the NDR are as follows: an index of food import dependency for the food sources that constitute each country's top 80 percent of caloric intake, as dependency is linked to international price volatility; the Gini coefficient, which measures the degree of inequality in each country (where 0 = perfect equality and 1 = total income concentration in a single individual) turned into a percentage; the rate of urbanization, with shifting lifestyles and food habits favoring the rise of convenience foods and the expansion of foreign corporations into fast food and junk food; the rate of female labor force participation, as this factor increases the likelihood of eating processed food and/or eating outside the home; and the index of economic globalization, which supplements the dependency index.

The globalization subindex is made of the following components: 50 percent is calculated by actual flows in trade (22 percent); foreign direct invest-

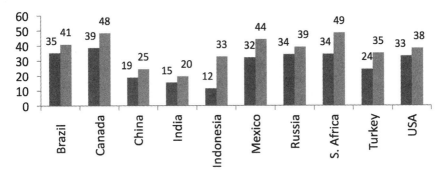

■ NDR 1985   ■ NDR 2007

Figure 7.2. Neoliberal diet risk in ten countries, 1985 and 2007. *Sources*: The import dependency index was constructed with data from FAOSTAT 2012a, b. The urbanization rate was derived from data from Index Mundi 2017. The economic globalization index was taken from KOF 2017 (1992 for Russia). For the Gini index, data are derived from World Bank 2017 for all but the United States and Canada: 1984 and 2008 for China, Indonesia, and Mexico; 1983 and 2005 for India; 1988 for Russia; 1993 and 2006 for South Africa; 1987 for Turkey. Gini for Canada is constructed with data from Statistics Canada 2017. Gini for the United States is from US Census Bureau 2012. Gini coefficients have been converted to Gini index by multiplying Gini coefficient × 100. Female labor force participation is derived from World Bank 2017: 1990 for China, 1981 and 2005 for India, 2008 for Indonesia, 1988 for Mexico, and 1992 for Russia.

ment, much of which involves investment in the food industry, and stocks (27 percent); portfolio investment (24 percent); and income payments to foreign nationals (27 percent). The other 50 percent is calculated by restrictions in the form of hidden import barriers (24 percent), mean tariff rate (28 percent), taxes on international trade as percent of current revenue (26 percent), and capital account restrictions (23 percent). While I generated the food dependency index from FAO data, the rest of the data come from a variety of sources. To the extent possible I used the same source for each index for each and all of the countries in my sample (figure 7.2 presents sources and further definitions of each index), except for the Gini coefficients, for which I relied on different sources for Canada and the United States; the rest of the Gini figures were all taken from the World Bank (2017).

Keeping with measurements developed by the United Nations Development Program (García Aguña and Kovacevic 2010), I aggregate the five components using the geometric mean to obtain the NDR. As a method of aggregation, the geometric mean has several advantages over the arithmetic average. Most importantly, it allows for better comparability of diverse indicators, even when their maximum values differ (García Aguña and Kovacevic 2010:10–11).

In calculating NDR I attempt to overcome the limitations of available measures, which tend to hide inequalities within countries. Available data on food supply in the FAOSTAT database are given in several measures of weight, dollar value, and calories per capita, but these are per capita averages. With the NDR I try to at least partially address this limitation by emphasizing measures that are likely to disproportionally affect the types of food available and accessible to lower- and middle-income classes. Centrally, each and all of the indices that make up the NDR are exclusively socioeconomic. This allows us to assess the NDR's validity by calculating its correlation with the body mass index (BMI), a strictly biophysical measure.

The NDR can be seen and understood as a measurement that has both construct and convergent validity (Bryman and Teevan 2005:59). Construct validity is said to exist when there is a good correspondence between the concept and its measurement, in this case between the NDR and the neoliberal diet as affecting primarily lower- and middle-income classes. There is also a case for convergent validity between NDR and the neoliberal diet. Such convergence is revealed by the strong correlation between two forms of measuring the NDR (arithmetic and geometric) and the BMI, one of the main biomedical indicators used in studies of food and hunger generally and overweight and obesity in particular. The BMI has its own problems as a measurement tool, especially to assess individuals (Guthman 2011), but it is an easily accessible and generally valid indicator to assess the weight status of general populations (Popkin 2009).

In my exploratory research to arrive at the NDR, I first constructed it using an arithmetic mean of its five components. I then ran the correlation between the NDR and BMI for the corresponding years and countries. I opted to calculate the NDR as a geometric mean, for reasons indicated above, and ran its correlation with the BMI. As it turns out, both NDR means have high positive correlations with the BMI (greater than 0.8), strengthening the case for convergent validity. I thus believe that the combination of the socioeconomic measures of food import dependency, inequality, urbanization, female labor force participation, and economic globalization constitutes a potent proxy for the risk of exposure to the neoliberal diet experienced by the working classes in each country.

As expected, all eight of my selected emerging countries had increases in the NDR between 1985 and 2007. Figure 7.2 presents the NDR for each country in alphabetical order. My calculations indicate that South Africa and Mexico have the greatest risk of exposure to the neoliberal diet among the emerging nations. South Africa scored the highest NDR (49) among emerging nations in 2007. As one of the main developing adopters of neoliberalism and with the highest degree of inequality, South Africa increased its import dependency in several top food sources as well as its vulnerability to international price fluctuations in food.

Mexico, Brazil, and Russia followed closely behind South Africa, with NDRs of 44, 41, and 39, respectively. The zealous incorporation of Mexico into the North American economic bloc, an increase in its dependency levels of basic food imports, and an increase in its female labor force participation rate—although still moderate, at 35 percent of the labor force—led the country to a higher risk of exposure to the neoliberal diet. For example, while Mexico's exports of fruits and vegetables to its NAFTA partners increased substantially, these foods did not make up much more than 2 to 3 percent of daily caloric intake in Canada and the United States. Conversely, by 2007 Mexico had become dependent on the importation of well above 20 percent of several top food sources, such as wheat (58 percent), pig meat (29 percent), maize (28 percent), and milk (22 percent).

Indonesia, China, and India had lower levels of NDR primarily because of their lower urbanization indices of 50, 42, and 30, respectively. Indonesia, however, leaped in NDR from 13 in 1985 to 35 in 2007; this dramatic increase of 175 percent is explained by a rise in Indonesia's import dependency level (from close to zero to almost 14 percent), a 122 percent increase in its index of economic globalization, and a 93 percent increase in its urbanization rates from 1985 to 2007. The next highest NDR increases were 46 percent for Turkey, 44 percent for South Africa, 38 percent for Mexico, and 32 percent for China.

CONCLUSION

The above data and analysis indicate a rising risk of neoliberal diet exposure for low- to middle-income working classes unable to afford the luxuries of a more expensive diet of fruits, vegetables, and meats. In keeping with scholarly literature on the nutrition transition, we can expect subsequent increases in the NDR and its associated adverse health impacts over time, barring some countervailing measures. As noted, my index is the most meaningful comparatively across time or between countries. My main goal is to show that the issue of overweight and obesity is not just a matter of choice or personal lifestyle. Rather, it is a structural matter that is causally related to how neoliberal globalization affects people differently depending on their country's level of NDR and a class-differentiated dietary convergence exacerbated by their economic class location within each country. Consequently, only a societal actor like the state can address the issue through means of better agricultural and food policies on the structural level and education and subsidies for a better diet in the short term. "What is to be done?" is the question I turn to in the book's conclusion.

Conclusion

WHAT IS TO BE DONE?

n this book I have offered a critique of neoliberal globalism as discourse, policy, and practice, especially for its results in agriculture and food trade liberalization across and within nations. I have presented an empirical analysis of the neoliberal diet and its relation to increasing trade dependency, inequality, and overweight. One of the leading goals of neoliberalism was to shift state responsibility for managing and protecting agricultural sectors to individual and especially to corporate economic actors. In the process, individuals were charged with bearing all or most responsibility for the courses of their lives, as the neoliberal state also ended most welfare policies (D. Harvey 2005). I have shown that the neoliberal diet has proliferated through all my sample countries, although at varying rates and intensities. In sharp contrast to the neoliberal and mainstream discourse of individual responsibility, I establish that the neoliberal diet is characterized by inequality of access to quality food. Most individuals do not have the choice of eating healthful foods. Unable to afford quality diets and with insufficient time to prepare healthful food, the working classes are the most exposed to this diet's low-cost yet energy-dense traits. Here I recap my main arguments and outline what is to be done to transcend the neoliberal food regime and its diet. The focus for change must be the food system itself but also structural income inequality. Social movements and civil society organizations must engage the state, in conjunction with supermarkets, in addressing both societal issues.

The four dynamic elements of the neoliberal food regime proposed here are the state, agribusiness multinationals, biotechnology, and supermarkets. Using and developing biotechnology to foster their own interests, ABMs have been the juggernaut in this food regime, but they could be controlled by the state. The issue is that not all states are equal, as they vary by the types of ruling classes that command their main social dynamics and the degree of resistance and contestation of subordinate groups and classes from below. I have established that Mexico, as the least developed of NAFTA partners, has taken the brunt of the adverse impacts of food and agricultural liberalization, which led to a different nature in social resistance to the neoliberal food regime. Social movements in Mexico took to the streets in protest, while in Canada and the United States social struggles took the form primarily of legal battles. Ultimately, when social movements had any degree of success in Mexico, however, it resulted in legal interventions, at least by the courts.

In addressing the US debate on diet and nutrition, I have contrasted the individualistic focus on food consumption with studies that consider structural realities of income inequality and how they affect food access and choice. Most participants in the debate, including critical food scholars, focus on the individual as the source of the problem and the point for intervention for a solution. Food industry advocates argue strenuously for individual responsibility and against regulation at all cost, lest we go into a nanny-state situation. For critical scholars, in contrast, preaching about eating better food is not sufficient to stem the advance of overweight and obesity. The individual responsibility discourse is thus elitist (Darmon and Drewnowsky 2015). But even critical food scholars who have produced valuable studies on food and income inequality propose solutions focused on the individual, such as subsidizing healthful food. So, the question seems to be whether to govern or not to govern food choices. I propose a different problematic, another way of looking at the issue and raising questions about it. The focus should not be on individual food choices, because they are limited by the structures of income inequality. Rather, the focus should be on the dominant economic actors producing food and on the system of income distribution. To illuminate the issues of overweight and obesity requires going beyond the individual to a societal agent that can help transcend the neoliberal food regime and its diet.

I widen the perspective from the United States to also consider its NAFTA partners, Canada and Mexico, and how the three countries have performed in food and agriculture. The comparison is valuable because it brings into focus neoliberal globalization taking place between two advanced capitalist countries and a developing country. Mexico also happens to be a nation whose technocrats and ruling classes adopted the neoliberal model wholeheartedly in the mid-1980s. Although the 1994 implementation of NAFTA is no doubt the crowning jewel of Mexico's neoliberal turn, the country's integration into the North American economy started silently but surely in the late 1980s (Otero 1995).

NAFTA did result in increasing trade over fivefold, as intended by the states, but this trade had divergent impacts in the three nations involved. Mexico developed a previously inexistent food import dependency, both in basic and luxury foods, while Canada and the United States became dependent on importing some luxury foods from Mexico. Fruits and vegetables constitute a mere 2 to 3 percent of average per capita food caloric intake in the wealthier countries, while in Mexico basic foods constitute over 40 percent of such intake. The results of joining the three NAFTA countries under the neoliberal paradigm has resulted in socioeconomic divergence, that is, increased inequality within countries, and class-differentiated convergence in diets; the rich have access to more diversified luxury foods, while the working classes are increasingly exposed to the energy-dense fare of the neoliberal diet. For developing countries, this pattern raises questions about the benefits of trade liberalization. I have argued that a food sovereignty program based on smallholders and medium-scale entrepreneurial farmers is likely to be a better option for them if food security is to be enhanced.

Mexico further exemplifies the perils of food import dependency, which has resulted in the country's loss of labor sovereignty; masses of its people had to leave Mexico, most of them to become unauthorized workers in the United States, in order to make a living. The migrant flow was consistent with bankrupting the peasantry, which historically oversaw the production of basic foods in Mexico, once the smallest-scale peasant growers were made to compete with heavily subsidized US farmers. In proportion to its population, Mexico was expelling about ten times more migrants than China or India in the early 2000s. The human rights situation for undocumented migrant workers in the United States has always been daunting and could worsen during the Trump administration. The vulnerable and precarious nature of agricultural work in North America has been documented by ethnographic and survey research. If a liberal ideal of a North American union that accepts the free flow of workers through the three member countries lies far into the future, my policy recommendation for Mexico is, again, to work on reenergizing its countryside along the lines of a food sovereignty and agroecological program.

To put Mexico's case into perspective I compare its two wealthy neighbors and a set of emerging economies: Brazil, China, India, Mexico, Russia, and Turkey. The point is to see how large, middle-income countries like these can either adopt neoliberal globalism or introduce some policies that attenuate its most pernicious social effects. In contrast to what some food regime scholars like McMichael (2009a) have suggested, that the North and South would become mutually dependent in food, I show that the situation is more nuanced. While the wealthier countries do become more dependent on the imports of luxury foods, emerging nations become more dependent on the import of basic foods. But no country in my sample displayed the grave levels of dependency of Mexico, followed at some distance by South Africa and Turkey, which also adopted neoliberal globalism. Food import dependency has enhanced food vulnerability, especially for the working classes, which become more exposed to energy-dense diets that are higher in fats and refined carbohydrates than more traditional fare. What has resulted from neoliberal globalism, therefore, is an uneven and combined dependency. Again, only a societal actor like the state can help society overcome the nutritional perils of the neoliberal diet.

Finally, I add empirical evidence with an expanded sample of countries to include Indonesia and Turkey, and I offer NDR as a new socioeconomic index to measure the risk of exposure to the neoliberal diet using five major components. My proposition is that the more a country is trade dependent, inequitable, and urbanized and has greater female labor-force participation and economic globalization, the more its people become exposed to the neoliberal diet risk. I do not defend traditional female roles in the household, but women have become integrated into the workforce without other household members also preparing food, an arrangement that contributes to a higher NDR. Even if household chores become more equitably distributed between genders, female wages are now required for working-class reproduction, indicating that there is less time for food preparation.

So, what is to be done? Liberal critics of the energy-dense diet have produced extremely useful empirical data and analysis about the food system and its main effects on the population. As mentioned, however, most of them sharply identify the individual as the locus for intervention to modify the quality of food consumption patterns. In the crudest form, this individual focus amounts to blaming the victim, in effect saying people are fat because they eat too much and exercise too little (Popkin 2009). Pollan overemphasizes the role of individual awareness and consumer responsibility in contending, "We need to invest more time, effort, and resources in providing for our sustenance . . . than most of us do today" (2008:145). He has lost sight of socioeconomic differences in the modern food system that limit the effectiveness of individual-based solutions. This individualistic stance leads Pollan and others to the naïve perspective that the powerful dynamics shaping the neoliberal food regime can be altered individually, an assumption that grossly undervalues the need for genuine structural change that requires collective efforts. Barry Popkin, Linda Adair, and Shu Wen Ng (2012), on the other hand, assume the role of experts, point out the problem, and outline solutions to be adopted by states around the world. Regarding sweetened soft drinks, Popkin and Corinna Hawkes (2016) recommend taxation, restrictions on marketing sugary foods to children, public awareness campaigns, and positive and negative front-of-pack labeling. Some of these measures may be welcome, if implemented, while others like taxing may have a regressive distributive effect. But the larger question is whether governments will implement any measures simply because experts tell them to, even as they face pressures from powerful, organized, deep-pocketed food industry lobby groups.

Some proposals against energy-dense food bring to the forefront corporate responsibility as a possible solution. Michael Moss (2013) has shown, however, that food processing companies have been aware of their role in creating overweight and have no real interest in making the changes required to reverse it. Indeed, corporate economic imperatives dictate that they stay the course, barring external pressures such as from state regulation. Paul Krugman (2015), a Nobel laureate in economics, has revealed that the food industry is a great contributor to the US Republican Party, which is not inclined toward state regulation. Smaller-scale political attempts to address the issue of obesity, prominently New York City Mayor Michael Bloomberg's failed effort to ban large sizes of beverages with high sugar concentration (Grynbaum 2013), indicate the myriad difficulties of consumption-focused approaches, particularly subnationally but even nationally.

Taxing junk food, as was done in Mexico with sugary soft drinks in 2013, further deepens inequalities, given that it is a regressive tax, especially in a country with limited availability of safe drinking water. Several cities in the United States have conducted referenda to tax sweetened soft drinks. By 2016, seven cities had done so. It remains to be seen whether this consumer approach to lowering energy-dense diets will have the desired effect. Predictably, the soft drink industry opposes any regulation and has lobbied heavily to oppose these referenda. It is possible that, as with binge drinking of alcoholic beverages, overall behavior does not change significantly with price increases or tax hikes. The same is likely to be the case with taxing junk food (Nelson 2014). Subsidies or incentives for low-income consumers to eat healthful food could be progressive (Darmon and Drewnowsky 2015). Yet, such policy recommendations are still focused on individual consumption. Are individual lifestyle choices enough to challenge the imperatives and compulsions of the neoliberal diet?

My suggestion is that we need much more research on how progressive social movements can nudge the state to lower inequality and change the food production system toward more nutritious contents. Redirecting state subsidies in production, for instance, would shift state priorities from strengthening corporate purveyors of the neoliberal diet to providing all citizens nutritious food. An example of a production-focused approach is to shift subsidies away from corn and soy producers and the food processing industry toward local produce growers that meet decent labor standards. Although it behooves the state as a societal actor to intervene in various ways, the mechanism is very important and a focus on reshaping production rather than individual consumption is required.

Large supermarket chains including Walmart could become allies in state interventions sensitized to the production focus approach, if we believe Walmart CEO Doug McMillon that the company advocates a triple bottom line for long-term capitalism, of financial, social, and ecological benefit. Interestingly, he and Walmart senior vice-president for sustainability Kathleen McLaughlin advocate that firms embed the values of the triple bottom line in their daily business operations at each level of responsibility (McLaughlin and McMillon 2015).

About food, Walmart's main product line, McLaughlin and McMillon (2015) state, "Our goal is to make the food system safer, more transparent, healthier, and more accessible—and to lower the 'true cost' of food for the environment as well as customers and farmers." On the global food system, they argue, "the system must evolve in a way that is sustainable for the environment and smallholder farmers around the world; the system also must be high-enough yielding to feed a growing world population." Even if this kind of intervention may be seen as part of Walmart's public relations strategy, it is a far cry from the nearly exclusive shareholder focus of companies like Monsanto that as input producers do not have to face consumers directly. How these concerns are shaped will depend largely on the ways in which bottom-up civil society organizations and the state intervene.

Conjunctural or short-term measures like education and subsidized consumption will help some people and social groups. That is a welcome outcome, but such measures by themselves will hardly alter the structures of inequality. On a world scale, to the extent that individual- or societal-level changes help reduce the intake of the energy-dense components of the neo-liberal diet in the United States, to that same extent agribusiness multi-nationals will intensify their efforts to further globalize the US diet. This is just what happened with the tobacco industry, and its parallels with Big Food have already been established (Brownell and Warner 2009; Hafez and Ling 2005). In my class analysis I have tried to show that, contrary to the individualistic focus, only a societal-level collective actor can hope to change inequality and obesogenic dietary trends and their health impacts.

Throughout the book, I have proposed that it will take bottom-up social movement pressure on the state from civil society to redirect its policies. It is important to recognize, however, that social movements are not uni-directional, either progressive or regressive. Their character is much more complex, as they deal not only with the state but also with countermovements that may represent interested parties in the food industry. States in general will try to satisfy or somehow pacify social movements, but they must also confront pressure from possible countermovements and perhaps more crucially from industry lobby groups that are usually very well funded. Moneyed counterefforts present an enormous challenge to grassroots social movements, which tend to have limited resources. It is quite likely that contentious issues will generate movements of both types, with progressive movements also generating countermovements (McAdam and Kloos 2014) or at least provoking reactions from the ferocious food industry lobby, which sometimes surreptitiously funds nongovernmental organizations doing the industry's financially interested bidding.

One example of the complexity of social movements has been mobilization in California to push for legislation requiring the labeling of genetically modified food such as soft drinks sweetened with high-fructose corn syrup produced with transgenic corn. In 2014 PepsiCo and Coca-Cola contributed about $20 million to counter the campaign, which ultimately lost. This brings up the colossal need to expurgate big money and companies from the political process so that ordinary citizens can choose what policies they would like their governments to implement. The challenge is immense because of the cynicism with which private lobbies fight such legal struggles by invoking freedom of speech rights or whatever other legal technicalities to maintain their interests.

Several enormous challenges should thus be clear. First, there is movement complexity; that is, not all food movements help advance progressive causes. Second, the odds are against succeeding in an extremely expensive fight with industry lobby groups, so movements must be prepared for that contingency. Third, the state also has complex patron-client relations with some popular movements, which must decide at what point their engagement with state officials compromises their movements' goals (Staggenborg and Ramos 2016). In such patron-client relations, grassroots movements may get some concession from the state in exchange for demobilizing. The most fundamental question for movements in this situation is whether demobilizing can be tactically prudent and the gains are worthwhile or if such compromise irremediably jeopardizes their autonomy from the state and therefore their strategic goals. Once its autonomy is compromised, a social movement will not likely regain its combativeness and mobilization for progressive change; it has fallen into the folds of bourgeois hegemony and quiescence (Otero 1999).

Fourth, progressive movements must be aware of other food movements in civil society, as some will be sympathetic but others may be hostile. For instance, social movements for the labeling of genetically modified food, while well intended, are firmly based on an individualistic approach and will also be buying a struggle with well-financed lobbies. Even if the movements succeed, the main beneficiaries of their successes may be the more affluent and educated social classes. Similarly, movements that aim to enhance the local content of food have usually been oblivious to the labor conditions under which such food is produced (Weiler, Otero, and Wittman 2016). My review of painstaking ethnographic studies documents the backbreaking nature of most work in the food and agriculture sector. In these sectors workers face conditions broadly characterized as dirty, dangerous, and difficult. In our study of farmworkers in British Columbia (Otero and Preibisch 2010), the late Kerry Preibisch and I add a fourth D, for devalued, as workers received compensation far below the wages local workers would accept for those jobs. Technically, said Mark Thompson, a University of British Columbia professor, it would be easy to recruit local workers — by doubling or tripling wages to compensate for the harsh conditions (in Otero and Preibisch 2010).

But then there's the structure of the food system. Farmers represent a roughly competitive sector in the sense that economics textbooks speak about competitiveness; the sector has such an abundance of producers that the actions of no single one of them can alter market conditions, especially prices. Market conditions include other aspects such as the relative sizes of sellers of agricultural inputs, buyers of agricultural goods and industrial processors, and distributors of food. Yet, farmers confront an oligopoly of a few large producers when purchasing inputs and an oligopsony of few large buyers when selling their harvests. Further up the food chain, the largest grain and produce traders face concentrated food industrializers, who in turn similarly confront behemoths like Walmart and Amazon, the final distributors to consumers. So, it is only the farming sector that is roughly competitive within the food system, even though its main trend since the 1980s is also clear: fewer and larger farms, as the minimum viable farm size keeps increasing.

This uncontrollable aspect of US farming has led to tremendous stress in farming communities. In a study by the US Centers for Disease Control and Prevention, "The data suggested that the suicide rate for agricultural workers in 17 states was nearly five times higher compared with that in the general population" (Weingarten 2017). The US farmer suicide crisis is not isolated; it is being replicated around the world. In France one farmer dies of suicide every two days. In India 270,000 farmers took their lives in large part due to indebtedness since 1995 (Weingarten 2017); the rise in suicides coincided with the introduction of Bt cotton and related indebtedness. After its fast-paced adoption of the crop but then the rising suicide rates, India is one of the few developing countries that have been disadopting transgenic crops (ISAAA 2016).

Given their relative weakness, small- and medium-scale farmers require support from government and civil society organizations, but those state and nonstate supporters should also monitor health and safety in working conditions, as workers are the most vulnerable class in the food system. Good working conditions and living wages should be secured for all workers in the food production chain, from farming through processing, distributing, and fast food restaurants. Many of the workers along the way, including those in Walmart, can subsist only thanks to state welfare programs. A policy goal for progressive social movements should thus be for employers, not the state, to pay the full wages of their workers, that is, sufficient pay for decent living. State welfare, which must exist in all healthy democracies, can then be focused on transitional necessities of the working class, as when people are between jobs; workers should have generous employment insurance so they do not have to end up accepting 4-D jobs any more. In envisioning "real utopias" (E. Wright 2010), a great policy to struggle for is basic income for all, as it would afford accomplishments in various areas of good living such as accessibility to better-quality food and freedom from the economic compulsion to work at any job, even if it's dirty, difficult, dangerous, and devalued. The multiplication of struggles not only means more fronts and work for social movements; it also means that a larger movement or coalition for food sovereignty and social justice must engage in a policy of alliances and articulations that can involve state officials sympathetic with the movement's goals.

What can be done from the top? Clearly, it is not enough to formulate a strategy for social movements, as their actions without the complement of state intervention can hardly succeed. Assuming, therefore, that the state can be democratized from below so that politicians govern by obeying the people, their constituencies, we can then take some advice from Thomas Piketty on how to reduce inequality. In sum, he says, "A capital tax is the most appropriate response to the inequality r > g as well as to the inequality of returns to capital as a function of the size of the initial stake" (2014:532). The United States has had one of the most progressive taxing systems in history, so Piketty's proposals have successful precedent behind them: "All told, over the period 1932–1980, nearly half a century, the top federal income tax rate in the United States averaged 81 percent" (507). Another example is that the top estate tax rate remained between 70 and 80 percent from 1930 to the 1980s, while in France and Germany the top rate never exceeded 30 to 40 percent except for the years 1946–1949 in Germany (507).

We also need to improve our understanding of how to study the food regime so as to better appreciate where its dynamic factors lie and what kind of collective action from below and above can be launched to improve access to healthful food. In sum, whether to analyze the food regime at a world scale or food systems at the domestic level, states continue to be central agencies in deploying neoregulation and policies that enhance neoliberalism — or in contesting it. Whether agreeing to participate (or not) in suprastate agreements or developing national legislation, states have been the key actors implementing neoregulation. States are also the key point of struggle to counter neoliberal globalism, as illustrated in the above examples, even if international solidarity is also a factor. How far such contestation must go before we transcend neoliberal globalism is presently unknowable or indeterminate (Lawrence 2017; Otero 2017). But subordinate groups and classes must believe that the dominant food regime is subject to contestation and win at least partial victories to continue the long-term struggle for an agro-ecological, sustainable food system.

References

AAI (Agribusiness Accountability Initiative). n.d. "Corporate Power in Livestock Production: How It's Hurting Farmers, Consumers, and Communities—and What We Can Do about It." Accessed 26 April 2012. http://www.ase.tufts.edu/gdae/Pubs/rp/AAI_Issue_Brief_1_3.pdf.

Acosta Córdova, Carlos. 2014. "La tierra prometida que nunca se alcanzó." *Proceso* (Mexico City), 5 January.

Aglietta, Michel. 1979. *A Theory of Capitalist Regulation: The US Experience.* London: New Left Books.

Akram-Lodhi, Haroon. 2012. "Contextualising Land Grabbing: Contemporary Land Deals, the Global Subsistence Crisis, and the World Food System." *Canadian Journal of Development Studies* 3 (3): 114–142.

Althaus, Dudly. 2013. "Mexico Takes Title of "Most Obese" from America." CBS News, 8 July. http://www.cbsnews.com/8301-202_162-57592714/mexico-takes-title-of-most-obese-from-america.

Amuna, Paul, and Francis B. Zortor. 2008. "The Epidemiological and Nutrition Transition in Developing Countries: Evolving Trends and Their Impact in Public Health and Human Development." *Proceedings of the Nutrition Society* 67:82–90.

Anderson, Kym. 2014. "Excise Taxes on Wines, Beer and Spirits: An Updated International Comparison." AAWE Working Papers, no. 170, October. American Association of Wine Economists. http://www.wine-economics.org.

Ansell, Aaron. 2014. *Zero Hunger: Political Culture and Antipoverty Policy in Northeast Brazil.* Chapel Hill: University of North Carolina Press.

Antonio, Robert J. 2014. "Piketty's Nightmare Capitalism: The Return of Rentier Society and De-Democratization." *Contemporary Sociology* 43 (6): 783–790.

AP (Associated Press). 2011. "Wisconsin Governor Passes Bill to Remove Collective Bargaining Rights." Reprint, *The Guardian*, 11 March. http://www.guardian.co.uk/world/2011/mar/11/wisconsin-collective-bargaining-rights?intcmp=239.

Appendini, Kirsten, 2014. "Reconstructing the Maize Market in Rural Mexico." *Journal of Agrarian Change* 14 (1): 1–25.

Araghi, Farshad. 2000. "The Great Global Enclosure of Our Times: Peasants and the Agrarian Question at the End of the Twentieth Century." In *Hungry for Profit: The Agribusiness Threat to Farmers, Food, and the Environment*, edited by F. Magdoff and J. Bellamy, 145–160. New York: Monthly Review Press.

———. 2003. "Food Regimes and the Production of Value: Some Methodological Issues." *Journal of Peasant Studies* 30 (2): 41–70.

Arnot, Bob. 2013. *The Aztec Diet: Chia Power; The Superfood That Gets You Skinny and Keeps You Healthy.* New York: HarperCollins.

Atkinson, Anthony B. 2015. *Inequality: What Can Be Done?* Cambridge, MA: Harvard University Press.

Baines, Joseph. 2015. "Fuel, Feed, and the Corporate Restructuring of the Food Regime." *Journal of Peasant Studies* 42 (2): 295–321.

Balsillie, Jim. 2017. "Raise a Glass to Canada's TPP Team for Standing Up to Corporate Bullies." *Globe and Mail*, 2 December.

Barndt, Deborah, ed. 1999. *Women Working the NAFTA Food Chain: Women, Food, and Globalization.* Toronto: Second Story.

Bartra, Armando. 2004. "Rebellious Cornfields: Toward Food and Labour Self-Sufficiency." In *Mexico in Transition: Neoliberal Globalism, the State, and Civil Society*, edited by Gerardo Otero, 18–36. London: Zed Books; Halifax, Canada: Fernwood.

Bartra, Armando, and Gerardo Otero. 2009. "Contesting Neoliberal Globalism and NAFTA in Rural Mexico: From State Corporatism to the Political-Cultural Formation of the Peasantry." In *Contentious Politics in North America: National Protest and Transnational Collaboration under Continental Integration*, edited by J. Ayres and L. Macdonald, 92–113. Houndmills, UK: Palgrave Macmillan.

Basok, Tanya. 2002. *Tortillas and Tomatoes: Transmigrant Mexican Harvesters in Canada.* Montreal: McGill-Queens University Press.

Bayer. 2016. "Bayer to Acquire Monsanto." News release, 14 September. https://www.advancingtogether.com/en/home.

Beaulac, Julie, Elizabeth Kristjansson, and Steven Cummins. 2009. "A Systematic Review of Food Deserts, 1966–2007." *Preventing Chronic Disease: Public Health Research, Practice, and Policy* 6 (3): A105.

Beingessner, Paul. 2004. "New Varieties Only Available to Farmers If They Pay Each Year." *CropChoice News*, 26 December. http://www.cropchoice.com/leadstrygmo122704.html.

Bell, Kirsten, and Judith Green. 2016. "On the Perils of Invoking Neoliberalism in Public Health Critique." *Critical Public Health* 26 (3): 239–243.

Bello, Walden. 2009 *Food Wars*, London: Verso.

Bernier, Maxime. 2007. "BIO 2007." Speech, 6 May. Delivered at Gowlings' Fifth Annual Brunch and Seminars, Boston. Accessed 28 November 2007 at Industry Canada, http://www.ic.gc.ca/; no longer available.

Bernstein, Henry. 2010. *Class Dynamics of Agrarian Change*. Halifax, Canada: Fernwood.

———. 2014. "Food Sovereignty via the 'Peasant Way': A Sceptical View." *Journal of Peasant Studies* 41 (6): 1031–1063.

———. 2016. "Agrarian Political Economy and Modern World Capitalism: The Contributions of Food Regime Analysis." *Journal of Peasant Studies* 43 (3–4): 611–647.

Beuchelt, Tina D., and Detlef Virchow. 2012. "Food Sovereignty or the Human Right to Adequate Food: Which Concept Serves Better As International Development Policy for Global Hunger and Poverty Reduction?" *Agriculture and Human Values* 29 (2): 259–273.

Bhurosy, Trishnee, and Rajesh Jeewon. 2014. "Overweight and Obesity Epidemic in Developing Countries: A Problem with Diet, Physical Activity, or Socioeconomic Status?" *Scientific World Journal* 1:7. Article 964236. http://dx.doi.org/10.1155/2014/964236.

Bjerga, Alan, and Lynn Thomasson. 2017. "Should Farmers Fear Him?" *Bloomberg Businessweek*, 20 February–5 March, 13–14.

Block, Jason, Richard A. Scribner, and Karen B. DeSalvo. 2004. "Fast Food, Race/Ethnicity, and Income: A Geographic Analysis." *American Journal of Preventive Medicine* 27 (3): 211–217.

BLS (US Department of Labor, Bureau of Labor Statistics). 2017a. "Union Members Summary." Economic news release, 26 January. Washington, DC: BLS. http://www.bls.gov/news.release/union2.nr0.htm.

———. 2017b. Consumer Expenditure Survey, 1972–1973, 1984, 1994, 2004, 2014. Washington, DC: BLS. https://www.bls.gov/cex/csxstnd.htm.

Bocquier, A., F. Vieux, S. Lioret, C. Dubuisson, F. Caillavet, and N. Darmon. 2015. "Socio-Economic Characteristics, Living Conditions, and Diet Quality Are Associated with Food Insecurity in France." *Public Health Nutrition* 18 (16): 2952–2961. https://doi.org/10.1017/S1368980014002912.

Bohn, Simone R. 2011. "Social Policy and Vote in Brazil: Bolsa Família and the Shifts in Lula's Electoral Base." *Latin American Research Review* 46 (1): 54–79.

Bonanno, Alessandro, and Douglas H. Constance. 2000. "Mega Hog Farms in the Texas Panhandle Region: Corporate Actions and Local Resistance." *Research in Social Movements, Conflicts, and Change* 22:83–110.

———. 2001. "Globalization, Fordism, and Post-Fordism in Agriculture and Food: A Critical Review of the Literature." *Culture and Agriculture* 23 (2): 1–15.

———. 2008. *Stories of Globalization: Transnational Corporations, Resistance, and the State*. University Park: Pennsylvania State University Press.

Borras, Saturnino M. Jr., Jennifer C. Franco, S. Ryan Isakson, Les Levidow, and Pietje

Vervest. 2015. "The Rise of Flex Crops and Commodities: Implications for Research." *Journal of Peasant Studies* 43 (1): 93–115.

Borras, Saturnino M. Jr., Ruth Hall, Ian Scoones, Ben White, and Wendy Wolford. 2011. "Towards a Better Understanding of Global Land Grabbing: An Editorial Introduction." *Journal of Peasant Studies* 38 (1): 209–216.

Brass, Tom. 2014. *Class, Culture, and the Agrarian Myth*. Leiden, Netherlands: Brill.

Brownell, Kelly D., and Kenneth E. Warner. 2009. "The Perils of Ignoring History: Big Tobacco Played Dirty and Millions Died: How Similar Is Big Food?" *Milbank Quarterly* 87 (1): 259–294.

Brunn, S., ed. 2006. *Wal-Mart World: The World's Biggest Corporation in the Global Economy*. New York: Routledge.

Bryman, Alan, and Teevan, James J. 2005. *Social Research Methods: Canadian Edition*. Oxford: Oxford University Press.

Burch, David, and Geoffrey Lawrence. 2005. "Supermarket Own Brands, Supply Chains, and the Transformation of the Agri-Food System." *International Journal of Sociology of Agriculture and Food* 13 (1): 1–18.

———, eds. 2007. *Supermarkets and Agri-Food Supply Chains: Transformations in the Production and Consumption of Foods*. Cheltenham, UK: Edward Elgar.

———. 2013. "Financialization in Agri-Food Supply Chains: Private Equity and the Transformation of the Retail Sector." *Agriculture and Human Values* 30:247–258.

Buttel, Frederick. 2001. "Some Reflections on Late Twentieth Century Agrarian Political Economy." *Sociologia Ruralis* 41 (2): 165–181.

Cage, S. 2008. "Food Prices May Ease Hostility to Gene-Altered Crops." Reuters, 9 July.

Calman, K. 2008. "Beyond the 'Nanny State': Stewardship and Public Health." *Public Health* 123 (1): e6–e10.

Cámara (Mexico, Cámara de Diputados del Congreso de la Unión). 2012. Ley Federal de Variedades Vegetales. Adopted 25 October 1996, revised 9 April 2012. http://www.diputados.gob.mx/LeyesBiblio/pdf/120.pdf.

Caraher, Martin, and Gill Cowburn. 2005. "Taxing Food: Implications for Public Health Nutrition." *Public Health Nutrition* 8 (8): 1242–1249.

Carlsen, Laura. 2004. "Conservation or Privatization? Biodiversity, the Global Market, and the Mesoamerican Biological Corridor." In *Mexico in Transition: Neoliberal Globalism, the State, and Civil Society*, edited by Gerardo Otero, 37–51. London: Zed Books; Halifax, Canada: Fernwood.

Carrington, Damian. 2011. "Food Is the Ultimate Security Need, New Map Shows." *The Guardian*, 31 August. http://www.guardian.co.uk/environment/damian-carrington-blog/2011/aug/31/food-security-prices-conflict#.

Castels, Stephen, and Mark J. Miller. 2003. *The Age of Migration: International Population Movements in the Modern World*. New York: Guilford.

Castillo, G. del. 1996. "NAFTA and the Struggle for Neoliberalism: Mexico's Elusive Quest for First World Status." In *Neoliberalism Revisited: Economic Restructuring and Mexico's Political Future*, edited by Gerardo Otero, 27–42. Boulder, CO: Westview.

CBAC (Canadian Biotechnology Advisory Committee). 2002. "Regulatory Structures and Processes." In *Improving the Regulation of Genetically Modified Foods and Other Novel Foods in Canada*, edited by CBAC. http://cbac-cccb.ca/epic/internet/incbac-cccb.nsf/en/Home.

———. 2004. "Completing the Biotechnology Regulatory Framework." Advisory memorandum. February. http://cbac-cccb.ca/epic/site/cbac-cccb.nsf/en/ah00436e.html.

CFIA (Canadian Food Inspection Agency). 2007. "Plants Evaluated for Environmental and Livestock Feed Safety." http://active.inspection.gc.ca/eng/plaveg/bio/pntvcne.asp.

———. 2012. "Modern Biotechnology: A Brief Overview." http://www.inspection.gc.ca/plants/plants-with-novel-traits/general-public/fact-sheets/overview/eng/1337827503752/1337827590597.

CBC News. 2006. "Canadian Wheat Board." *CBC News in Depth: Agriculture*, 6 December. http://www.cbc.ca/news/background/agriculture/cwb.html.

———. 2009. "3-Death Crash Inquest Told Previous Inquest 'Ignored.'" 9 December. http://www.cbc.ca/canada/british-columbia/story/2009/12/09/bc-highway-van-crash-inquest-sinclair.html.

———. 2012. "Mushroom Farm Coroner's Jury Urges Training, Inspections." 16 May. http://www.cbc.ca/news/canada/british-columbia/story/2012/05/16/bc-mushroom-farm-inquest-recommendations.html.

CFS (Center for Food Safety). 2005. *Monsanto vs. U.S. Farmers*. Washington, DC: Center for Food Safety.

Chandrasekaran, M., Soorej M. Basheer, Sreeja Chellappan, P. Karthikeyan, and K. K. Elyas. 2013. "Food Processing Industries: An Overview." In *Valorization of Food Processing By-Products*, edited by M. Chandrasekaran, 3–34. Boca Raton, FL: CRC.

Chayanov, Alexander. V. 1974. *La organización de la unidad económica campesina*. Buenos Aires: Nueva Visión.

Chioda, Laura, João M. P. De Mello, and Rodrigo R. Soares. 2016. "Spillovers from Conditional Cash Transfer Programs: Bolsa Família and Crime in Urban Brazil." *Economics of Education Review* 54 (October): 306–320.

Christensen, Vibeke T., and Richard M. Carpiano. 2014. "Social Class Differences in BMI among Danish Women: Applying Cockerham's Health Lifestyles Approach and Bourdieu's Theory of Lifestyle." *Social Science and Medicine* 112:12–21.

Chung, Chanjin, and Samuel. L. Myers. 1999. "Do the Poor Pay More for Food? An Analysis of Grocery Store Availability and Food Price Disparities." *Journal of Consumer Affairs* 33 (2): 276–296.

CIA (US Central Intelligence Agency). 2016. "North America: Mexico." *The World Factbook*. https://www.cia.gov/Library/publications/the-world-factbook/fields/2048.html.

Citizenship and Immigration Canada. 2012. *Canada Facts and Figures 2011 Immigration Overview: Permanent and Temporary Residents*. Ottawa: Citizenship and Immigration Canada.

Clapp, Jennifer. 2014. "Food Security and Food Sovereignty: Getting Past the Binary." *Dialogues in Human Geography* 4 (2): 206–211.

Clapp, Jennifer, and Doris Fuchs. 2009. *Corporate Power in Global Agrifood Governance.* Cambridge, MA: MIT Press.

Coburn, David. 2004. "Beyond the Income-Inequality Hypothesis: Class, Neo-Liberalism, and Health Inequalities." *Social Science and Medicine* 58:41–56.

Codex Alimentarius. International Food Standards. 1995. World Health Organization and UN Food and Agriculture Organization. http://www.fao.org/docrep/003/x7 354e/x7354e02.htm.

COFEPRIS (Mexico, Comisión Federal para la Protección contra los Riesgos Sanitarios). 2005. "Productos biotecnológicos para consumo humano que se han evaluado y aceptado para su comercialización en México." http://www.cofepris.gob.mx/pyp /biotec/OMG.pdf.

Cohen, Jean-Michel. 2013. *The Parisian Diet: How to Reach Your Right Weight and Stay There.* Translated by Anne McDowall. Paris: Flammarion.

Cohrs, J. C., and Stelzl, M. 2010. "How Ideological Attitudes Predict Host Society Members' Attitudes toward Immigrants: Exploring Cross-National Differences." *Journal of Social Issues* 66 (4): 673–694.

Alisha Coleman-Jensen, Matthew P. Rabbitt, Christian A. Gregory, and Anita Singh. 2017. Household Food Security in the United States in 2016, ERR-237, U.S. Department of Agriculture, Economic Research Service.

Colen, Lisbeth, and Johan Swinnen. 2011. "Beer Drinking Nations: The Determinants of Global Beer Consumption." AAWE Working Papers, no. 79. American Association of Wine Economists. http://www.wine-economics.org.

Common Dreams Progressive Newswire. 2006. "Farmers, Ranchers, and Consumers Challenge GM Alfalfa: Lawsuit Says USDA Failed to Address Public Health, Environmental and Economic Risks in Approving Commercial Release." 16 February. http://www.commondreams.org.

CONAPO (Mexico, Consejo Nacional de Población). 2011. "República Mexicana: Indicadores demográficos 1990–2050." http://www.conapo.gob.mx/index.php?opti on-com_content&view=article&id=125&Itemid=193.

Concheiro Bórquez, Luciano, and Roberto Diego Quintana. 2001. *Una perspectiva campesina del mercado de tierras ejidales: análisis comparativo de siete estudios de caso.* Mexico City: Casa Juan Pablos.

Concheiro Bórquez, Luciano, and Francisco López Bárcenas, eds. 2006. *Biodiversidad y conocimiento tradicional en la sociedad rural: Entre el bien común y la propiedad privada.* Mexico City: Centro de Estudios para el Desarrollo Rural Sustentable y la Soberanía Alimentaria; Cámara de Diputados, LX Legislatura.

CONEVAL (Consejo Nacional de Evaluación de la Política de Desarrollo Social). 2012. "Avances y retos de la política de desarrollo social en México 2012." http:// www.coneval.org.mx/Informes/Evaluacion/Avances%20y%20Retos%202012/Ay R12_11%205%20-%20Publicaci%C3%B3n%20(29%20ago%2012).pdf.

———. 2015. "Evolución de las dimensiones de la pobreza 1990–2014." http://www

.coneval.org.mx/Medicion/EDP/Paginas/Evolucion-de-las-dimensiones-de-la
-pobreza-1990-2014-.aspx.

Constance, Douglas H. 2009. "Contested Globalization of the Agrifood System: A Missouri School Analysis of Sanderson Farms and Seaboard Farms in Texas." *Southern Rural Sociology* 24 (2): 48–86.

Cornelius, Wayne, and David Myhre, eds. 1998. *The Transformation of Rural Mexico: Reforming the Ejido Sector*. La Jolla: Center for US-Mexican Studies, University of California, San Diego.

Corona, Rodolfo, and Rodolfo Tuirán. 2006. "Magnitud aproximada de la migración mexicana a Estados Unidos." Paper presented at Congreso Internacional de Migración, Alcances y Límites de las Políticas Migratorias, October, Mexico City.

Cypher, James M., and Raúl Delgado-Wise. 2010. *Mexico's Economic Dilemma: The Developmental Failure of Neoliberalism*. Lanham, MD: Rowman and Littlefield.

Darmon, Nicole, and Adam Drewnowski. 2008. "Does Social Class Predict Diet Quality?" *American Journal of Clinical Nutrition* 87:1107–1117.

———. 2015. "Contribution of Food Prices and Diet Cost to Socioeconomic Disparities in Diet Quality and Health: A Systematic Review and Analysis." *Nutrition Reviews* 73 (10): 643–660.

Davies, Mike. 2001. *Late Victorian Holocausts: El Niño Famines and the Making of the Third World*. London: Verso.

Delgado, Christopher L. 2003. "Rising Consumption of Meat and Milk in Developing Countries Has Created a New Food Revolution." *Journal of Nutrition* 133 (11): 3907S–3910S.

Delgado-Wise, Raúl, and James M. Cypher. 2007. "The Strategic Role of Mexican Labor under NAFTA: Critical Perspectives on Current Economic Integration." *Annals of the American Academy of Political and Social Science* 601 (1): 119–144.

De Schutter, Olivier. 2009. "The Meatification of Diets and Global Food Security." UN Special Rapporteur on the Right to Food, speech to the European Parliament, 3 December. http://www.europarl.europa.eu/climatechange/doc/speeche_Mr_de_schutter.pdf.

Desmarais, Annette Aurélie. 2007. *La Vía Campesina: Globalization and the Power of Peasants*. Halifax, Canada: Fernwood.

———. 2008. "The Power of Peasants: Reflections on the Meanings of La Vía Campesina." *Journal of Rural Studies* 24 (2): 138–149.

Dixon, Jane. 2009. "From the Imperial to the Empty Calorie: How Nutrition Relations Underpin Food Regime Transitions." *Agriculture and Human Values* 26:321–333.

Dosi, Giovanni. 1984. *Technical Change and Industrial Transformation*. London: Macmillan.

Drewnowski, Adam. 2009. "Obesity, Diets, and Social Inequality." *Nutrition Reviews* 67 (supplement): S36–S39.

Drewnowski, Adam, and Nicole Darmon. 2005. "The Economics of Obesity: Dietary Energy Density and Energy Cost." *American Journal of Clinical Nutrition* 82 (supplement): 265S–273S.

Drewnowski, Adam, A. V. Moudon, J. Jiao, A. Aggarwal, H. Charreire, and B. Chaix. 2014. "Food Environments and Socioeconomic Status Influence Obesity Rates in Seattle and in Paris." *International Journal of Obesity* 38:306–314.

Drewnowski, Adam, and Barry M. Popkin. 1997. "The Nutrition Transition: New Trends in the Global Diet." *Nutrition Reviews* 55 (2): 31–43.

Drewnowski, Adam, and S. E. Specter. 2004. "Poverty and Obesity: The Role of Energy Density and Energy Costs." *American Journal of Clinical Nutrition* 79 (1): 6–16.

Dubowitz, Tamara, Melonie Heron, Chloe E. Bird, Nicole Lurie, Brian K. Finch, Ricardo Basurto-Davila, Lauren Hale, and Jose J. Escarce. 2008. "Neighborhood Socioeconomic Status and Fruit and Vegetable Intake among Whites, Blacks, and Mexican Americans in the United States." *American Journal of Clinical Nutrition* 87 (6): 1883–1891.

Eaton, Emily. 2013. *Growing Resistance: Canadian Farmers and the Politics of Genetically Modified Wheat*. Winnipeg: University of Manitoba Press.

Echánove Huacuja, Flavia. 2013. "Agricultural Policy and the Feed Industry in Mexico." *Mexican Studies/Estudios Mexicanos* 29 (1): 61–84.

EcoNexus and Berne-Declaration. 2013. "Agropoly: A Handful of Corporations Control World Food Production." http://www.econexus.info/sites/econexus/files/Agropoly_Econexus_BerneDeclaration.pdf.

The Economist. 2002. "Mexico's Farmers: Floundering in a Tariff-Free Landscape." 28 November, 31–32. http://www.economist.com/node/1471549.

———. 2007. "Smaller Shares, Bigger Slices." 4 April. http://www.economist.com/node/8959966.

———. 2011. "Workers (and Business) Unite!" 27 August. http://www.economist.com/node/21526915.

———. 2012. "Fights about Fairness." 21 November. https://www.economist.com/news/21566292-zanny-minton-beddoes-says-debate-2013-should-be-over-role-statenot-just-tax-fights.

———. 2013. "Hot Air: Are Models That Show the Economic Effects of Climate Change Useless?" 5 October, 78.

———. 2016. "Too Much of a Good Thing." 26 March. https://www.economist.com/news/briefing/21695385-profits-are-too-high-america-needs-giant-dose-competition-too-much-good-thing.

Edelman, Marc. 2014. "Food Sovereignty: Forgotten Genealogies and Future Regulatory Challenges." *Journal of Peasant Studies* 41 (6): 959–978.

Ellerman, David. 2005. "Labour Migration: A Developmental Path or a Low-Level Trap?" *Development in Practice* 15 (5): 617–630.

EPA (US Environmental Protection Agency). 2003. "EPA's Regulation of Biotechnology for Use in Pest Management." http://www.epa.gov/oppbppd1/biopesticides/reg_of_biotech/eparegofbiotech.htm.

Escobar, Christine. 2011. "The Tale of rBGH Milk, Monsanto and the Organic Backlash." *Huffington Post*, 25 May. https://www.huffingtonpost.com/christine-escobar/the-tale-of-rbgh-milk-mon_b_170823.html.

ETC Group. 2005a. "Oligopoly, Inc. 2005: Concentration in Corporate Power." ETC Group Communique, no. 91 (December). http://www.etcgroup.org/en/materials /publications.html?pub_id=42.

———. 2005b. "Global Seed Industry Concentration-2005." ETC Group Communique, no. 90 (September/October). http://www.mindfully.org/Farm/2005/Global -Seed-Industry6sep05.htm.

Fader, Marianela, Dieter Gerten, Michael Krause, Wolfgang Lucht, and Wolfgang Cramer. 2013. "Spatial Decoupling of Agricultural Production and Consumption: Quantifying Dependences of Countries on Food Imports due to Domestic Land and Water Constraints." *Environmental Research Letters* 8 (1): 1–15.

Fagan, Drew. 1994. "Ministers Cite NAFTA Benefits Pact 'Will Create Jobs,' Kantor Says in Mexico City." *Globe and Mail*, 15 January. http://search.proquest.com.proxy .lib.sfu.ca/docview/385184918?accountid=13800.

Fairbairn, Madeleine. 2010. "Framing Resistance: International Food Regimes and the Roots of Food Sovereignty." In *Food Sovereignty: Reconnecting Food, Nature and Community*, edited by Hannah Wittman, Annette Aurélie Desmarais, and Nettie Wiebe, 15–32. Halifax, Canada: Fernwood.

———. 2014. "'Like Gold with Yield': Evolving Intersections of Farmland and Finance." *Journal of Peasant Studies* 41 (5): 777–795.

Fairbairn, Madeleine, Jonathan Fox, S. Ryan Isakson, Michael Levien, Nancy Peluso, Shahra Razavi, Ian Scoons, and K. Sivaramakrishan. 2014. "Introduction: New Directions in Agrarian Political Economy." *Journal of Peasant Studies* 41 (5): 653–666.

Fairey, David, Christina Hanson, Glenn MacInnes, Arlene Tigar McLaren, Gerardo Otero, Kerry Preibisch, and Mark Thompson. 2008. *Cultivating Farmworkers' Rights: Ending the Exploitation of Immigrant and Migrant Farmworkers in BC*. Vancouver: Canadian Centre for Policy Alternatives, BC Office; Justicia for Migrant Workers; Progressive Intercultural Community Services; BC Federation of Labour.

FAO (Food and Agriculture Organization of the United Nations). 2000. *Multilateral Trade Negotiations on Agriculture: A Resource Manual*. Rome: FAO.

———. 2003. *Trade and Food Security: Conceptualising the Linkages*. Rome: FAO.

———. 2004. *The State of Agricultural Commodity Markets*. Rome: FAO.

———. 2005. *The State of Food and Agriculture*. Rome: FAO.

———. 2006. "Food Security." Policy Brief, no. 2 (June). http://www.fao.org/forestry /13128-0e6f36f27e0091055bec28ebe830f46b3.pdf.

———. 2008. *An Introduction to the Basic Concepts of Food Security*. Rome: FAO.

———. 2012. "Food Security Statistics." http://www.fao.org/economic/ess/ess-fs/en.

———. 2013. "The State of Food and Agriculture." http://www.fao.org/docrep/018/i33 00e/i3300e.pdf.

———. 2014. "World Food Situation: FAO Food Price Index." http://www.fao.org/wor ldfoodsituation/foodpricesindex/en.

———. 2016. "Mexico: Country Fact Sheet on Food and Agriculture Policy Trends." August. http://www.fao.org/3/a-i6006e.pdf.

———. 2017a. "Canada." http://www.fao.org/countryprofiles/index/en/?iso3=CAN.

————. 2017b. "United States." http://www.fao.org/countryprofiles/index/en/?iso3 =USA.

FAOSTAT. 2007. Commodity Balances. http://faostat3.fao.org/download/FB/BC/E.

————. 2012a. Consumer Price Indices. http://faostat.fao.org/site/683/DesktopDefa ult.aspx?PageID=683#ancor.

————. 2012b. Food Balance. Data for each nation for 1985 and 2007. http://faostat.fao .org/site/368/default.aspx#ancor.

————. 2015a. Animal products data. http://faostat.fao.org/site/610/DesktopDefault .aspx?PageID=610#ancor.

————. 2015b. Crop data. http://faostat.fao.org/site/609/DesktopDefault.aspx?Page ID=609#ancor.

————. 2017a. Consumer Price Indices. http://www.fao.org/faostat/en/#data/CP.

————. 2017b. Crops and Livestock Products. http://www.fao.org/faostat/en/#data /TP.

————. 2017c. Food Supply—Crops Primary Equivalent. http://fao.org/faostat/en /#data/CC.

————. 2017d. Food Supply—Livestock and Fish Primary Equivalent. http://fao.org /faostat/en/#data/CL.

————. 2017e. Livestock Primary. http://www.fao.org/faostat/en/#data/QL.

————. 2017 f. Suite of Food Security Indices. http://www.fao.org/faostat/en/#data /FS.

————. 2017g. Trade Indices. http://www.fao.org/faostat/en/#data/TI.

FAO, WFP, and IFAD. (Food and Agriculture Organization, World Food Program, and International Fund for Agricultural Development). 2012. *The State of Food Insecurity in the World 2012: Economic Growth Is Necessary but Not Sufficient to Accelerate Reduction of Hunger and Malnutrition*. Rome: FAO. http://www.fao.org/docrep/016 /i3027e/i3027e.pdf.

Fekete, Jason. 2011. "Free-Trade Frenzy." (Toronto) *National Post*, 27 December.

Fetzer, J. S. 2000. "Economic Self-Interest or Cultural Marginality? Anti-immigration Sentiment and Nativist Political Movements in France, Germany, and the USA." *Journal of Ethnic and Migration Studies* 26 (1): 5–23.

Fitting, Elizabeth. 2008. "Importing Corn, Exporting Labor: The Neoliberal Corn Regime." In *Food for the Few: Neoliberal Globalism and Biotechnology in Latin America*, edited by Gerardo Otero, 135–158. Austin: University of Texas Press.

————. 2011. *The Struggle for Maize: Campesinos, Workers, and Transgenic Corn in The Mexican Countryside*. Durham, NC: Duke University Press.

Food Processing. 2015. "Food Processing's Top 100." http://www.foodprocessing.com /top100/index.html.

Foster, John Belamy. 2000. *Marx's Ecology: Materialism and Nature*. New York: Monthly Review Press.

————. 2009. *The Ecological Revolution: Making Peace with the Planet*. New York: Monthly Review.

Fowler, Cary, and Pat Mooney. 1990. *Shattering: Food, Politics, and the Loss of Genetic Diversity*. Tucson: University of Arizona Press.

Fox, Rebekah, and Graham Smith. 2011. "Sinner Ladies and the Gospel of Good Taste: Geographies of Food, Class, and Care." *Health and Place* 17 (2): 403–412.

Freeman, Andrea. 2007. "Fast Food: Oppression through Poor Nutrition." *California Law Review* 95 (6): 2221–2259.

Friedmann, Harriet. 1982. "The Political Economy of Food: The Rise and Fall of the Postwar International Food Order." *American Journal of Sociology* 88 (supplement): S248–S286.

———. 1992. "Distance and Durability: Shaky Foundations of the World Food Economy." *Third World Quarterly* 13 (2): 371–383.

———. 1993. "The Political Economy of Food: A Global Crisis." *New Left Review* 197 (January–February): 29–57.

———. 1995. "Food Politics: New Dangers, New Possibilities." In *Food and Agrarian Orders in the World-Economy*, edited by Philip McMichael, 15–34. Westport, CT: Greenwood.

———. 1999. "Remaking Traditions: How We Eat, What We Eat, and the Changing Political Economy of Food." In *Women Working the NAFTA Food Chain: Women, Food, and Globalization*, edited by Deborah Barndt, 36–60. Toronto: Second Story.

———. 2005. "From Colonialism to Green Capitalism: Social Movements and Emergence of Food Regimes." *Research in Rural Sociology and Development* 11:227–264.

———. 2009. "Feeding the Empire: The Pathologies of Globalized Agriculture." *Socialist Register* 41:124–143.

Friedmann, Harriet, and Philip McMichael. 1989. "Agriculture and the State System: The Rise and Decline of National Agricultures, 1870 to the Present." *Sociologia Ruralis* 29 (2): 93–117.

Friedmann, Harriet, and Amber McNair. 2008. "Whose Rules Rule? Contested Projects to Certify 'Local Production for Distant Consumers.'" *Journal of Agrarian Change* 8 (2–3): 408–434.

Friends of the Earth International. 2009. *Who Benefits from GM Crops? Feeding the Biotech Giants, Not the World's Poor*. Report, no. 116 (February). http://www.foei.org /en/resources/publications/annual-report/annual-report-2009/what-we-achiev ed-in-2009/communications/publications-materials-audiovisual/who-benefits -from-gm-crops.

Furtado, Celso. 1976. *Economic Development of Latin America: Historical Background and Contemporary Problems*. 2nd ed. Translated by Suzette Macedo. New York: Cambridge University Press.

Galbraith, James K. 2012. *Inequality and Instability: A Study of the World Economy Just before the Great Crisis*. Oxford: Oxford University Press.

Gambrell, Dorothy. 2016. "Trade Give and Take." *Bloomberg BusinessWeek*, 21–27 November, 18.

García Aguña, Clara, and Milorad Kovacevic. 2010. "Uncertainty and Sensitivity Analysis of the Human Development Index." (UN Development Program) *Human Development Research Paper* 47:1–65. http://hdr.undp.org/sites/default/files/hdrp_2010 _47.pdf.

Gereffi, Gary, and Michelle Christian. 2009. "The Impacts of Wal-Mart: The Rise and

Consequences of the World's Dominant Retailer." *Annual Review of Sociology* 35: 573–591.

Gereffi, Gary, and Miguel Korzenievikz. 1994. *Commodity Chains and Global Capitalism.* Wesport, CT: Greenwood.

Gereffi, Gary, Joonkoo Lee, and Michelle Christian. 2009. "US-Based Food and Agricultural Value Chains and Their Relevance to Healthy Diets." *Journal of Hunger and Environmental Nutrition* 4 (3): 357–374.

Gillam, Carey. 2007. "Monsanto Profit Beats Estimates, Raises Outlook." Reuters, 4 April. https://www.reuters.com/article/us-food-monsanto-earns/monsanto-profit-beats-estimates-raises-outlook-idUSWEN610420070404.

Glenna, Leland L., and Daniel R. Cahoy. 2009. "Agribusiness Concentration, Intellectual Property, and the Prospects for Rural Economic Benefits from the Emerging Biofuel Economy." *Southern Rural Sociology* 24 (2): 111–129.

Glewwe, Paul, and Ana Lucia Kassouf. 2012. "The Impact of the *Bolsa Escola/Família* Conditional Cash Transfer Program on Enrollment, Dropout Rates, and Grade Promotion in Brazil." *Journal of Development Economics* 97 (2): 505–517.

Glover, D. 2010a. "The Corporate Shaping of GM Crops as a Technology for the Poor." *Journal of Peasant Studies* 37 (1): 67–90.

———. 2010b. "Exploring the Resilience of Bt Cotton's 'Pro-Poor Success Story.'" *Development and Change* 41 (6): 955–981.

———. 2010c. "GM crops: Still Not a Panacea for Poor Farmers." *Appropriate Technology* 37 (3): 19–29.

———. 2010d. "Is Bt Cotton a Pro-Poor Technology? A Review and Critique of the Empirical Record." *Journal of Agrarian Change* 10 (4): 482–509.

Gomes, Marcel. 2015. "Globalization and Concentration in Brazil's Agri-Food System." *Monitor (Repórter Brasil)* 1 (1): 1–6.

Gómez González, Irma. 2016. "A Honey-Sealed Alliance: Mayan Beekeepers in the Yucatán Peninsula versus Transgenic Soybeans in Mexico's Last Tropical Forest." *Journal of Agrarian Change* 16 (4): 728–736.

González, Humberto. 2013. "Especialización productiva y vulnerabilidad agroalimentaria en México." *Comercio Exterior* 63 (2): 21–36.

González Amador, R., and D. Brooks. 2007. "México: El mayor expulsor de migrantes, dice el BM." *La Jornada* (Mexico City), 16 April. http://www.jornada.unam.mx/2007/04/16/index.php?section=politica&article=003n1pol.

González Chávez, Humberto, and Alejandro Macías Macías. 2007. "Vulnerabilidad alimentaria y política agroalimentaria en México." *Desacatos: Revista de Antropología Social* 25:47–78.

Goodman, David., and Michael Watts. 1994. "Reconfiguring the Rural or Fording the Divide? Capitalist Restructuring and the Global Agro-Food System." *Journal of Peasant Studies* 22 (1): 1–49.

Gordon, Cynthia, Marnie Purciel-Hill, Nirupa R. Ghai, Leslie Kaufman, Regina Graham, and Gretchen Van Wye. 2011. "Measuring Food Deserts in New York City's Low-Income Neighborhoods." *Health and Place* 17:696–700.

Gramsci, Antonio. 1971. *Selections from the Prison Notebooks*. Edited and translated by Quintin Hoare and Geoffrey Nowell Smith. New York: International.

Grandia, Liza. 2014. "Modified Landscapes: Vulnerabilities to Genetically Modified Corn in Northern Guatemala." *Journal of Peasant Studies* 41 (1): 79–105.

Greenpeace. 2007. "US GM Rice Contaminate World Rice Supplies." GM Contamination Register. http://www.gmcontaminationregister.org/index.php?content=nw _detail2.

Grynbaum, Michael. 2013. "Judge Blocks New York City's Limits on Big Sugary Drinks." *New York Times*, 11 March. http://www.nytimes.com/2013/03/12/nyreg ion/judge-invalidates-bloombergs-soda-ban.html.

Gunther, Marc. 2007. "Attack of the Mutant Rice." *Fortune*, 9 July, 74. http://money .cnn.com/magazines/fortune/fortune_archive/2007/07/09/100122123/index.htm.

Guptill, Amy E., Denise A. Copelton, and Betsy Lucal. 2013. *Food and Society: Principles and Paradoxes*. Cambridge, UK: Polity.

Gürcan, Efe Can. 2011. "Food Crisis and Beyond: Locating Food-Sovereign Alternatives in a Post-Neoliberal Context." *Kasarinlan: Philippine Journal of Third World Studies* 26 (1–2): 482–496.

———. 2013. "Cuban Agriculture and the Four Pillars of Food Sovereignty Policies: Beyond Civil Society–Centric and Globalist Paradigms." *Latin American Perspectives* 41 (4): 129–146.

Guthman, Julie. 2004. *Agrarian Dreams: The Paradox of Organic Farming in California*. Berkeley: University of California Press.

———. 2007a. "Can't Stomach It: How Michael Pollan et al. Made Me Want to Eat Cheetos." *Gastronomica* 7:75–79.

———. 2007b. "Commentary on Teaching Food: Why I Am Fed Up with Michael Pollan et al." *Agriculture and Human Values* 24:261–264.

———. 2007c. "The Polanyian Way? Voluntary Food Labels as Neoliberal Governance." *Antipode* 39:456–478.

———. 2011. *Weighing In: Obesity, Food Justice, and the Limits of Capitalism*. Berkeley: University of California Press.

Guthman, Julie, and Melanie DuPuis. 2006. "Embodying Neoliberalism: Economy, Culture, and the Politics of Fat." *Environment and Planning D: Society and Space* 24: 427–448.

Hafez, Navid, and Pamela M. Ling. 2005. "How Philip Morris Built Marlboro into a Global Brand for Young Adults: Implications for International Tobacco Control." *Tobacco Control* 14 (4): 262–271.

Håkansson, A., Håkan S. Andersson, and Yvonne Grafeldt. 2015. "Diet Inequality Prevails among Consumers Interested and Knowledgeable in Nutrition." *Food and Nutrition Research* 59 (1). http://dx.doi.org/10.3402/fnr.v59.27601.

Harrington, J., A. P. Fitzgerald, R. Layte, J. Lutomski, and M. Molcho. 2011. "Sociodemographic, Health, and Lifestyle Predictors of Poor Diets." *Public Health Nutrition* 14 (12): 2166–2175.

Harvey, David. 2005. *A Brief History of Neoliberalism*. Oxford: Oxford University Press.

Harvey, Fiona, and George Parker. 2008. "Top UK Scientist Pushes for GM Crops." *Financial Times*, 8 July.

Harvey, Neil. 1996. "Rural Reforms and the Zapatista Rebellion: Chiapas 1988–95." In *Neoliberalism Revisited: Economic Restructuring and Mexico's Political Future*, edited by Gerardo Otero, 187–208. Boulder, CO: Westview.

Hawkes, Corinna. 2006. "Uneven Dietary Development: Linking the Policies and Processes of Globalization with the Nutrition Transition, Obesity, and Diet-Related Chronic Diseases." *Globalization and Health* 2 (4): 1–18.

Hawkes, Corinna, Bettina Gerken Brazil, Inês Rugani Ribeiro de Castro, and Patrícia Constante Jaime. 2016. "How to Engage across Sectors: Lessons from Agriculture and Nutrition in the Brazilian School Feeding Program." *Revista de Saúde Pública* 50(47). At https://www.researchgate.net/publication/306049495_How_to_engage _across_sectors_lessons_from_agriculture_and_nutrition_in_the_Brazilian_Sch ool_Feeding_Program.

Heller, Lorraine. 2007. "Organic Dairy Farmers Join Battle against GM Alfalfa." Nutra-Ingredients.com. 20 April. https://www.nutraingredients-usa.com/Article/2007/04 /20/Organic-dairy-farmers-join-battle-against-GM-alfalfa.

Hellman, Judith Adler. 2008. *The World of Mexican Migrants: The Rock and the Hard Place*. New York: New Press.

Hendrickson, Mary K., and William D. Heffernan. 2002. "Opening Spaces through Relocalization: Locating Potential Resistance in the Weaknesses of the Global Food System." *Sociologia Ruralis* 42 (4): 347–369.

———. 2005. "Concentration of Agricultural Markets." University of Missouri, Department of Rural Sociology. February. http://www.agribusinesscenter.org/docs /Kraft_1.pdf.

Hennebry, Jenna L. 2008. *International Agricultural Migration and Public Health: Examining Migrant Farm Worker Health and the Public Health Implications of Agricultural Temporary Migration*. Ottawa: Public Health Agency of Canada.

Hennebry, Jenna L., Kerry Preibisch, and Janet McLaughlin. 2010. *Health Across Borders—Health Status, Risks and Care among Transnational Migrant Farm Workers in Ontario*. Toronto: CERIS (Centre of Excellence for Research on Immigration and Settlement), Ontario Metropolis Centre.

Herring, Ronald. 2007. "Stealth Seeds: Bioproperty, Biosafety, Biopolitics." *Journal of Development Studies* 43 (1): 130–157.

Hewitt de Alcántara, Cynthia. 1978. *Modernización de la agricultura mexicana*. Mexico City: Siglo XXI.

Hisano, Shuji 2005. "Critical Observation on the Mainstream Discourse of Biotechnology for the Poor." *Tailoring Biotechnologies* 1 (2): 81–105.

Hisano, Shuji, and Simone Altoé. 2008. "Brazilian Farmers at a Crossroads: Biotech Industrialization of Agriculture or New Alternatives for Family Farmers? In *Food for the Few: Neoliberal Globalism and Biotechnology in Latin America*, edited by Gerardo Otero, 243–265. Austin: University of Texas Press.

Holland, Dawn. 2012. "The Impact of Transitional Arrangements on Migration in the

Enlarged EU." *FMW: Online Journal on Free Movement of Workers* 4:18–25. http://www.ru.nl/publish/pages/714306/issue_4.pdf.

Holmes, Seth M. 2013. *Fresh Fruit, Broken Bodies: Migrant Workers in the United States.* Berkeley: University of California Press.

Holt-Giménez, Eric, ed. 2011. *Food Movements Unite! Strategies to Transform Our Food Systems.* San Francisco: Food First.

Holt-Giménez, Eric, and Raj Patel, with Annie Shattuck. 2009. *Food Rebellions! Crisis and the Hunger for Justice.* San Francisco: Pambazuka/Food-First Books/Grassroots International.

Holt Giménez, Eric, and Annie Shattuck. 2011. "Food Crises, Food Regimes, and Food Movements: Rumblings of Reform or Tides of Transformation?" *Journal of Peasant Studies* 38 (1): 109–144.

Horton, Sarah Bronwen. 2016. *They Leave Their Kidneys in the Fields: Illness, Injury, and Illegality among U.S. Farmworkers.* Berkeley: University of California Press.

Howard, Charlotte. 2012. "The Big Picture." *The Economist*, 15 December. http://www.economist.com/news/special-report/21568065-world-getting-wider-says-charlotte-howard-what-can-be-done-about-it-big.

Howard, Philip H. 2014. "Too Big to Ale? Globalization and Consolidation in the Beer Industry." In *The Geography of Beer: Regions, Environment, and Society*, edited by Mark W. Patterson and Nancy Hoalst Pullen, 155–165. New York: Springer.

———. 2016. *Concentration and Power in the Food System: Who Controls What We Eat?* London and New York: Bloomsbury.

Index Mundi. 2017. Data portal. http://www.indexmundi.com.

INEGI (Mexico, Instituto Nacional de Estadística, Geografía e Informática). 1985. "Encuesta Nacional de Ingresos y Gastos de los Hogares 1984 (ENIGH). Tabulados básicos." http://www.beta.inegi.org.mx/proyectos/enchogares/regulares/enigh/tradicional/1984/default.html.

———. 2007. "Encuesta Nacional de Ingresos y Gastos de los Hogares 2006 (ENIGH). Tabulados básicos." http://www.beta.inegi.org.mx/proyectos/enchogares/regulares/enigh/tradicional/2006/default.html.

———. 2013. "Encuesta Nacional de Ingresos y Gastos de los Hogares 2012 (ENIGH). Tabulados básicos." http://www.beta.inegi.org.mx/proyectos/enchogares/regulares/enigh/tradicional/2012/default.html.

ISAAA (International Service for the Acquisition of Agri-biotech Applications). 2006. "Global Status of Commercialized Biotech/GM Crops: 2006." Executive summary, ISAAA Brief no. 35-2006. http://www.isaaa.org/resources/publications/briefs/35/executivesummary/default.html.

———. 2016. "Brief 52: Global Status of Commercialized Biotech/GM Crops: 2016." ISAAA Brief no. 52. http://www.isaaa.org/resources/publications/briefs/52/download/isaaa-brief-52-2016.pdf.

Issaoui-Mansouri, Kheira. 2010. "Souveraineté alimentaire: Un concept en émergence." [Food sovereignty: an emerging concept] *Possibles* 34 (1–2): 14–29.

Ita, Ana de. 2007. *Catorce años de TLCAN y la crisis de la tortilla.* Special report for Programa de las Americas, 11 November. Washington, DC: Center for International Policy.

James, Clive. 2000. "Global Status of Commercialized Transgenic Crops: 1999." ISAAA Brief no. 17. Ithaca, NY: International Service for the Acquisition of Agri-biotech Applications (ISAAA). http://www.isaaa.org/Resources/publications/briefs/17/download/isaaa-brief-17-2000.pdf.

———. 2004. "Preview: Global Status of Commercialized Biotech/GM Crops: 2004." ISAAA Brief no. 32-2004. http://www.isaaa.org.

———. 2005. "CropBiotech Update Special Edition. Highlights of ISAAA Brief No. 34-2005: Global Status of Commericalized Biotech/GM Crops, 2005." ISAAA. 11 January. http://www.isaaa.org/kc/bin/briefs34/cbu/index.htm.

———. 2014. "Global Status of Commercialized Biotech/GM Crops: 2014." ISAAA Brief no. 49, executive summary.

James, W. P. 2008. "The Fundamental Drivers of the Obesity Epidemic." *Obesity Reviews* 9:6–13.

Jansen, Kees, and Aarti Gupta. 2009. "Anticipating the Future: 'Biotechnology for the Poor' as Unrealized Promise?" *Futures* 41 (7): 436–445.

Jarosz, Lucy. 2009. "Energy, Climate Change, Meat, and Markets: Mapping the Coordinates of the Current World Food Crisis." *Geography Compass* 3 (6): 2065–2083.

———. 2011. "Defining World Hunger: Scale and Neoliberal Ideology in International Food Security Policy Discourse." *Food, Culture, and Society: An International Journal of Multidisciplinary Research* 14 (1): 117–139.

Jepson, Wendy E., Christian Brannstrom, and Renato S. de Sousa. 2008. "Brazilian Biotechnology Governance: Consensus and Conflict over Genetically Modified Crops." In *Food for the Few: Neoliberal Globalism and Biotechnology in Latin America*, edited by Gerardo Otero, 217–242. Austin: University of Texas Press.

Jessop, Bob. 2007. *State Power: A Strategic-Relational Approach*. Cambridge, MA: Polity.

Johnston, Joseé, and Shyon Baumann. 2010. *Foodies: Democracy and Distinction in Gourmet Foodscape*. New York: Routledge.

Justicia for Migrant Workers. 2013. "About Us." http://www.justicia4migrantworkers.org/justicia_new.htm.

Kenney, M. 1986. *Biotechnology: The University-Industrial Complex*. New Haven, CT: Yale University Press.

Klepek, James. 2012. "Against the Grain: Knowledge Alliances and Resistance to Agricultural Biotechnology in Guatemala." *Canadian Journal of Development Studies* 33 (3): 310–325.

Kloppenburg, Jack R. Jr. 1988. *Seeds and Sovereignty: The Use and Control of Plant Genetic Resources*. Durham, NC: Duke University Press.

———. 2004. *First the Seed: The Political Economy of Plant Biotechnology*. 2nd ed. Madison: University of Wisconsin Press.

KOF (Swiss Economic Institute). 2017. Economic Globalization Index. http://globalization.kof.ethz.ch.

Koplan, Jeffrey P., Catharyn T. Liverman, and Vivica I. Kraak. 2005. "Preventing Childhood Obesity: Health in Balance: Executive Summary." *Journal of American Dietetic Association* 105 (1): 131–138.

Krugman, Paul. 2015. "Pepperoni Turns Partisan." *New York Times*, 6 March. http://www.nytimes.com/2015/03/06/opinion/paul-krugman-pepperoni-turns-partisan.html.

Lapegna, Pablo. 2016. *Soybeans and Power: Genetically Modified Crops, Environmental Politics, and Social Movements in Argentina*. New York: Oxford University.

Lara, José Bell. 2007. "Cuban Socialism in the Face of Globalisation." In *Imperialism, Neoliberalism and Social Struggles in Latin America*, edited by Richard Alan Dello Buono and José Bell Lara, 145–172. Leiden, Netherlands: Brill.

Larson, Nicole I., Mary T. Story, and Melissa C. Nelson. 2009. "Neighborhood Environments: Disparities in Access to Healthy Foods in the U.S." *American Journal of Preventative Medicine* 36 (1): 74–81.

Lawrence, Geoffrey. 2014. "Financialization." *Journal of Peasant Studies* 41 (3): 421–426.

———. 2017. "Re-Evaluating Food Systems and Food Security: A Global Perspective." *Journal of Sociology* 53 (4): 774–796.

Lean, Geoffrey. 2008. "Multinationals Make Billions in Profit Out of Growing Global Food Crisis." *The Independent*. 4 May. Reprint, Common Dreams, https://www.commondreams.org/news/2008/05/04/multinationals-make-billions-profit-out-growing-global-food-crisis.

Lee, Hedwig. 2011. "Inequality as an Explanation for Obesity in the United States." *Sociology Compass* 5 (3): 215–232.

Lee, Jamie. 2008. "GM Crops May Be Answer to Food Crisis: Ecologist." (Singapore) *Business Times*. Reprint, Wild Singapore, 30 June, http://wildsingaporenews.blogspot.ca/2008/06/gm-crops-may-be-answer-to-food-crisis.html#.WicuDLQ-fjA.

Lee, Joonkoo, Gary Gereffi, and Janet Beauvais. 2012. "Global Value Chains and Agrifood Standards: Challenges and Possibilities for Smallholders in Developing Countries." *Proceedings of the National Academy of Sciences* 109 (31): 12326–12331.

Le Heron, Richard and Michael Roche. 1995. "A 'Fresh' Place in Food's Space." *Area* 27 (1): 23–33.

Lind, David, and Elizabeth Barham. 2004. "The Social Life of the Tortilla: Food, Cultural Politics, and Contested Commodification." *Agriculture and Human Values* 21 (1): 47–60.

Lipietz, Alain. 1987. *Mirages and Miracles: The Crisis of Global Fordism*. Translated by D. Macey. London: Verso.

Lomborg, Bjorn. 2009. "Another 'Green Revolution.'" (Toronto) *National Post*, 25 March.

MacIntyre, U. E., H. S. Kruger, C. S. Venter, and H. H. Vorster. 2002. "Dietary Intakes of an African Population in Different Stages of Transition in the North West Province, South Africa: The THUSA Study." *Nutrition Research* 22:239–256.

Maffetone, Philip B., Ivan Rivera-Dominguez, and Paul B. Laursen. 2017. "Overfat Adults and Children in Developed Countries: The Public Health Importance of Identifying Excess Body Weight." *Frontiers in Public Health* 5:1–11. https://doi.org/10.3389/fpubh.2017.00190.

Magnan, André. 2016. *When Wheat was King: The Rise and Fall of the Canada-UK Grain Trade*. Vancouver, BC: UBC Press.

Maio, Fernando de. 2014. *Global Health Inequities: A Sociological Perspective*. Basingstoke, UK: Palgrave Macmillan.

Marchant, G. 1988. "Modified Rules for Modified Bugs: Balancing Safety and Efficiency in the Regulation of Deliberate Release of Genetically Engineered Microorganisms." *Harvard Journal of Law and Technology* 1 (Spring): 163–208. http://jolt.law.harvard.edu/articles/pdf/01HarvJLTech163.pdf.

Markin, Rom J. 1968. *The Supermarket: An Analysis of Growth, Development, and Change*. Rev. ed. Pullman: Washington State University Press.

Martin, Andrew. 2015. "Inside the Powerful Lobby to Fight for Your Right to Eat Pizza." *Bloomberg BusinessWeek*, 3 March. http://www.bloomberg.com/news/features/2015-03-03/junk-food-s-last-stand-the-pizza-lobby-is-not-backing-down.

Martin, Sarah J., and Jennifer Clapp. 2015. "Finance for Agriculture or Agriculture for Finance?" *Journal of Agrarian Change* 15 (4): 549–559.

Martínez-Gómez, Francisco, Gilberto Aboites-Manrique, and Douglas Constance. 2013. "Neoliberal Restructuring, Neoregulation, and the Mexican Poultry Industry." *Agriculture and Human Values* 30:495–510. https://doi.org/10.1007/s10460-013-9431-0.

Marx, Karl. 1977. *Capital: A Critique of Political Economy*. Volume 1. Translated by Ben Fowkes. London: Penguin.

Mascarenhas, Michael, and Lawrence Busch. 2006. "Seeds of Change: Intellectual Property Rights, Genetically Modified Soybeans and Seed Saving in the United States." *Sociologia Ruralis* 46 (2): 122–138.

Mason, Katherine. 2012. "The Unequal Weight of Discrimination: Gender, Body Size, and Income Inequality." *Social Problems* 59 (3): 411–435.

McAdam, Doug, and Karina Kloos. 2014. *Deeply Divided: Racial Politics and Social Movements in Post-War America*. Oxford: Oxford University Press.

McAfee, Kathy. 2008. "Exporting Crop Biotechnology: The Myth of Molecular Miracles." In *Food for the Few: Neoliberal Globalism and Biotechnology in Latin America*, edited by Gerardo Otero, 61–90. Austin: University of Texas Press.

McKenna, Barrie. 2012. "Canadian Beef Exports in Rapid Decline." *Globe and Mail*, 10 September.

McLaren, Lindsay. 2007. "Socioeconomic Status and Obesity." *Epidemiologic Reviews* 29:29–48.

McLaughlin, Janet. 2009. "Trouble in Our Fields: Health and Human Rights among Mexican and Caribbean Migrant Farm Workers in Canada." PhD diss., Department of Anthropology, University of Toronto, Toronto.

McLaughlin, Kathleen, and Doug McMillon. 2015. "Business and Society in the Coming Decades." Commentary, April. McKinsey and Company. http://www.mckinsey.com/insights/strategy/Business_and_society_in_the_coming_decades?cid=other-eml-alt-mip-mck-oth-1504.

McMichael, Philip. 1992. "Tensions between National and International Control of the World Food Order: Contours of a New Food Regime." *Sociological Perspectives* 35 (2): 343–365.

———. 2004. "Biotechnology and Food Security: Profiting on Insecurity." In *Global tensions: Challenges and Opportunities in the World Economy*, edited by L. Beneria and S. Bisnaith, 137–153. New York: Routledge.

———. 2005. "Global Development and the Corporate Food Regime." *Research in Rural Sociology and Development* 11:265–299.

———. 2009a. "A Food Regime Analysis of the 'World Food Crisis.'" *Agriculture and Human Values* 26 (4): 281–295.

———. 2009b. "A Food Regime Genealogy." *Journal of Peasant Studies* 36 (1): 139–169.

McMichael, Philip, and Harriett Friedmann. 2007. "Situating the 'Retailing Revolution.'" In *Supermarkets and Agri-Food Supply Chains: Transformations in the Production and Consumption of Foods*, edited by David Burch and Geoffrey Lawrence, 291–319. Cheltenham, UK: Edward Elgar.

Migrant Workers Alliance for Change. 2013. "Our Demands." http://www.migrant workersalliance.org/about-us/demands.

Miller, Adrian. 2013. *Soul Food: The Surprising Story of an American Cuisine, One Plate at a Time*. Chapel Hill: University of North California Press.

Mincer, Jacob. 1962. "Labor Force Participation of Married Women: A Study of Labor Supply." In *Aspects of Labor Economics*, edited by the National Bureau of Economic Research, 63–105. Princeton, NJ: Princeton University Press.

Mintz, Sidney. 1985. *Sweetness and Power: The Place of Sugar in Modern History*. New York: Penguin.

Mitchell, Sheona, and Dorothy Shaw. 2015. "The Worldwide Epidemic of Female Obesity." *Best Practice and Research Clinical Obstetrics and Gynaecology* 29 (3): 289–299. https://doi.org/10.1016/j.bpobgyn.2014.10.002.

Monsanto. 2005. *2005 Annual Report*. https://monsanto.com/investors/reports/archiv ed-annual-reports.

———. 2007. "Monsanto Sees Record Sales in Fiscal Year 2007; Seeds and Traits Business Contributes to Strong Fourth Quarter and Year-End Results." News release. https://monsanto.com/news-releases/monsanto-sees-record-sales-in-fiscal-year -2007-seeds-and-traits-business-contributes-to-strong-fourth-quarter-and-year -end-results.

Monteiro, Carlos A., Jean-Claude Moubarac, G. Gagnon, S. W. Ng, and Barry Popkin. 2013. "Ultra-Processed Products Are Becoming Dominant in the Global Food System." *Obesity Reviews* 14 (supplement 2): 21–28.

Monteiro, Carlos, Erly Moura, Wolney Conde, and Barry Popkin. 2004. "Socioeconomic Status and Obesity in Adult Populations of Developing Countries: A Review." *Bulletin of the World Health Organization* 82 (12): 940–946.

Montgomery, D. R. 2007. *Dirt: The Erosion of Civilizations*. Berkeley: University of California Press.

Moodie, Rob, David Stuckler, Carlos Monteiro, Nick Sheron, Bruce Neal, Thaksaphon Thamarangsi, Paul Lincoln, and Sally Casswell. 2013. "Profits and Pandemics:

Prevention of Harmful Effects of Tobacco, Alcohol, and Ultra-Processed Food and Drink Industries." *The Lancet* 381:670–679.

Moore, Jason. 2010. "Agricultural Revolutions in the Capitalist World-Ecology, 1450–2010." *Journal of Agrarian Change* 10 (3): 389–413.

Moran, W., G. Blunden, M. Workman, and A. Bradly. 1996. "Family Farmers, Real Regulation, and the Experience of Food Regimes." *Journal of Rural Studies* 12 (3): 245–258.

Moreno-Brid, Juan Carlos, and Jaime Ros. 2009. *Development and Growth in the Mexican Economy: A Historical Perspective*. Oxford: Oxford University Press.

Morland, Kimberly, Steve Wind, Ana Diez Roux, and Charles Poole. 2002. "Neighborhood Characteristics Associated with the Location of Food Stores and Food Service Places." *American Journal of Preventive Medicine* 22 (1): 23–29.

Morrison, Rosanna M., Jean C. Buzby, and Hodan F. Wells. 2010. "Guess Who's Turning 100? Tracking a Century of American Eating." *Amber Waves* (USDA) 8 (1 March): 1. https://www.ers.usda.gov/amber-waves/2010/march/guess-who-s-tu rning-100tracking-a-century-of-american-eating.

Morton, Adam David. 2011. *Revolution and State in Modern Mexico: The Political Economy of Uneven Development*. Lanham, MD: Rowman and Littlefield.

Morton, Peter. 1999. "Polishing the NAFTA Image Five-Year-Old Pact: Despite Growth in Trade, Misgivings Remain." (Toronto) *National Post*, 22 April.

Moss, Michael. 2013. *Salt, Sugar, Fat: How the Food Giants Hooked Us*. New York: Random House Trade Paperbacks.

Motta, Renata. 2016. *Social Mobilization, Global Capitalism, and Struggles over Food*. New York: Routledge.

Moubarac, Jean-Claude, Ana Paula Bortoletto Martins, Rafael Moreira Claro, Renata Bertazzi Levi, Geoffrey Cannon, and Carlos Augusto Monteiro. 2012. "Consumption of Ultra-Processed Foods and Likely Impact On Human Health: Evidence from Canada." *Public Health Nutrition*. 16 (12): 2240–2248.

Mukherjee, S. 2012. "India Emerges as World's Top Rice Exporter." *Business Standard* (New Delhi), 5 May. http://www.business-standard.com/india/news/india -emerges-as-world039s-top-rice-exporter/473452.

Munn-Venn, Trefor, and Paul Mitchell. 2005. *Biotechnology in Canada: A Technology Platform for Growth*. December. Conference Board of Canada. http://publications .gc.ca/collection_2007/cbac-cccb/Iu199-10-2005E.pdf.

Nagatada, Takanayagi. 2006. "Global Flows of Fruit and Vegetables in the Third Food Regime." *Journal of Rural Community Studies* 102:25–41.

National Academies of Sciences, Engineering, and Medicine. 2016. *Genetically Engineered Crops: Experiences and Prospects*. Washington, DC: National Academies Press. https://doi.org/10.17226/23395.

Nelson, Jon P. 2014. "Binge Drinking, Alcohol Prices, and Alcohol Taxes: A Systematic Review of Results for Youth, Young Adults, and Adults from Economic Studies, Natural Experiments, and Field Studies." AAWE Working Papers, no. 146. American Association of Wine Economists. http://www.wine-economics.org.

Nestle, Marion. 2006. *What to Eat*. New York: North Point.

———. 2010. *Safe Food: The Politics of Food Safety*. Berkeley: University of California Press.

———. 2013. *Food Politics: How the Food Industry Influences Nutrition and Health*. Rev. ed. Berkeley: University of California Press.

Notimex. 2009. "Subieron 15% los alimentos básicos y cayó 30% el consumo." *La Jornada* (Mexico City). 7 January. http://www.jornada.unam.mx/2009/01/07/index .php?section=economia&article=022n2eco.

Novek, J. 2003. "Intensive Hog Farming in Manitoba: Transnational Treadmills and Local Conflicts." *Canadian Review of Sociology and Anthropology* 40 (1): 3–26.

O'Connor, Anahad, and Margot Sanger-Katz. 2016. "Soda Taxes Gain Acceptance, City by Revenue-Hungry City." *New York Times*, 27 November.

Oliveira, Gustavo de L. T., and Mindi Schneider. 2014. *The Politics of Flexing Soybeans in Brazil and China*. Think Piece Series on Flex Crops and Commodities, no. 3 (September). Amsterdam: Transnational Institute Agrarian Justice Program. https:// www.tni.org/files/download/flexcrops03.pdf.

Ontario Provincial Police. 2012. "Update—Multi Fatal OPP Investigation." News release, 8 February. http://www.newswire.ca/news-releases/update———multi -fatal-opp-investigation-509590851.html.

Ó Riain, Seán. 2000. "States and Markets in an Era of Globalization." *Annual Review of Sociology* 26:187–213.

O'Sullivan, John. 2016. "The World Economy: An Open and Shut Case." *The Economist*, 1 October. https://www.economist.com/news/special-report/21707833-consensus -favour-open-economies-cracking-says-john-osullivan.

Otero, Gerardo 1995. "Mexico's Political Future(s) in a Globalizing Economy." *Canadian Review of Sociology and Anthropology* 32 (3): 319–343.

———. 1998. "Atencingo Revisited: Political Class Formation and Economic Restructuring in Mexico's Sugar Industry." *Rural Sociology*. 63 (2): 272–299.

———. 1999. *Farewell to the Peasantry? Political Class Formation in Rural Mexico*. Boulder, CO: Westview.

———, ed. 2004. *Mexico in Transition: Neoliberal Globalism, the State and Civil Society*. London: Zed Books; Halifax, Canada: Fernwood.

———, ed. 2008. *Food for the Few: Neoliberal Globalism and Biotechnology in Latin America*. Austin: University of Texas Press.

———. 2011. "Neoliberal Globalization, NAFTA, and Migration: Mexico's Loss of Food and Labor Sovereignty." *Journal of Poverty* 15 (4): 384–402.

———. 2012. "The Neoliberal Food Regime in Latin America: State, Agribusiness Transnational Corporations, and Biotechnology." *Canadian Journal of Development Studies* 33 (3): 282–294.

———. 2013. "The Neoliberal Food Regime and Its Crises: State, Agribusiness Transnational Corporations, and Biotechnology." In *The Neoliberal Regime in the Agri-Food Sector: Crisis, Resilience, and Restructuring*, edited by Stephen A. Wolf and Alessandro Bonanno, 225–244. London: Earthscan/Routledge.

———. 2017. "Contesting Neoliberal Globalism: A Comment on 'Re-evaluating Food Systems and Food Security: A Global Perspective.'" *Journal of Sociology* 53 (4): 797–799.

Otero, Gerardo, and Cornelia B. Flora. 2009. "Sweet Protectionism: State Policy and Employment in the Sugar Industries of the NAFTA Countries." In *NAFTA and the Campesinos: The Impact of NAFTA on Small-Scale Agricultural Producers in Mexico and the Prospects for Change*, edited by Juan M. Rivera, Scott Whiteford, and Manuel Chávez, 63–88. Scranton, PA: University of Scranton Press.

Otero, Gerardo, and Hayley Jones. 2010. "Biofuels or Biofools: A Socio-Ecological Critique of Agrofuels." Paper presented at the International Congress of the Latin American Studies Association, 6–9 October, Toronto.

Otero, Gerardo, and Heidi Jugenitz. 2006. "Forging New Democracies: Indigenous Struggles for Autonomy." In *Not for Sale: Decommodifying Public Life*, edited by Gordon Laxer and Denis Soron, 169–186. Peterborough, Canada: Broadview.

Otero, Gerardo, and Pablo Lapegna. 2016. "Transgenic Crops in Latin America: Expropriation, Negative Value and the State." *Journal of Agrarian Change* 16 (4): 665–674.

Otero, Gerardo, and Gabriela Pechlaner. 2005. "Food for the Few: The Biotechnology Revolution in Latin America" *Canadian Journal of Development Studies* 26 (4): 867–887.

———. 2008. "Latin American Agriculture and Biotechnology: Temperate Dietary Pattern Adoption and Unsustainability." In *Food for the Few: Neoliberal Globalism and Biotechnology in Latin America*, edited by Gerardo Otero, 31–60. Austin: University of Texas Press.

———. 2009. "Is Biotechnology the Answer? The Evidence from North America." *NACLA Report on the Americas*, May/June, 27–31.

Otero, Gerardo, Gabriela Pechlaner, and Efe Can Gürcan. 2013. "The Political Economy of 'Food Security' and Trade: Uneven and Combined Dependency." *Rural Sociology* 78 (3): 263–289.

———. 2015. "The Neoliberal Diet: Fattening Profits and People." In *The Routledge Handbook of Poverty and the United States*, edited by Stephen Nathan Haymes, María Vidal de Haymes, and Reuben Jonathan Miller, 472–479. London: Routledge.

Otero, Gerardo, Gabriela Pechlaner, Efe Can Gürcan, and Giselle Liberman. 2015. "The Neoliberal Diet and Inequality in the United States." *Social Science and Medicine* 142:47–55.

Otero, Gerardo, Gabriela Pechlaner, Giselle Liberman, and Efe Can Gürcan. 2018. "Food Security, Obesity, and Inequality: Measuring the Risk of Exposure to the Neoliberal Diet." *Journal of Agrarian Change* (forthcoming).

Otero, Gerardo, Manuel Poitras, and Gabriela Pechlaner. 2008. "Political Economy of Agricultural Biotechnology in North America: The Case of rBST in La Laguna, Mexico." In *Food for the Few: Neoliberal Globalism and Biotechnology in Latin America*, edited by Gerardo Otero, 159–188. Austin: University of Texas Press.

Otero, Gerardo, and Kerry Preibisch. 2010. *Farmworker Health and Safety: Challenges for British Columbia*. Vancouver, Canada: WorkSafeBC. http://www.sfu.ca/content/dam/sfu/people/otero/Otero-and-Preibisch-Final-Nov-2010.pdf.

————. 2015. *Citizenship and Precarious Labour in Canadian Agriculture*. Policy Report, November. Canadian Centre for Policy Alternatives. https://www.policyalternatives .ca/publications/reports/citizenship-and-precarious-labour-canadian-agriculture.

PBS. 1998. *Fat*. TV documentary. *Frontline*, 3 November.

Pampel, Fred C., Justin T. Denney, and Patrick M. Krueger. 2012. "Obesity, SES, and Economic Development: A Test of the Reversal Hypothesis." *Social Science and Medicine* 74:1073–1081.

Panitch, Leo, and Sam Gindin. 2012. *The Making of Global Capitalism: The Political Economy of American Empire*. London: Verso.

Passel, Jeffrey S., and D'Vera Cohn. 2009. *A Portrait of Unauthorized Immigrants in the United States*. Washington, DC: Pew Hispanic Center.

Patel, Raj C. 2007. *Stuffed and Starved: Markets, Power and the Hidden Battle for the World Food System*. London: Portobello.

————. 2009. "What Does Food Sovereignty Look Like?" *Journal of Peasant Studies* 36 (3): 663–706.

————. 2012. *Stuffed and Starved: The Hidden Battle for the World Food System*. Brooklyn, NY: Melville House.

Pavitt, Keith. 2001. "Public Policies to Support Basic Research: What Can the Rest of the World Learn from US Theory and Practice? (And What They Should Not Learn)." *Industrial and Corporate Change* 10 (3): 761–779.

Pearse, Andrew C. 1980. *Seeds of Plenty, Seeds of Want: Social and Economic Implications of the Green Revolution*. Oxford, UK: Clarendon; New York: Oxford University Press.

Pechlaner, Gabriela. 2007. "Beyond the Science of Agricultural Biotechnology: Corporate Technology, Law and Local Control over Food Production." PhD diss., Simon Fraser University.

————. 2012a. *Corporate Crops: Biotechnology, Agriculture, and the Struggle for Control*. Austin: University of Texas Press.

————. 2012b. "GMO-Free America? Mendocino County and the Impact of Local Level Resistance to the Agricultural Biotechnology Paradigm." *International Journal of the Sociology of Agriculture and Food* 19 (3): 445–464.

Pechlaner, Gabriela, and Gerardo Otero. 2008. "The Third Food Regime: Neoliberal Globalism and Agricultural Biotechnology in North America." *Sociologia Ruralis* 48 (4): 351–371.

————. 2010. "The Neoliberal Food Regime: Neoregulation and the New Division of Labor in North America." *Rural Sociology* 75 (2): 179–208.

————. 2015. "The Neoliberal Diet and Inequality: Differentiated Convergence in NAFTA." In *Handbook of the International Political Economy of Agriculture and Food*, edited by Alessandro Bonanno and Lawrence Busch, 131–155. Cheltenham, UK: Edward Elgar.

Peck, Jamie. 2010. *Constructions of Neoliberal Reason*. Oxford: Oxford University Press.

Pérez Castañeda, Juan Carlos, and Horacio Mackinlay. 2015. "¿Existe aún la propiedad social agraria en México?" *Polis* 11 (1): 45–82.

Pérez Escamilla, Rafael, Salvador Villalpando, Teresa Shamah-Levy, and Ignacio Méndez-Gómez Humarán. 2014. "Household Food Insecurity, Diabetes, and

Hypertension among Mexican Adults: Results from Ensanut 2012." *Salud Pública de México* 56 (S1): 62–70.

Peschard, Karine. 2012. "Unexpected Discontent: Exploring New Developments in Brazil's Transgenic Controversy." *Canadian Journal of Development Studies* 33 (3): 326–337.

Pickett, K., S. Kelly, E. Brunner, T. Lobstein, and R. Wilkinson. 2005. "Wider Income Gaps, Wider Waistbands? An Ecological Study of Obesity and Income Inequality." *Journal of Epidemiology and Community Health* 59 (8): 670–674.

Piketty, Thomas. 2014. *Capital in the Twenty-First Century*. Cambridge, MA: Harvard University Press.

POED (Netherlands, Ministry of Foreign Affairs, Policy and Operations Evaluation Department). 2012. "Improving Food Security: Emerging Evaluation Lessons." *Evaluation Insights* 5 (January). Organization for Economic Co-operation and Development (OECD). http://www.oecd.org/derec/50313960.pdf.

Poitras, Manuel. 2008. "Social Movements and Techno-Democracy: Reclaiming the Genetic Commons." In *Food for the Few: Neoliberal Globalism and Biotechnology in Latin America*, edited by Gerardo Otero, 267–287. Austin: University of Texas Press.

Polanyi, Karl. 1944. *The Great Transformation*. New York: Rinehart.

Pollan Michael. 2006. *The Omnivore's Dilemma: A Natural History of Four Meals*. New York: Penguin.

———. 2008. *In Defense of Food: An Eater's Manifesto*. New York: Penguin.

———. 2012. "Vote for the Dinner Party." *New York Times Magazine*, 14 October, 62–64.

———. 2016. "Big Food Strikes Back." *New York Times Magazine*, 6 October, 40–83.

Pooley, Eric, and Philip Revzin. 2011. "Hungry for a Solution." *Bloomberg BusinessWeek*, 7–9 February.

Popkin, Barry M. 1998. "The Nutrition Transition and Its Health Implications in Lower-Income Countries." *Public Health Nutrition* 1 (1): 5–21.

———. 2009. *The World Is Fat: The Fads, Trends, Policies, and Products That Are Fattening the Human Race*. New York: Avery.

———. 2014. "Nutrition, Agriculture, and the Global Food System in Low and Middle Income Countries." *Food Policy* 47:91–96.

Popkin, Barry M., Linda S. Adair, and Shu Wen Ng. 2012. "The Global Nutrition Transition and the Pandemic of Obesity in Developing Countries." *Nutrition Reviews* 70:3–21.

Popkin, Barry M., and Corinna Hawkes. 2016. "Sweetening of the Global Diet, Particularly Beverages: Patterns, Trends, and Policy Responses." *Lancet Diabetes and Endocrinology* 4:174–186.

Portes, Alejandro. 2009. "Migration and Development: Reconciling Opposite Views." *Ethnic and Racial Studies* 32 (1): 5–22.

Portes, Alejandro, and Josh DeWind. 2004. "A Cross-Atlantic Dialogue: The Progress of Research and Theory in the Study of International Migration." *International Migration Review* 38 (3): 828–851.

Preibisch, Kerry, and Gerardo Otero. 2014. "Does Citizenship Status Matter in Canadian Agriculture? Workplace Health and Safety for Migrant and Immigrant Workers." *Rural Sociology* 79 (2): 174–199.

Potato Gene. 2005. "Syngenta's Unapproved GM Maize Variety." The Potato Gene Engineering Network. https://research.cip.cgiar.org/confluence/display/potatogene/Syngentas+unaproved+GM+maize+variety+bt10.

Rama, Ruth. 2015. "Foreign Multinational Enterprises in the Food and Beverages Industries of the BRICS." In *Structural Change and Industrial Development in the BRICS*, edited by Wim Naudé, Adam Szirmai, and Nobuya Haraguchi, 294–323. Oxford: Oxford University Press.

Rasella, Davide, Rosana Aquino, Carlos A. T. Santos, Rômulo Paes-Sousa, and Mauricio L. Barreto. 2013. "Effect of a Conditional Cash Transfer Programme on Childhood Mortality: A Nationwide Analysis of Brazilian Municipalities." *The Lancet* 382 (9886): 57–64.

Rayner, Geoff, Corinna Hawkes, Tim Lang, and Walden Bello. 2006. "Trade Liberalization and the Diet Transition: A Public Health Response." *Health Promotion International* 21 (S1): 67–74.

Reardon, Thomas, Christopher Barrett, Julio A. Berdegué, and Johan F. M. Swinnen. 2009. "Agrifood Industry Transformation and Small Farmers in Developing Countries." *World Development* 37 (11): 1717–1727.

Reardon, Thomas, and C. Peter Timmer. 2012. "The Economics of the Food System Revolution." *Annual Review of Resource Economics* 4:225–264. https://doi.org/10.1146/annurev.resource.050708.144147.

Reardon, Thomas C., Peter Timmer, Christopher B. Barrett, and Julio Berdegué. 2003. "The Rise Of Supermarkets in Africa, Asia, and Latin America." *American Journal of Agricultural Economics* 85 (5): 1140–1146.

Reforma. 2008. "Amenaza alza de alimentos estabilidad." 16 April. http://www.reforma.com/internacional/articulo/437/873059.

Regmi, Anita. 2001. "Changing Structure of Global Food Consumption and Trade." International Agriculture and Trade Outlook (WRS-01-1). May. Washington, DC: USDA Economic Research Services. https://www.ers.usda.gov/publications/pub-details/?pubid=40319.

Reutlinger, Shlomo, and Jack van Holst Pellekaan. 1985. *Ensuring Food Security in the Developing World: Issues and Options.* Washington, DC: World Bank.

———. 1986. *Poverty and Hunger: Issues and Options for Food Security in Developing Countries.* World Bank Policy Study no. 9275. Washington, DC: World Bank. http://documents.worldbank.org/curated/en/974281468325297392/pdf/multi-page.pdf.

Ribas, Vanesa. 2016. *On the Line: Slaughterhouse Lives and the Making of the New South.* Berkeley: University of California Press.

Richter-Tate, Caleb. 2012. "Surviving Modern Agriculture in Nebraska: Organizational Strength and Sustainability." PhD diss., Universidad Autónoma de Zacatecas, Mexico.

Rickard, Bradley J., Olivier Gergaud, Shuay-Tsyr Ho, and Wengjing Hu. 2014. "Trade Liberalization in the Presence of Domestic Regulations: Impacts of the Proposed

EU-U.S. Free Trade Agreement on Wine Markets." AAWE Working Papers, no. 173, November. American Association of Wine Economists. http://www.wine -economics.org/dt_catalog/aawe-working-paper-no-173-economics.

Robinson, William. 2008. *Global Capitalism and Latin America*. Baltimore, MD: Johns Hopkins University Press.

Rodrik, Dani. 2016. "Put Globalization to Work for Democracies." *New York Times*, September 18.

———. 2017. "The Fatal Flaw of Neoliberalism: It's Bad Economics." *The Guardian*. 14 November. https://www.theguardian.com/news/2017/nov/14/the-fatal-flaw-of -neoliberalism-its-bad-economics.

Roig-Franzia, Manuel. 2007. "A Culinary and Cultural Staple in Crisis: Mexico Grapples with Soaring Prices for Corn—and Tortillas." *Washington Post*, 27 January. http://www.washingtonpost.com/wp-dyn/content/article/2007/01/26/AR200701 2601896.html.

Rose, Donald, and Rickelle Richards. 2004. "Food Store Access and Household Fruit and Vegetable Use among Participants in the US Food Stamp Program." *Public Health Nutrition* 7 (8): 1081–1088.

Rosset, Peter. 2009. "Food Sovereignty in Latin America: Confronting the 'New' Crisis." *NACLA Report on the Americas*, May/June, 16–21.

Ruhs, M., and P. Martin. 2008. "Numbers vs. Rights: Trade-offs and Guest Worker Programs." *International Migration Review* 42 (1): 249–265.

Runsten, David, Richard Mines, and Sandra Nichols. 2013. "Immigration Reform and Labor Requirements in Manually-Skilled Industries: A Market Approach." Policy Brief no. 2013-1, February. Community Alliance with Family Farmers. http://caff .org/wp-content/uploads/2010/07/North-american-visa-white-paper-022613.pdf.

Russel, Karl, and Danny Hakim. 2016. "Broken Promises of Genetically Modified Crops." *New York Times*, 29 October. http://www.nytimes.com/interactive/2016 /10/30/business/gmo-crops-pesticides.html?_r=0.

San Vicente Tello, Adelita. 2015. "Una disputa civilizatoria: La lucha en México contra el maíz transgénico. El caso de la 'Demanda Colectiva.'" *Revista del ITESO* (Instituto Tecnológico y de Estudios Superiores de Occidente, Guadalajara, Mexico).

San Vicente Tello, Adelita, and Jaime Morales Hernández. 2015. "La demanda colectiva contra el maíz transgénico: Ciudadanía y soberanía alimentaria." Vía Orgánica. 30 September. http://viaorganica.org/la-demanda-colectiva-contra-la-siembra-de -maiz-transgenico-ciudadania%E2%80%A8y-soberania-alimentaria.

Sandborn, Tom. 2009. "Setback for Historic Effort to Unionize Guest Farm Workers." *The Tyee* (Vancouver, Canada), 29 June. http://thetyee.ca/News/2009/06/29/Farm UnionSetback.

Schneider, Mindi. 2011. *Feeding China's Pigs: Implications for the Environment, China's Smallholder Farmers and Food Security*. Institute for Agriculture and Trade Policy. 17 May. https://www.iatp.org/documents/feeding-china%E2%80%99s-pigs-implica tions-for-the-environment-china%E2%80%99s-smallholder-farmers-and-food.

———. 2014. "Developing the Meat Grab." *Journal of Peasant Studies* 41 (4): 613–633. https://doi.org/10.1080/03066150.2014.918959.

Schrecker, Ted. 2016. "'Neoliberal Epidemics' and Public Health: Sometimes the Word Is Less Complicated than It Appears." *Critical Public Health* 26 (5): 477–480.

Schrecker, Ted, and Clare Bambra. 2015. *How Politics Makes Us Sick: Neoliberal Epidemics.* Houndmills, UK: Palgrave Macmillan.

Schwartzman, Kathleen. 2012. *The Chicken Trail: Following Workers, Migrants, and Corporations across the Americas.* Ithaca, NY: Cornell University Press.

ScienceDaily. 2007. "Mayday 23: World Population Becomes More Urban Than Rural." 25 May. https://www.sciencedaily.com/releases/2007/05/070525000642.htm.

Scoffield, H. 2004. "Biotech Giant Backs Off on Wheat." *Globe and Mail*, 11 May.

Scoffield, H., and M. Strauss. 2008. "Against the Grain." *Globe and Mail*, 17 April.

Scoones, Ian. 2002. "Can Agricultural Biotechnology Be Pro-Poor? A Sceptical Look at the Emerging 'Consensus.'" *IDS [International Development Studies] Bulletin* 3 (4): 114–119.

———. 2008. "Mobilizing against GM Crops in India, South Africa, and Brazil." *Journal of Agrarian Change* 8 (2–3): 315–344.

Scrinis, Gyorgy. 2008. "On the Ideology of Nutritionism." *Gastronomica: The Journal of Food and Culture* 8 (1): 39–48.

———. 2013. *Nutritionism: The Science and Politics of Dietary Advice.* New York: Columbia University Press.

Sen, Amartya. 2011. "Quality of Life: India vs. China." *New York Times Book Review*, 13 May. http://www.davidmlast.org/POE320-2012/Week_1_files/Sen-Quality%20of%20Life%20India%20vs.%20China,%20NYRB.pdf.

Statistics Canada. 2017. "Gini Coefficients of Adjusted Market, Total and After-Tax Income, Canada and Provinces." Statistics Canada. CANSIM table 206-0033. http://www5.statcan.gc.ca/cansim/a26?lang=eng&id=2060033&p2=33.

Serageldin, I., and D. Steeds. 1997. *Rural Well-Being: From Vision to Action.* Washington, DC: World Bank.

Shaw, Hillary. 2006. "Food Deserts: Towards the Development of a Classification." *Geografiska Annaler: Series B, Human Geography* 88B (2): 231–247.

Simon, Michele. 2006. *Appetite for Profit: How the Food Industry Undermines Our Health and How to Fight Back.* New York: Nation Books.

Sklair, Leslie. 1989. *Assembling for Development: The Maquila Industry in Mexico and the United States.* Boston: Unwin Hyman.

———. 2002. *Globalization: Capitalism and Its Alternatives.* Oxford: Oxford University Press.

Smith, Bren. 2014. "Don't Let your Children Grow Up to Be Farmers." *New York Times*, Sunday Review, 9 August. http://www.nytimes.com/2014/08/10/opinion/sunday/dont-let-your-children-grow-up-to-be-farmers.html?emc=eta1&_r=0.

Smith, Gary. 2002. "Farmers Are Getting Plowed Under: With Tariffs Disappearing, U.S. Exports to Mexico May Soar." *BusinessWeek*, 18 November, 31–32.

Snyder, Richard. 2001. *Politics after Neoliberalism: Reregulation in Mexico.* New York: Cambridge University Press.

Sonnino, Roberta, Camilo Lozano Torres, and Sergio Schneider. 2014. "Reflexive Governance for Food Security: The Example of School Feeding in Brazil." *Journal of Rural Studies* 36:1–12.

Spark, Arlene. 2014. "U.S. Agricultural Policies and the U.S. Food Industry: Production to Retail." In *Local Food Environments: Food Access in America*, edited by K. B. Morland, 29–61. Boca Raton, FL: CRC.

Sparks, Mark. 2011. "Building Healthy Public Policy: Don't Believe the Misdirection." *Health Promotion International* 26 (3): 259–262.

Sreenivasan, Gauri, with Jean Christie. 2002. "Intellectual Property, Biodiversity, and the Rights of the Poor." Trade and Poverty Series, paper 3. Ottawa: Canadian Council for International Co-Operation. https://www.iatp.org/sites/default/files/Intellectual_Property_Biodiversity_and_the_Rig.htm.

Staggenborg, Suzanne, and Howard Ramos. 2016. *Social Movements*. 3rd ed. Don Mills, Canada: Oxford University Press.

Stark, O., and D. E. Bloom. 1985. "The New Economics of Labor Migration." *American Economic Review* 75 (2): 173–178.

Stédile, Joao Pedro, and Horacio Martins de Carvalho. 2011. "People Need Food Sovereignty." In *Food Movements Unite!*, edited by Eric Holt-Giménez, 21–34. Oakland, CA: Food First Books.

Stiglitz, Joseph E. 2013. *The Price of Inequality*. New York: Norton.

———. 2014. "Inequality Is Not Inevitable." *New York Times*, Sunday Review, 29 June, 1, 7.

Streiner, David L., John Cairney, and Geoffrey R. Norman. 2015. *Health Measurement Scales: A Practical Guide to Their Development and Use*. 5th ed. Oxford: Oxford University Press.

Striffler, Steve. 2005. *Chicken: The Dangerous Transformation of America's Favorite Food*. New Haven, CT: Yale University Press.

Stuesse, Angela. 2016. *Scratching Out a Living: Latinos, Race, and Work in the Deep South*. Berkeley: University of California Press.

Taber, Jane. 2014. "The Dilemma between Healthy Eating and Staying above the Poverty Line." *Globe and Mail*, 19 October. http://www.theglobeandmail.com/life/health-and-fitness/health/the-dilemma-between-healthy-eating-and-staying-above-the-poverty-line/article21150445.

Taylor, J. Edward. 1999. "The New Economics of Labor Migration and the Role of Remittances in the Migration Process." *International Migration* 37 (1): 63–88.

Teubal, Miguel. 2008. "Genetically Modified Soybeans and the Crisis of Argentina's Agriculture Model." In *Food for the Few: Neoliberal Globalism and Biotechnology in Latin America*, edited by Gerardo Otero, 189–216. Austin: University of Texas Press.

Thirlaway, Kathryn, and Dominic Upton. (2009). *The Psychology of Lifestyle: Promoting Healthy Behaviour*. London: Routledge.

Thomson, Anne, and Manfred Metz. 1998. *Implications of Economic Policy for Food Security: A Training Manual*. Rome: FAO. http://www.fao.org/DOCREP/004/X3936E/X3936E00.HTM.

Thow, Anne Marie. 2009. "Trade Liberalization and the Nutrition Transition: Mapping the Pathways for Public Health Nutritionists." *Public Health Nutrition* 12 (11): 2150–2158.

Tilly, Charles. 1998. *Durable Inequality*. Berkeley: University of California Press.

Tomaskovic-Devey, Donald, and Ken-Hou Lin. 2011. "Income Dynamics, Economic Rents, and the Financialization of the U.S. Economy." *American Sociological Review* 76 (4): 538–559.

Tomlinson, Kathy. 2013. "RBC Replaces Canadian Staff with Foreign Workers." *CBC News*, 6 April. http://www.cbc.ca/news/canada/british-columbia/rbc-replaces -canadian-staff-with-foreign-workers-1.1315008.

Toro-Gonzalez, Daniel. 2015. "The Beer Industry in Latin America." AAWE Working Papers, no. 177. American Association of Wine Economists. http://www.wine -economics.org/dt_catalog/aawe-working-paper-no-177-business.

Trotsky, Leon. 1934. *The History of the Russian Revolution*. Translated by Max Eastman. London: V. Gollanca.

Turrent Fernández, Antonio, Timothy A. Wise, and Elise Garvey. 2012. "Achieving Mexico's Maize Potential." Global Development and Environment Institute Working Paper no. 12-03, Medford, MA: Tufts University.

TWN (Third World Network). 2005. "Developing Countries Propose That TRIPS Should Require Patent Applications on Genetic Resources/Traditional Knowledge Should Prove Benefit Sharing." TWN Info Services on WTO and Trade Issues, 18 March. http://www.twn.my/title2/twninfo189.htm.

United Food and Commercial Workers of Canada and Agriculture Workers Alliance. 2011. *The Status of Migrant Farm Workers in Canada 2010–2011*. Rexdale: United Food and Commercial Workers of Canada.

Urmetzer, Peter. 2005. *Globalization Unplugged: Sovereignty and the Canadian State in the Twenty-First Century*. Toronto: University of Toronto Press.

US Census Bureau. 2012. *Income, Poverty, and Health Insurance Coverage: 2011*. Washington, DC: Economics and Statistics Administration, US Department of Commerce. https://www.census.gov/newsroom/releases/pdf/20120912_ip_%20slides_noplot points.pdf.

———. 2017. *Trade in Goods with Mexico*. Washington, DC: Economics and Statistics Administration, US Department of Commerce. https://www.census.gov/foreign -trade/balance/c2010.html#2016.

USDA (US Department of Agriculture). 2005. *Audit Report: Animal and Plant Health Inspection Service Controls over Issuance of Genetically Engineered Organism Release Permits*. Audit 50601-Te, December. USDA Office of Inspector General, Southwest Region. https://www.usda.gov/oig/webdocs/50601-08-TE.pdf.

———. 2012. "Grain: World Markets and Trade." Foreign Agriculture Service, circular series FG 90-12, September. http://www.fas.usda.gov/psdonline/circulars /grain.pdf.

———. 2016. "Global Food Industry." Washington, DC: USDA Economic Research Service (ERS). http://www.ers.usda.gov/topics/international-markets-trade/glo bal-food-markets/global-food-industry.aspx.

———. 2017a. "Adoption of Genetically Engineered Crops in the U.S." ERS. https://www .ers.usda.gov/data-products/adoption-of-genetically-engineered-crops-in-the-us.

———. 2017b. "Canada Trade and FDI." ERS. https://www.ers.usda.gov/webdocs /charts/63303/canda-image11.png?v=42571.

———. 2017c. "Mexico Trade and FDI." ERS. https://www.ers.usda.gov/webdocs /charts/56395/strong_growth.jpg?v=42996.

———. 2017d. "Total Product Sales in Various Categories of Top Four Firms (Percentage Share)." ERS. http://www.ers.usda.gov/topics/international-markets-trade /global-food-markets/global-food-industry.aspx.

———. 2017e. "U.S. Food Imports." ERS. https://www.ers.usda.gov/data-products /us-food-imports/us-food-imports/#Source countries of U.S. food imports.

USTR (US Office of the Trade Representative). 2017. "Mexico: U.S.-Mexico Trade Facts." https://ustr.gov/countries-regions/americas/mexico.

Vallgårda, Signild. 2015. "Governing Obesity Policies from England, France, Germany and Scotland." *Social Science and Medicine* 147:317–323.

van der Ploeg, Jan Douwe. 2008. *The New Peasantries: Struggles for Autonomy and Sustainability in an Era of Empire and Globalization*, Abingdon, UK: Earthscan.

———. 2014. "Peasant-Driven Agricultural Growth and Food Sovereignty." *Journal of Peasant Studies* 41 (6): 999–1030.

Vaver, D. 2004. "Canada's Intellectual Property Framework: A Comparative Overview." *Intellectual Property Journal* 17:125–188.

Vergara-Camus, Leandro. 2014. *Land and Freedom: The MST, the Zapatistas, and Alternatives to Neoliberalism*. London: Zed Books.

von Braun, Joachim. 2007. *The World Food Situation: New Driving Forces and Required Actions*. Food Policy Report 18. Washington, DC: International Food Policy Research Institute.

Walker, A. R., F. Adam, and B. F. Walker. 2001. "World Pandemic of Obesity: The Situation in Southern African Populations." *Public Health* 115:368–372.

Walker, Renee E., Christopher R. Keane, and Jessica G. Burke. 2010. "Disparities and Access to Healthy Food in the United States: A Review of Food Deserts Literature." *Health and Place* 16 (5): 876–884.

Walsh-Dilley, Marygold. 2009. "Localizing Control: Mendocino County and the Ban on GMOs." *Agriculture and Human Values* 26:95–105.

Weiler, Anelyse M., Gerardo Otero, and Hannah Wittman. 2016. "Rock Stars and Bad Apples: Moral Economies of Alternative Food Networks and Precarious Farm Work Regimes." *Antipode* 48 (4): 1–23.

Weingarten, Debbie. 2017. *The Guardian*. "Why Are American Farmers Killing Themselves in Record Numbers?" 6 December. https://www.theguardian.com/us-news /2017/dec/06/why-are-americas-farmers-killing-themselves-in-record-numbers.

Weis, Tony. 2013a. *The Ecological Hoofprint: The Global Burden of Industrial Livestock*. London: Zed Books.

———. 2013b. "The Meat of the Global Food Crisis." *Journal of Peasant Studies* 40 (1): 65–85.

Weisbrot, Mark, Stephan Lefebvre, and Joseph Sammut. 2014. *Did NAFTA Help Mexico? An Assessment after 20 Years.* Center for Economic and Policy Research. http://cepr.net/publications/reports/nafta-20-years.

Weiss, Linda. 1997. "Globalization and the Myth of the Powerless State." *New Left Review* 225:3–27.

Western, Bruce, and Jake Rosenfeld. 2011. "Unions, Norms, and the Rise in U.S. Wage Inequality." *American Sociological Review* 76 (4): 513–537.

WHO (World Health Organization). 2009. *Global Health Risks: Mortality and Burden of Disease Attributable to Major Health Risks.* http://www.who.int/healthinfo/global _burden_disease/GlobalHealthRisks_report_full.pdf.

———. 2015. "Noncommunicable Diseases." Fact sheet, updated January 2015. http:// www.who.int/mediacentre/factsheets/fs355/en.

WHO/FAO (World Health Organization/Food and Agriculture Organization of the United Nations). 2003. *Diet, Nutrition, and the Prevention of Chronic Diseases: Report of a Joint WHO/FAO Expert Consultation.* WHO Technical Report Series, no. 916. Geneva: WHO/FAO. http://apps.who.int/iris/bitstream/10665/42665/1/WHO _TRS_916.pdf.

Wiley, Lindsay F., Michael L. Berman, and Doug Blanke. 2013. "Who's Your Nanny? Choice, Paternalism, and Public Health in the Age of Personal Responsibility." *Journal of Law, Medicine, and Ethics* 41 (supplement 1): 88–91.

Williams-Forson, Psyche A. 2006. *Building Houses out of Chicken Legs: Black Women, Food, and Power.* Chapel Hill: University of North Carolina Press.

Wilkinson, John. 2009. "The Globalization of Agribusiness and Developing World Food Systems." *Monthly Review*, September, 38–50.

Winders, Bill. 2009a. "The Vanishing Free Market: The Formation and Spread of the British and US Food Regimes." *Journal of Agrarian Change* 9 (3): 315–344.

———. 2009b. *The Politics of Food Supply: U.S. Agricultural Policy in the World Economy.* New Haven, CT: Yale University Press.

———. 2017. *Grains.* Malden, MA: Polity.

Winson, Anthony. 1992. *The Intimate Commodity: Food and the Development of the Agro-Industrial Complex in Canada.* Toronto: Garamond.

———. 2013. *The Industrial Diet: The Degradation of Food and the Struggle For Healthy Eating.* Vancouver, Canada: UBC Press.

Winson, Anthony, and Jin Young Choi. 2016. "Dietary Regimes and the Nutrition Transition: Bridging Disciplinary Domains." *Agriculture and Human Values* 34 (3): 559–572. https://doi.org/10.1007/s10460-016-9746-8.

Wise, Timothy A. 2014. "Monsanto Meets Its Match in the Birthplace of Maize." *Triple Crisis: Global Perspectives on Finance, Development and Environment*, 12 May. http:// triplecrisis.com/monsanto-meets-its-match-in-the-birthplace-of-maize.

Wittman, Hannah, and Jennifer Blesh. 2017. "Food Sovereignty and Fome Zero: Connecting Public Food Procurement Programmes to Sustainable Rural Development in Brazil." *Journal of Agrarian Change.* 17 (1): 81–105. https://doi.org/10.1111 /joac.12131.

Wittman, Hannah, Annette Aurélie Desmarais, and Nettie Wiebe. 2010. "The Origins and Potential of Food Sovereignty." Introduction to *Food Sovereignty: Reconnecting Food, Nature, and Community*, edited by Hannah Wittman, Annette Aurélie Desmarais, and Nettie Wiebe, 1–14. Halifax, Canada: Fernwood.

Wolf, Eric. 1966. *Peasants*. Englewood Cliffs, NJ: Prentice-Hall.

Wolf, Steven A., and Frederick Buttel. 1996. "The Political Economy of Precision Farming." *American Journal of Agricultural Economics* 78 (December): 1269–1274.

World Bank. 2001. *Response to the Proposal of the WTO Net-Food Importing Countries*. Washington, DC: World Bank.

———. 2017. "GINI Index." World Bank estimate. https://data.worldbank.org/indicator/SI.POV.GINI.

Wright, Erik. 2010. *Envisioning Real Utopias*. London: Verso.

Wright, Tom. 2005. "U.S. Fines Swiss Company over Sale of Altered Seed." *New York Times*, 9 April. http://www.nytimes.com/2005/04/09/business/worldbusiness/09syngenta.html.

WTO (World Trade Organization). 1994. "Trade-Related Aspects of Intellectual Property Rights." http://www.wto.org/english/docs_e/legal_e/27-trips_01_e.htm.

Zahniser, Steven, Edwin Young, and John Wainio. 2005. "Recent Agricultural Policy Reforms in North America." Report WRS-05-03, April. Washington, DC: USDA, ERS. http://www.ers.usda.gov/publications/WRS0503/wrs0503.pdf.

Index

Note: page numbers in italics represent information included in tables or figures.

competition: competitive vs. comparative advantage, 155; against globalized agriculture, 39; vs. industry concentration, 11–12, *13*; for one crop by multiple industries, 50–51. *See also* concentration in agrifood industry

complex carbohydrates, decrease in diets, 87, 88

concentration in agrifood industry: vs. competition, 11–12, *13*, 177, 194–195; examples of, 9–10, 18, 40; global profiles of, *55*; of land ownership, 73–74; and Mexican exporters, 134. *See also* agribusiness multinationals (ABMs)

construct validity, 184

consumer responsibility vs. inequalities of choice, 187–188, 190–191. *See also* food choice inequalities, overviews

consumption trends. *See* expenditure and consumption trends

contamination issues, 65

convenience foods. *See* processed foods

convenience stores, 83–84, 173

Convention on Biological Diversity (CBD) of UN, 62–63

convergent validity, 184

Coordinated Framework for the Regulation of Biotechnology, 64

corn, transgenic: concentration of industry processors of, 18, 40; for ethanol production, 27, 50–51, 131, 152; expansion of, 11, 60, 152; movements against, 41–43; and poultry industry, 115; regulation of, in Mexico, 75, 76, 77–78, 130; regulatory failures, 65. *See also* high-fructose corn syrup

"corporate" food regime, 37, 151

cotton, transgenic, 11, 60, 67, 72, 152, 195

dangerous work. *See* injuries, on-job; working/living conditions for laborers

deaths, on-job, 142

dependency, unequal and combined, 151–160, 169. *See also* import dependency

deregulation vs. neoregulation, 28, 39–40

diets under food regimes. *See* food regimes

"differential profit," 6

disease. *See* nutrition-related disease

distribution, inequality in, 46, 48–49

diversity, biological. *See* biodiversity

diversity, food source, 108, 109, 160–166

Doha Development Round, WTO negotiations, 38, 61, 154

domestic agriculture. *See* small-scale farming

Eaton, Emily, 71

ecology/agroecology, 20–21, 46, 71–72, 155, 181, 189, 196

economic issues: employment/unemployment, 32, 144–146, 147; globalization and disarticulation of local economies, 128–129, 182; growth vs. return on capital, 29; income inequality, 105, 128, 134 (*see also* wealth inequality); wage "theft" of migrant workers, 140, 146; world food prices, internalization of, 107–108, 112, 151, 157, 158. *See also* food price crisis; wealth inequality

Economist, 12, 90, 128, 130

education, social movements for, 19–20

ejidos (communal lands), 73

El Campo No Aguanta Más, 77

emerging economies. *See* BRIC(S)/BRICSTIM countries

employment/unemployment, 32, 144–146, 147

endocrine-disruptive chemicals, 5

energy-balance model, 2, 3–4, 5

energy-dense foods, definitions, 1, 8, 80–81

entrepreneurial farming, 47–48. *See also* small-scale farming

Environment Canada, 69

epigenetics and obesity, 5–6

ethanol, 27, 50–51, 131, 152

expenditure and consumption trends: by economic class, 82–84, 91–98, 178, *179*, *180*; and evolution of neoliberal diet, 6, 84–91; and import dependency, 160–166; Mexico case study in, 118–122; in